DATE DUE

RUSSIAN RESEARCH CENTER STUDIES, 62

Icon and Swastika

Icon and Swastika

The Russian Orthodox Church
under Nazi and Soviet Control

Harvey Fireside

HARVARD UNIVERSITY PRESS

CAMBRIDGE, MASSACHUSETTS

1971

The Russian Research Center of Harvard University is supported by a grant from the Ford Foundation. The Center carries out interdisciplinary study of Russian institutions and behavior and related subjects.

Library of Congress Catalog Card Number 70–123567

SBN 674–44160–5

Printed in the United States of America

Distributed in Great Britain by Oxford University Press, London

To Rose Levenberg

Foreword by
Paul B. Anderson

Once in talking with Sir Bernard Pares at the School of Slavonic and Eastern European Studies of the University of London, he remarked that between the mountains of Wales and the Urals there is no hill higher than six hundred feet. Having crossed this area many times, I know that, were it not for the change in village scenes and the great rivers, it might be uninteresting territory for a casual traveler. Yet the contrary holds if the visitor has a bent for history, especially the great decisive moments in the millennium of relations between the Slavic East, basically Byzantine Orthodox, and the Catholic-Protestant West.

In 1920 I drove out of Warsaw and in half an hour came to the forward Polish positions facing the Bolshevik armies. Two months later there were the bivouacs of the two hundred thousand interned Russians who had been driven by the Poles through the Mazurian lakes into East Prussia. A year later came the streams of refugees from Soviet famine; I met them at Baranovitse and Rovno, where the Polish-Soviet frontier had been established well to the east of the Curzon line at Brest-Litovsk. In the spring of 1939 I visited the ancient fortress there; the frescoes in the little chapel depicted the historic scenes as the city fell to one side or the other, to Russians or to Poles. In the last fifty years the frontier has shifted five times. Religion, or antireligion, can be seen as a major element behind each change.

Dr. Fireside provides us with a valuable study of the way in which religion was manipulated on the Eastern front in World War II by the Germany army and occupying administration. My own preview of German policy occurred on a visit to Berlin during the Nazi period, when I saw Bishop Seraphim Lade several times and also visited the beautiful

Russian Orthodox Cathedral which the German state had helped the émigré Church to erect. As the Nazi armies moved into Russian territory beyond Brest-Litovsk, they helped the Orthodox to open churches, most of which had been closed by the Soviets, in the same way. As Dr. Fireside explains, the Nazis made use of Bishop Lade and émigré clergy in their efforts to replace priests by then dead or exiled to the Far East.

The author's review of Nazi policy is preceded by two relevant chapters on the background of Soviet religious policy, and on the nature of Russian Orthodoxy. Both are vast fields, with much documentary evidence available and many sorts of evaluating opinion to draw upon. It will therefore not be surprising if some readers object to the interpretation given in Dr. Fireside's brief summary; his ideas are stimulating indeed.

Nor is documentation lacking on events and policies of the actual years of German occupation. A wealth of material is available from the Nuremberg trial, from war memoirs, and from the studies conducted by Harvard University teams among refugees immediately after the close of the war. All sources agree that the German administration of occupied territories was chaotic. The author's analysis of the conflicting policies of seven major Nazi agencies—military, security, and civil—helps greatly to see how bewildered the population must have been, and how even a return to Communist rule must have seemed preferable for some.

There are varied opinions, among scholars, too, on the manner and extent to which Soviet policy on religion in the war and the postwar period was affected by Nazi policy and practice during the occupation. Numerous conversations with leading Russian hierarchs, both in the Soviet Union and abroad, would on the whole lead me to support the author's thesis that Stalin was influenced greatly by the fact that religion still existed even after terrible atheistic drives, and that it could come to life even under the rigors of Nazi occupation. Fortunately for the Russian Orthodox Church, he did not adopt the Nazi policy of arbitrarily favoring now one, now another, claimant to Church authority, but instead came out clearly in favor of the Patriarchate. The bishops and many of the clergy who were active under the Germans fled with the retreating Nazi armies. Let us hope that a further study will follow these wartime Orthodox leaders to their new fields of endeavor—often in competition with one another—in Canada, Australia, and the United States.

Having visited Metropolitan Dionisius, head of the Polish Orthodox Church, several times before the war, I went to see him again in 1946.

He related the courtesy of the Russian high command in returning him from his refuge in Austria to resume office in Warsaw. On another visit, in 1948, I was told by someone at the door that the Metropolitan could see no one. In fact, he was under house arrest and was soon deprived of office.

Dr. Fireside writes of the broad operations of the Moscow Patriarchate in dealing with heads of other Orthodox Churches and with Western non-Orthodox churches, and of the 1948 decision not to affiliate with the World Council that was rescinded before formal entry in 1961. This, of course, is well beyond the period of German occupation or even of Soviet expansion westward. The author's closing section, however, brings out the fact that the foreign relations and peace efforts of the Moscow Patriarchate share the characteristics of Soviet foreign policy; he ventures to say that perhaps this "junior partnership" relationship has had a beneficial effect on the domestic life of the Orthodox Church in the Soviet Union. He feels that both Church and state are strongly patriotic, and that this may be a factor in ensuring the maintenance of religious life in the Soviet Union.

Contents

Preface

An analysis of the experiences of the Russian Orthodox Church under German occupation in World War II afforded an opportunity to explore, in the form of a comparative case study, the systems of Soviet and Nazi social controls and the degree of popular compliance each was able to attain. Such a study might provide insights into the strains of the Stalinist system, as indicated by the reaction of some sixty million people during the hiatus after Soviet power had vanished and before Nazi repression had made itself felt. It could also be considered something like a sociopolitical experiment spanning the period from June 1941 to July 1944, in which religious organizations under Nazi rule represented the "experimental group" and those remaining under Soviet rule the "control group." Finally, it might shed light on the nature of the Soviet decision-making process, since the religious revival that swept the German-occupied areas was evidently related to the subsequent shift in Soviet policy which brought about accommodation between regime and Church in September 1943.

It soon became apparent why this specific topic had been treated peripherally, if at all, in previous studies both of the Church and of the German occupation. For one thing, the institution being investigated proved to be not one church but a number of Orthodox factions—a half dozen in the Ukraine alone—with the antecedents and structure peculiar to each determining its set of responses. For another, German policy in this field turned out, on closer examination, to resemble the rationalizations of planners in Berlin rather than the welter of conflicting directives and improvisational gestures by which at least seven Nazi agencies sought to fit the religious question into their respective missions. It would, therefore, be impossible to arrive at a single, definitive answer to the central inquiry: How effectively did the German administrators exploit religious tensions created by the Soviet system? Still, by piecing together the fragmentary data, one might hope to offer tentative conclusions on the two major variables.

Instead of approaching the subject head-on, it seemed more suitable to take an indirect approach, so that relevant experiences and ideological preconceptions of all the actors could first be viewed in perspective. Thus, excursions into the roles of regional church groups and into the attitudes of German officials for whom religious regulation was an incidental affair might yield clues to help explain resurgence of the Church on a grand scale. Introductory chapters would have to supply background on an institution that had survived two decades of the Soviet regime's cyclical but inexorable drive toward atheism, as well as on the German decision-makers who brought to their Russian assignment attitudes shaped by dealing with the churches of their homeland. Finally, the yardstick by which "effective exploitation" might be measured had to provide two parameters. First, the efforts of German agencies had to be gauged by the degree to which they enabled each unit to perform its immediate function in the short run. Then, they had to be re-examined in terms of how much allegiance they engendered for the occupation power, without which any long-run political rule would have been obviated except at gunpoint.

A good deal has been written about church experiences under the Soviet and Nazi regimes. It might well be questioned, therefore, whether brief reference to such sources would not have sufficed. The decision to present this material anew in three background chapters reflected a feeling that previous writing had presented documents and other data from the viewpoint of historians who shrank from drawing conclusions about the political nature of the institution they were describing. By covering the old ground with the tools of political sociology, one might hope to engender new insights about the rationale of totalitarian decision-making in a comparative context. The actions of individual churchmen could then be seen not as isolated examples of bravery or cowardice, opportunism or principle, but rather as patterns of response to institutional pressures.

There were additional reasons for an extensive introduction to an account of the Church under German occupation. Each vital element of the story was linked to the experiences of the previous generation: the religious frustrations of the people in the occupied territories, the widespread church revival, the resistance of most congregations to Nazi exploitation, the factional disputes among rival clerics, the interrelation between church and nationalist movements. Further, the major actors were keenly aware that theirs was a subplot of a larger drama. Thus, a German administrator knew that the options in dealing with local church groups were circumscribed by the demands of Nazi ideology, and he knew the anticipated response from religious bodies in the Reich and the capital that Soviet propagandists and partisans would be able to make of his actions—beyond the net gain or loss in advancing objectives in his immediate jurisdiction. In like fashion, the men in the Kremlin in carving out a new role for the Church drew upon their ideological sets, their intelligence data on what was happening in the occupied areas, and their assessment of the religious tenacity and political reliability of Russian believers.

A German official's failure to follow up initial successes of a liberal religious policy and a Soviet move to capitalize on it would appear as arbitrary tactical exchanges unless the introductory chapters placed them in a broader setting. Only then might it become clear whether such moves kept to lines established in preceding years. Because the most dramatic change transpired in Stalin's policies, it was of special interest to determine the degree to which they diverged from the Marx-Engels-Lenin approach to religion. In tracing these connections, it became necessary to fill gaps in the existing literature, which has never systematically analyzed this strand of Communist ideology. As regarded the Nazis, again a background section was required to at least offer a summary account of German church experiences that still await full-length scholarly treatment. Only by tracing Soviet and Nazi religious policies to their origins could it become apparent which aspects of them in the wartime period constituted improvisations, which variations on older themes.

The most appropriate method of study seemed to be a historical approach: exploring probable cause-and-effect relations in the data with a minimum of preconceived hypotheses. The limited original sources—German documents scattered in various archives, isolated accounts of Russian and German eyewitnesses, and the hundreds of interview protocols gathered in 1950–51 by the Harvard Refugee Interview Project—had to be collated and evaluated critically. Any biases or self-serving statements would have to be disallowed. A similar corrective factor was required for German and Soviet policy statements on religion generally, since the explicit rationale of each often covered crucial underlying motivations. With these reservations governing the use of sources, it appeared advisable to allow for theories to follow patterns of data, rather than vice versa. As much as possible, objectivity and rigor of investigation would have to dictate categorization of fragmentary materials. An extra share of speculation might be in order, however, for the final chapter on the "New Religious Policy" in the Soviet Union, in order to bring the study to bear on questions of current social controls and to suggest an answer regarding the regime's ability to manipulate the ideological framework to suit its practical purposes.

It should be noted that I am neither Russian nor Orthodox and have no particular ax to grind on the politics under discussion. Still, one man's detachment may be another's bias. For example, it may infuriate some readers to be confronted with evidence that a number of priests proved all too human in succumbing to the temptation of giving in to demands of Nazi Reichsleiter, as they had to Soviet commissars on occasion. No attempt has been made to excuse or condemn them for such actions. They are, simply, described as accurately as possible and in the light of all the extreme pressures that motivated them. It remains to the reader to speculate whether others might have played such difficult parts in a different fashion.

The Harvard Refugee Interview Project first drew my attention to the usefulness of data on the German occupation of Russia in World War II as a means of exploring the Soviet social controls that were detached for a three-year period. I owe a great deal to the advice and encouragement of four of the project's specialists: Dr. Alex Inkeles, under whom I worked as research assistant at the Russian Research Center; Dr. Merle Fainsod, who guided my studies of Soviet politics; Dr. David Gleicher, whom I helped to classify the interview protocols; and, perhaps most of all, Dr. Alexander Dallin, Harvard consultant on research into the occupation and later director of Columbia University's Russian Institute, who provided not only many valuable insights through writings and conversations on the occupation era, but also the urging I needed to follow this study to its final stage. I am further indebted to Dr. Dallin for generously allowing me the use of his files, with their store of hitherto unpublished information. Thanks are also due the New York State Education Department's Office of Foreign Area Studies for a grant enabling me, as visiting scholar at Columbia in 1967–68, to track down the more elusive sources.

Further, I wish to acknowledge assistance of the staff at Columbia's Archive of East European and Russian History, which granted access to its manuscript collection and permission for citation. Like appreciation is due the Yivo Institute for Jewish Research for making available its files of original German documents, as well as the National Archives for supplying microfilms of captured German records. Additional materials were furnished by the able library staffs at Harvard and Columbia Universities, the World Jewish Congress, and the Slavonic Divisions of the Library of Congress and the New York Public Library.

A special measure of gratitude is reserved for Dr. George Ginsburgs, my adviser at the Graduate Faculty of Political and Social Science of the New School for Social Research, for his patience, counsel, and wit. To help the reader keep straight the confusing cast of Orthodox Church clerics, I have followed Dr. Ginsburgs' suggestion and appended a glossary of the prelates in order of their appearance in the text. Including the many variants of their names would only have compounded the confusion, so reference is limited to the most commonly used names, with surnames or Russian equivalents of Ukrainian and Belorussian clergy added in parentheses. The transliteration system is a simplified form of that used by the United States Geographic Board, with diacritical marks and palatalization signs omitted.

Harvey Fireside

Ithaca
February 1970

Glossary of Orthodox Church Prelates

In Order of Appearance in the Text

Tikhon—elected Patriarch in 1917, failed to rouse resistance to the Soviets, arrested in 1922 and "confessed" his political errors after his release in 1923, died in 1925.

Sergius—became locum tenens or Acting Patriarch in 1925, arrested in 1926 and 1927, after his release promised political obedience to the regime, weathered two Soviet antireligious campaigns, called for resistance to the German invasion, organized Church contributions to the war effort, evacuated to Ulyanovsk 1941–1943, elected to the Patriarchy after his return to Moscow and a historic interview with Stalin, died in 1944.

Alexis—Metropolitan of Leningrad during wartime siege, decorated for his part in the city's defense, became Acting Patriarch in 1944, elected Patriarch in 1945, reorganized the Church administration with the help of new seminaries and clerics from areas retaken by the Soviets, issued pro-Stalin appeals and statements in support of Soviet policy.

Nikolai—obtained submission of Ukrainian hierarchs to the Patriarchy after Soviet seizure of eastern Poland in 1939, became Metropolitan of Kiev after fleeing from Germans, issued patriotic appeals from Moscow during the war and served on War Crimes Commission, became the foreign policy spokesman of the Church in 1945, died in 1961.

Seraphim—émigré bishop selected by the Nazis to head all Orthodox parishes in the Third Reich, confirmed by the anti-Soviet Karlovtsi Synod in Yugoslavia, tried to extend his influence into the occupied territories, restricted to his Berlin diocese after 1940 except for a special Church conference in Vienna in 1943.

Sergius the Younger—named Exarch of the Baltic states after their occupation by the Soviets in 1940, concealed himself to avoid evacuation, supported the Nazis but maintained nominal allegiance to the Patriarchate, built an active Church organization extending beyond the limits of his diocese, murdered in 1944 probably by a German security squad.

Szepticky—Metropolitan of the Uniate Church in the Ukraine, restricted by the Germans to the Polish General-Gouvernement, died in 1944.

Panteleimon—Exarch of Belorussia after Soviet occupation of western area in 1939, picked by Germans to head Belorussian Autocephalous Church in 1941, exiled in 1942 but recalled a year later to reorganize the Church.

Dionisius—Metropolitan of the Polish Autocephalous Church, tried to influence Orthodox organizations in Ukraine and Belorussia during occupation era, displaced by pro-Soviet bishop in 1948.

Vasily Lipkovsky—organizer of Ukrainian Autocephalous Church which made him a bishop in 1921, ordained many unqualified clerics until Soviets forced him out in 1928, followers known as Lipkovtsy left with clerical status in doubt.

Polykarp—Bishop of Lutsk under Polish Autocephalous Church since 1932, in 1941 with urging of Dionisius re-established Ukrainian Autocephalous Church (UAPTs) of which he became "Administrator," fled to West Germany and defrocked by émigré bishops in 1945, though later headed European section of UAPTs in exile.

Alexei—Bishop in eastern Ukraine, as senior churchman in 1941 became Metropolitan and acting head of Autonomous Ukrainian Church while keeping nominal allegiance to the Patriarchate, opposed to UAPTs, assassinated by extremists in 1943.

Alexander—Archbishop of Pinsk and senior primate of Belorussia, helped Polykarp set up UAPTs in 1941, briefly headed Belorussian Autocephalous Church.

Hilarion—Ukrainian nationalist in 1918–1919 regimes, later philologist in Polish area, became Archbishop of Kholm in 1940, during occupation funneled nationalist clerics into eastern Ukraine and promoted UAPTs.

Palladius—old-time Ukrainian nationalist who became Bishop of Lemko in 1940, then of Cracow, active in UAPTs.

Mstyslav—Stephen Skrypnik, active as politician in Poland, then as publisher with German approval in 1941, became Bishop of Pereiaslav in 1942 and one of most ardent nationalists in UAPTs.

Fotius—former Soviet spy in Poland, became Bishop of Vinnitsa in 1942, dislodged with difficulty by Polykarp in 1943 after having won local German support.

Feofil—long-time schismatic, allowed to build independent church organization by Germans and make himself Metropolitan of Kharkov in 1941, joined UAPTs in 1942, excommunicated by Patriarch in 1944.

Platon—Bishop of Rovno, one of strongest Nazi sympathizers in UAPTs with close ties to Bandera partisans.

Manuil—Bishop of Vladimir Volynsk, switched from UAPTs to Autonomous Ukrainian Church, assassinated 1943 by Bandera band.

Panteleimon (Rudyk)—named Bishop of Lvov after Soviet occupation of West Ukraine in 1939, loyal to Autonomous Church in 1941, fought with UAPTs over control of Kiev diocese, succeeded Alexei in 1943.

Gennady—sent by UAPTs to become Bishop of Dnepropetrovsk, backed by German commissar and local Ukrainian nationalists against Autonomous Church organization.

Vladimir Benevsky—head of Poltava Church Administration, reorganized city's religious life under occupation, gave official thanks to Germans.

Icon and Swastika

1

The Background of
Soviet Religious Policy

When the German overlords were planning their conquest of the eastern reaches that would supply them with indentured servants for the master race, they had to admit into the strategic councils psychological as well as military experts. The wartime strategy called for blitzkrieg, the kind of lightning advance that had already put the bulk of Western Europe under the swastika. Assuming that victory against the Soviets could be snatched with like speed, German civilian administrators would be faced with a gigantic task in the newly conquered area. Hundreds of millions of future colonial subjects had to be provided for.

The waiting Aryan governors knew that the mentality of their future subjects was not the blank slate that would have been the ideal medium on which to inscribe the New Order. In order to harness the Slavs to the engines of the Third Reich, some account—no matter how grudging—would have to be taken of their past hopes and frustrations. Likewise, on the grander plane of the future Teutonic empire, before new social and political institutions could be erected according to Hitler's master plan, a massive job of demolition and reconstruction would have to be performed on the structures that had persisted through the past twenty-three years of Soviet rule.

In both these respects, the church policy of the German occupiers was bound to be affected by the religious needs of their subjects, for these had been conditioned by a generation of Communist practice. What such needs and practice were must be borne in mind as an immediate backdrop to the occupation drama that will furnish an essential contrast against which to view German policy and practice—the extent to which the Germans attempted to undo or parallel Soviet institutions

1

and controls. An overview of the preceding period will also throw light
on the object that German administrators would try to shape to their
purpose: what was the condition of the Church at the eve of the war?
Was it too emasculated to resist any of the new strictures to be imposed
on it? Or, did it have reservoirs of strength which might swell it into a
redoubtable force for the Germans to reckon with, perhaps even a rallying point for the frustrations of Nazi as well as Communist rule?

RELIGION AND REACTION

From the voluminous and easily accessible literature on the Russian
Orthodox Church, data can be culled that suggest certain hypotheses
about the political sociology of religion in Russia. Though the facts are
known, the story has so far been told only in episodic form by historians.
The potential contribution of the following analysis lies in drawing
conclusions from the data, particularly as these highlight the Church as
a social institution interacting with the governmental bureaucracy. To
my knowledge, this is a novel attempt to view features of the Orthodox
organization as response patterns to political pressure.

First, the Church since the early eighteenth century had uncomplain-
ingly done yeoman service on the ship of state. It had no modern record
of opposition to the regime's course, though that course might, in the
opinion of some Church leaders, be heading for disaster. Instead, its
prime role was that of willing handmaiden, receiving the material and
status benefits of an established religion, acquiescing in the personnel
and policy directives received from political decision-makers. Whenever
called upon, it stood ready to anoint the legitimacy of the state and to
rationalize the latest repressions of the government. Its power, which
was considerable, generally lay unexpended. An occasional churchman,
the most notorious being Rasputin, might aspire to primacy in the ante-
chambers of the autocratic court, but he was the exception. The more
consistent stance of the Church in the halls of state was one of passivity;
power strivings were seemingly displaced within the institution itself—
turned inwardly by the hierarchs into factional or personal struggles for
pre-eminence. If such a hypothesis is warranted, it goes far to make
understandable the rather short-lived hostility of the Church to the
Soviet regime, its persistent attempts at the accommodation finally found
in wartime alliance with its self-declared archenemies, and what to some
observers has been a series of moves into a position of abject political
servility.

Viewed in this light, the factional battles that span Soviet church history in the prewar period are also easier to fathom. Until the decisive intervention of the state sealed the issue, each churchman contending for the patriarchal throne could sustain his claim, on whatever shred of legitimate basis he found at hand, and try to bluff out his rivals. This leads to the second hypothesis: that power within the Church was substantiated by traditional, rather than by charismatic or rational, means. The apex of the hierarchy is populated not by the spell-binding prophet or the supple bureaucrat, but by the aged monastic priest from the upper class with extensive university and seminary education and a lifetime of experience in the lower echelons, where greater store was laid on theological lore than on social skills, including administrative talent. Such a man would prove no match for either commissar or Gauleiter; he might also be hard put to deal with an occasional charlatan aspiring to high church office; he would have to rely on tested defenses—canon law, time, and patience.

Centuries of traditional exercise of power could be expected to fossilize communications and administrative practice within an institution. In the case of the Russian Orthodox Church, when the word was given by prelates at the apex of the structure it percolated down slowly and fitfully to the typical village congregation at the bottom; any return flow was negligible. These two strata occupied two different worlds, and, while both shared a common interest in maintenance of the faith, in virtually all other ways their roles diverged. The sumptuously accoutred bishop, a monastic swathed in the mysteries of ancient ritual, stood versts apart from the peasant world of the married priest, who as often as not tilled his own fields, dickered with his parishioners over baptismal fees, or drowned his frustrations in the vodka bottle.[1] At times of chaos, with sections of the country cut off by civil war or foreign occupation, it is not unexpected to find that parts of this body existed independently of the head; after regenerating their own centers of authority, they might even feel relief at the removal of central church pressures and respond with a surprising burst of vigor. At other times of general political repression of religious activity, the semi-autonomous life of individual congregations could persist remarkably unchanged, making the discovery of a "catacomb church" by some observers somewhat of a misnomer. In relation to Church headquarters in Moscow, the small village flock might often have regarded itself as occupying the ecclesiastical catacombs.

In line with previous assumptions about a church both politically and administratively wedded to the status quo, a third hypothesis offers the view of it as a conservative social force. Conservatism, an inherent resistance to change, is a notoriously relative matter, but it seems to have a specific bearing here to the Church's self-conception, its ideology, as well as to its interactions with other institutions. The last ambassador of France to the Russian Court, Maurice Paléologue, shared many attitudes of the Petrograd aristocratic circles in which he moved. Yet on February 28, 1917, his memoirs carry the following caustic entry: "All who study the history and theology of the Russian Orthodox Church, 'the True Church of Christ,' realize that its essential characteristics are its conservative instincts, the immutable rigidity of its creed, reverence for canon law, the importance of forms and rites, routine devotions, sumptuous ceremonial, an imposing hierarchy and humble, blind submission on the part of the faithful."[2] Those who strayed from the path, seventeenth-century schismatics and contemporary, more radical "sectarians," tended to end up in extreme positions of their own, with an ultra-individualistic, disorganized style that Paléologue summarized as "absolute anarchy."

Looking inwardly, the Church cast a jaundiced eye on any attempts at reform. Priding itself on its calcefied traditions, it disparaged Western Christianity for its changeableness.[3] Whether in the matter of conducting services in the vernacular rather than the time-hallowed Church Slavonic or of grudging a mite of self-determination to the congregations, the prelates insisted on looking backward. They relied entirely on the authoritarian solution. Even when change was thrust upon them, as in the upheaval of the October Revolution, their reaction was retrogressive: reverting from the synodal form of administration of the past two centuries to the patriarchal office swept away by Peter the Great in 1721. If a grass-roots demand for reform seized sizable areas of the country, the orthodox hierarchy stood its ground, using the weapons of recrimination and anathema, forcing the reformers into an untenable position as schismatics, most of all counting on the enthusiasm for change to die down among a flock of believers conditioned to ritualized prayer and obedience. Inevitably, a few years later, a couple of decades—it didn't really matter—the factional leaders grew weary of the unequal battle and came around repentant to seek readmission to the Mother Church, which usually let them back into the fold with their titles intact, as if the whole affair had been a youthful prank.

During tsarist times, conservatism was reinforced by the social groups with which the Church was allied: the nobility and upper bureaucracy at the top, the peasantry at the base. Notably absent were the catalysts of change: the bulk of the intelligentsia at the higher reaches, the increasingly important industrial proletariat at the lower. Liberal, let alone radical, forces were not so much arrayed against the Church as alienated from it. It had little to offer them, so they gave it the cold shoulder or, at worst, shrugged it off as one more of the deadweights carried on the bowed backs of the people. As for social pronouncements of church leaders, they stayed within the narrow confines set by such civil administrators as Pobedonostsev, Ober Procurator of the Holy Synod during the reign of the last two tsars and symbol of obscurantism. Liberalism in politics, according to such guidelines, was as reprehensible as democratization in church doctrine.

THE WAYS OF SURVIVAL

That this static social institution was able to maintain itself at all—more than that, keep up an establishment of 130 bishops, some 50,000 priests and 80,000 monks and nuns in 1914[4]—calls for further comment. Of course, an interpretation of this latest pre-World War I statistic from reports of the Ober Procurator depends on whether one sees it as genuine indication of vitality or merely as the last flush of a moribund establishment. A review of most impartial commentaries makes us incline to the latter option, which is buttressed by the relative ease with which the new Communist regime could deal with an at first implacably hostile Church —shifting from a policy of entirely ignoring its challenge to one of limitations of scope, then harassment and finally open persecution, without ever encountering a general show of popular revolt. Indeed, the initial strategy of the hierarchs was predicated on weakness, since the demonstrations they organized in the city streets were meant to provoke Red soldiers into taking a toll of martyrs large enough for a nationwide crusade against the regime. True, there were other prelates to be found blessing the weapons of the White Guard armies during the years of civil war, but even they failed to arouse the masses and thereby also attested to the fundamental weakness of the Church base. The churchmen who could be so glaringly ignored then were in an impossible negotiating position: boxed into a political nonworld, having made compromise unthinkable with foes they had anathematized, they left themselves only the draconic choice of official extinction or total submission.

The legacy of conservatism had depleted the arsenal of political weapons available to the embattled Church, stripped it of its defenders, robbed it of the flexible responses demanded by the revolutionary situation. Gone now were the faithful nobles and assiduous bureaucrats who had been its shield, terrorized and disrupted the peasantry that had been its sinews. Here and there a village stood ready to rally round its priest against the pillaging Red Guards, but such jacqueries were isolated. Their emotion was too short-lived and shallow to furnish the grounds for organized resistance. Too many of the first open clashes were about church property, which the new regime was trying to seize, for the peasants to be convinced that defense of silver ornaments was worth the risk of their lives. It proved more convenient to rely on heavenly wrath to catch up with the perpetrators of sacrilege than to snatch up one's pitchfork.

Undoubtedly a deeper reason for the dearth of popular martyrs lies in the gulf between people and Church. At a simple level this was reflected in the bickering that surrounded the local priest—quarrels about his exorbitant fees or his rights as a landowner, suspicions of his drunkenness and corruption. In the popular view, he was also linked somehow to the sumptuary trappings of the prelates, subsidized like them from the coffers of an autocratic state. He was part and parcel of an establishment which, except for an occasional renegade like Father Gapon leading the marchers on Bloody Sunday of 1905, sought to fasten the yoke yet more securely on the necks of the people—an institution whose ideology made it answer the primordial cries for peace and land with admonitions to keep fighting and remain content with the old. Sermons that had automatically been cast into the mold of quietude could not instantly be reshaped into calls for action. A church anchored in the status quo was unable to fathom the depth of, let alone build a programmatic bridge to, the streams of the country's economic and social frustrations.

And yet the Church lingered on. Not only were patriarch and politburo eventually reconciled, but the rapprochement uncovered the flocks of believers who had remained steadfast and now overflowed reopened chapels and reconsecrated shrines, even oversubscribed in large numbers the vacancies in the new seminaries. Again a problem of interpreting this tenacity of religious belief must be faced. Mere habit inculcated into childish minds before the age of reason does not offer a satisfying answer. Why did parents bother? Why did many of the children not jettison their faith when they grew aware of the negative status it carried in Soviet life?

Communist ideologists, using as a springboard the social Darwinism of Engels, would jump to the prediction of godless generations meeting the dawn of Communism, having discarded their faith like a maladaptive vestigial organ after sufficiently long exposure to the classless conditions of socialist society. In thus circumventing the problem, however, they have transposed it into a nonpragmatic framework. Who can check how long will be long enough? The enlightenment drive in the Soviet Union has littered recent history with false forecasts; the Militant Atheist League pronounced a death sentence over the Church in the thirties, yet it continues as a viable institution three decades later.

Equally unconvincing rings the suggestion of some anthropologists, taking another leaf from Engels, who conclude that Russian religion at some primitive level satisfies the demands for nature-worship of the Russian peasant. Major church holidays may relate to the seasonal cycle which dominates the life of tillers of the soil—the vernal rebirth of Eastertime, for instance. But what attracts the peasant, admittedly the most devout of the believers, to a daily or weekly service? Why did the drive for "godless collective farms" of presumably rational socialist farmers fizzle out? Further, how can the ever new reports of religious observance in the cities by workers, even professionals (notably an Alleluyeva), a couple of generations or more removed from the countryside be explained?

Nicholas Timasheff has pointed to the beauty of the divine service itself as providing "the strongest attraction to the Russian Orthodox Church."[5] The elaborate ceremonial, especially the glorious songs, are said to offer a respite from the ugliness of Soviet local "cultural institutions." If that were the case, however, a beautification program for village Houses of Culture would strike a deathblow at the faith. The roots seem to go deeper, though this does not gainsay the connection between bureaucratic drabness at marriage registration offices and the widespread preference of young couples for a church ceremony, for example. Soviet officials have shown that they appreciate the effect by literally rolling out red carpets for civil nuptials and adding recorded music in an obvious effort to meet the competition.

The people's psychological thirst for religion appears to embrace, beyond a craving for esthetic rewards of the service, a search for symbolic rewards, in part substitute, in part supplement for the meager material rewards offered by the Soviet system so far. At least the average Russian consumer hangs a considerable distance below the "new class" of the political and professional elite when it comes to priorities for better housing, clothes, and luxuries. Yet in his church he can enjoy spiritual benefits, including the promise of eternal rewards that are barred to his social betters by official sanction. In this realm he is king. He is able to envisage himself master of his destiny, a prospect apparently worth the price of state-sponsored caricatures of his "superstitions."

But at the same time the Russian churchgoer is more than an individual whom official ideologists denounce as a spiritual dope addict. He belongs to a whole cult of fellow addicts. Here may well lie a clue to the social nexus for the hardiness shown by beleaguered congregations. The collectivization and industrialization drives launched by Stalin in the late twenties brought in their wake a vast disruption of traditional social patterns. To a great extent the society was atomized, with individuals uprooted from their extended family and community relations to fill slots in the rosters of collective farm or factory, their work depersonalized to specialized functions paid by the hour or piece instead of continuing in the old work cycle of the small farmer or craftsman, their locally limited world shattered by the demands of "horizontal and vertical mobility" that might deposit them and their immediate kin in the metallurgical plant of a new city like Magnitogorsk or a pioneer kolkhoz in Siberia. Their children, too, would no longer follow the traditional family occupations but go far from the hearth to prepare for their careers.

Against such social storms the religious congregation provides a buffer. Its very existence bears witness to the persistence of the community below the surface of the economic plan in which the person figures as a production statistic, perennially short of his output quota. The brotherhood of believers is exemplified around the baptismal font where the infant is accepted into the fold, surrounded by family, godparents, and the remainder of the congregation; Soviet society is typified in the factory or farm brigade where money and honors go to the worker who outperforms his fellows, the Stakhanovite who stands on the shoulders of hundreds of plodders. The sociological terms of the contrast are *Gemeinschaft* and *Gesellschaft*, the status of ascription versus that of achievement or, in a nontechnical formulation, the security of an individual knowing he belongs without question versus his frantic scramble for a place in the competition of society's many markets. In a sense, the Church promises to everyman what the Party does to a relative few, and it casts its spell of kinship without fear of purge or denunciation. It has no niche for the ambitious who would rise in the ranks, if need be over the prone bodies of a rival clique.

The societies of "the chosen" in Church and Party offer some surprisingly similar psychological rewards to their faithful. The members of each, once past initiation rites, are expected to remain for life, departing only "feet first" unless an order from the authoritarian center banishes them for infraction of organizational commandments. Each of the two orders has its scriptures, its canon saints whose relics are revered by pilgrims, and its rogues' gallery of schismatics. In each the primary channel of communication is downward, conveying instructions, whether in pastoral letter or Central Committee directive, that require unquestioning obedience. Both have a ritual of confession followed by acts of penance as a central obligation of their practicing members. Finally, they share, to some degree, a claim for universal dominance—in the "Third Rome" image of the Church and the socialist world headquarters of the Party, as well as in a utopian future held out to believers in compensation for the host of contemporaneous privations.

Naturally, during the Soviet era the scope of the Party has expanded, that of the Church shrunk. The Church has been largely stripped of its educational, charitable, social, and politically influential functions and has held only conditional title to a much reduced inventory of property. The Party, on the other hand, exerts the decisive power in all social institutions—to an extent that has been aptly characterized as akin to a board of directors of the entire country.[6] The status difference between Party and Church thus boils down to an ideological monopoly facing a *lumpenproletariat*. The haves loom over the have-nots. They can kick and scoff at them, threaten them with imminent extinction, snatch what shreds of legitimacy have been left them—better yet, they can occasionally gratify their egos by granting some limited rights to the religious suppliants and garnering odes to their benevolence in return. Although its dogma assures the Party that, in the process of constructing Communism, it will automatically be rid of the spiritually benighted, in the meantime it might even begin to get used to having them around, living examples of an outworn past, for purposes of amusement and of furnishing object lessons in how not to succeed. By the end of the thirties, at least, they had been rendered harmless; at that point they could even be mustered for special menial tasks in support of the system, but any such bargain would clearly be struck between unequal partners: talk of a concordat[7] completely misses the realities of power in a situation matching leviathan with sacrificial lamb.

Whatever truce was achieved was bound to be unstable. An implicit part of the bargain between Party and Church was that the former retained all rights of unilateral abrogation, the latter only a tenuous claim to survival at the sufferance of its masters. The antireligious dogma of the Party was not negotiable, so that a rise in the status of believers was restricted to the minimal. Party members and a scattering of non-members who were ideologically reliable maintain their pre-emptive claim to all leading positions in the administration, professions, and other cadres; the Party elite continues to claim the lion's share of decision-making and supervisory functions throughout society. And Church membership remains incompatible with the occupation of such status according to official standards; conversely, a devout believer still finds the doors to advancement shut unless he can practice his faith sub rosa, with the attendant hazard of being found out eventually.

MARXIST DOGMA AND THE OPIUM HABIT

Karl Marx launched his broadsides against religion in the 1840's; Frederick Engels refined the attack and gave it some sociological underpinnings in the 1870's; Vladimir Ilich Lenin had absorbed their teaching and was adding marginal notes relating them to contemporary conditions in Russia by the 1900's.

Each of the three oracles of Communism pronounced a curse on religion, not simply as an antiscientific doctrine, but specifically as the narcotic used in Machiavellian fashion by the forces of reaction upon their victims to deaden the blows of the exploiters' knout. Christianity celebrated the patient bearing of adversity; what was worse, it made a virtue of turning the other cheek. Behind each capitalist there was a priest spreading unction; they formed, indeed, an unholy alliance draining the proletarian of his willpower as well as of his lifeblood. In order to weld together a revolutionary workers' party, one had to rouse the people from their torpor of piety and not only turn them away from religion, but marshal them to storm the palisades of faith that fortified the citadel of the bourgeoisie.

This theme runs through the writings of all three grand masters of Communism. Marx's opening salvo in 1844 marked the line of attack along which all later polemics would fly: "The struggle against religion is, therefore, indirectly a struggle against *that world* whose spiritual aroma is religion. *Religious* suffering is at the same time an *expression* of real suffering and a *protest* against real suffering. Religion is the sigh of the oppressed creature, the sentiment of a heartless world, and the soul of soulless conditions. It is the *opium* of the people. The abolition of religion as the *illusory* happiness of men is a demand for their *real* happiness."[8] Subsequent forays, whether by him or Engels or Lenin, only elaborated the theme, footnoting it to refer to particular conditions in Germany, France, England, or Russia or to credit its genesis to the French encyclopedists and distinguish it from the cruder deviations of Ludwig Feuerbach and Eugen Dühring. Yet, having unmasked the cleric as an archenemy of the proletariat, all three ideologues surprisingly wasted very little ammunition on him.

Antireligious passages lace enough writings of Marx and Engels for a publisher to have brought them out in book form; likewise for Lenin, but the editors of both volumes had to include quite a bit of incidental material to pad them out.[9] And even then it is clear that neither work harbors a single major essay or a full-dress presentation of critical theory on the subject. Both are beset by a basic logical inconsistency: religion generally induces a harmful narcotic state in the working class, but under extraordinary circumstances in past times and present the cross has been held aloft by revolutionaries. The exceptions—ranging from communistic early Christians to the leaders of the Peasant War in the early sixteenth century, from the Levelers of Cromwellian England to the Christian socialists of present-day Europe and even to a Father Gapon of 1905 Russia—leave the crude tenet in shambles. How can an antiscientific illusion have advanced the cause of progress, a soporific have spurred its victims into action?

Fundamental Marxist theory is aware of the question, yet the answer is wanting. An ambivalent diagnosis of the divine disease—now wholly evil, now mysteriously beneficial—stops the communist doctors to a society of "addicts" from prescribing radical withdrawal. The opium habit, they insist, is not to be stamped out by fiat but to be gradually extinguished when the revolution has created conditions for its replacement by proper socialist habits. Like other forms of exploitation in bourgeois institutions, the church will wither away with the ultimate resolution of the class struggle in the utopia of communism. Marx, Engels, and Lenin, in their writings on religion, reserve their sharpest invective for the crude deviations of materialists like Eugen Dühring whose approach is much more straightforward: a radical remedy, abolition of religion, as a political platform.

Orthodox Marxists, once they have slapped the priest in the face by a calculatedly insulting epithet, seem to hesitate—as if it might be a mistake, after all, to expend too much force on a protagonist armed only with an error-ridden Bible. Their pause also suggests that a general attack would be out of order when the opponent may only have extended his hand in friendship. Behind the banner of religion marches not a lockstep army, but a motley retinue of the disestablished as well: dissenters, schismatics, sectarians, and untouchables like Jews. The revolutionary party of the downtrodden cannot easily stuff all of them into the same sack as followers of the state-sponsored Church. To do so would mean endorsement of the policy of Bismarck's *Kultur-kampf* against German Catholics or the persecutions and pogroms countenanced by the tsar's ministers.

Marx and company end up drawing much finer distinctions in their analysis of religion than do their implacably atheist contemporaries among European socialists. The greater finesse in theory is grounded in tactical requirements. They are obviously aware that their fairly feeble movement could never attract the minions needed to storm the barricades if it drove away all those who clung to their faith as one of a few inviolable treasures. They know they have to forge a party of disparate elements or they may end up with just another philosophical debating club. Here, as in other twists of the Marxist line, the snarls are attributable to programmatic needs.

The Communist Manifesto in 1847–48 charges that "the parson has ever gone hand in hand with the landlord" and discounts any egalitarian movement he may lead. In Marx's and Engels' early phrasing, "Christian socialism is but the holy water with which the priest consecrates the heartburnings of the aristocrat."[10] The nobleman's internal complaints apparently derive from the defeat his feudal class sustained a century before at the hands of "the then revolutionary bourgeoisie." It was the latter class that undermined the claims of established churches with "ideas of religious liberty and freedom of conscience" not in accord with any immutable principle of justice, but with its ethics of the marketplace; that is, it thereby "merely gave expression to the sway of free competition within the domain of knowledge."[11]

Christian socialism is discussed under the heading of "reactionary socialism," since the priest as agent of the aristocrat is presumably trying to reverse the historical clock, to worm his way back to the place of social eminence from which he was toppled by the bourgeoisie. In these efforts he does not play the part of an independent variable in the historical process, but of camp follower to a party in the class struggle. His realm is merely a sector of the superstructure—at that, of one which disintegrated a hundred years before. Marx and Engels can entirely dispense with his anachronistic reappearance on the scene during the euphoric days preceding the 1848 revolutions.

This was also the time when Marx was contributing to a Brussels newspaper a vitriolic column on German conservatism with the following intrasigent catechism:

> The social principles of Christianity justified the slavery of Antiquity, glorified the serfdom of the Middle Ages and equally know, when necessary, how to defend the oppression of the proletariat, although they make a pitiful face over it.
>
> The social principles of Christianity preach the necessity of a ruling and an oppressed class, and all they have for the latter is the pious wish the former will be charitable . . .
>
> The social principles of Christianity declare all vile acts of the oppressors against the oppressed to be either the just punishment of original sin and other sins or trials that the Lord in his infinite wisdom imposes on those redeemed.
>
> The social principles of Christianity preach cowardice, self-contempt, abasement, submission, dejection, in a word all the qualities of the *canaille;* and the proletariat, not wishing to be treated as *canaille*, needs its courage, its self-feeling, its pride and its sense of independence more than its bread.
>
> The social principles of Christianity are sneakish and the proletariat is revolutionary.
>
> So much for the social principles of Christianity.[12]

And, one may add, so much for the self-confidence of 1847.

Two decades of European reaction had followed by the time *Das Kapital* appeared, and neither there nor in other post-1848 writings of Marx or Engels were the strident notes of the early countercrusade heard again. Marx's magnum opus declares that "the religious world is but the reflex of the real world,"[13] a much muted refrain of the old battle cry. The dominant theme had been softened and embellished, calling for variations when touching on different religions in varying social contexts. Marx concluded this passage on religion by calling for a critique of the subject relating it to its materialist substratum, the production process. The evolutionary method developed by Darwin, he suggested, could aptly be applied.

Engels responded to the hint of his mentor a decade later, in 1878, in a polemic against one of the many "vulgarizers and distorters" who by that season had become fair game for the guardians of true communism. "Herr Dühring" is roundly taken to task for spinning Marx's early anticlericalism to its logical conclusion: including in his socialist platform a plan for total abolition of the church. What might have been deemed a virtue thirty years before had by now become a sin—first of ignoring new conditions, especially the anti-Catholic legislation promulgated in Prussia in May 1873. Dühring "out-Bismarcks Bismarck," says Engels, because his proposals would be directed "not merely against Catholicism, but against all religion."[14] Secondly, he has committed the sin of historical misinterpretation and impatience unworthy of a true socialist by provoking action where none is needed. Instead of realizing that iron laws of evolution forecast the automatic extinction of religion once the era of bourgeois exploitation is over, Dühring "cannot wait until religion dies a natural death."

Engels contends that a policy based on such misunderstanding can only backfire. Dühring "sets his gendarmes of the future on religion and thereby gives it a longer lease of life by martyrdom." The implications of the new theological Darwinism are quietist—waiting for the priest to dig his own grave—where the early charge of Marx had been activist. In the process, the garb of the clerical enemy is shown to be no longer all black but an indeterminate shade of gray, depending upon circumstances. Early Christianity displays as a central positive feature a belief in the equality of all men, although according to Engels it degrades that egalitarianism by casting it into a negative form "of an equal taint of original sin." Such a version, naturally suited to the beliefs "of slaves and the oppressed," was relegated to the closet when hierarchical distinctions were established within a church that had achieved legitimacy and begun its persecution of pagans and heretics. The rise of the bourgeoisie, however, brought a resurgence of the demand for equality by the newly disadvantaged class of proletarians that dogged its steps. "This was first made in a religious form and was based upon early Christianity . . . as was particularly the case at first, in the Peasants' War . . ."[15] .

Engels waxes even more eloquent in the praise of folk heroes among the Christian opium addicts in his 1894–1895 essays "On the History of Early Christianity," which open with a surprising note of appreciation:

> The history of early Christianity has notable points of resemblance with the modern working-class movement. Like the latter, Christianity was originally a movement of oppressed people; it first appeared

as the religion of slaves and emancipated slaves, of poor people deprived of all rights, of peoples subjugated or dispersed by Rome. Both Christianity and the workers' socialism preach forthcoming salvation from bondage and misery; Christianity places this salvation in a life beyond, after death, in heaven; socialism places it in this world, in a transformation of society. Both are persecuted and baited, their adherents are despised and made the objects of exclusive laws . . . And in spite of all persecutions, nay, even spurred on by it, they forge victoriously, irresistibly ahead.[16]

To some students of Marxism such qualified appreciation counts for little. They would deprecate it as a temporary tack en route to the unchanged goal of an atheistic society. That kind of analysis, however, relies on circular logic—forcing all data around its foregone conclusion, the inflexibility of Communist doctrine. In quite another area, Soviet foreign policy, it insists on the primacy of the drive for world domination, interpreting coexistence as only a subterfuge for continued imperialist expansion by the Kremlin. It further denies the validity of the Sino-Soviet rift, affirming that not far below the stormy surface the foundations of "the Communist bloc" lie undisturbed. The trouble with such a model of the implacable enemy is not only its dogmatism, rationalizing all data into its closed system, but also in its failure to appreciate the causes and significance of altered Communist policies. In a sense, it depends on reification of doctrine, making it appear to exist independently of those who formulate it and reshape it to conform to new exigencies.

For present purposes, it is helpful to dispense with such a Platonic idea world in interpretations of Communist ideology and instead to focus on the very real sources and effects of programmatic change. Even what is termed a tactical shift or a difference of degree can matter quite a lot when Christian socialists, for example, are approached by the Party as potential collaborators rather than arraigned as class enemies— just as it has mattered whether Moscow sends out trade missions or an order for a renewed blockade of Berlin. For purposes of understanding, possibly predicting, Communist strategy, it is best to dispense with the image of the Marxist mastermind who juggles a variety of disparate programs intent on the ultimate success of his act. If he did exist, for one thing he would be able to point to a much more consistent record of achievements; for another, he would surpass human understanding of his ultra-Machiavellian method.

Marx and Engels are much more comprehensible when reduced to
a scale where doubts, contradictions, and changes of mind are possible
than on the ideal plane where all their words and deeds fall perfectly
into place. The "abolition of religion" that Marx posited in 1844 became
a doctrinal encumbrance in the Europe of the 1870's and could be
relegated to the distant evolutionary future; by the 1890's it had turned
out to be anti-Marxist heresy. At that juncture, Engels decided that
Communists and Christian socialists were marching from similiar starting positions, traveling parallel roads beset by like dangers, heading
for a common destination. The only tangible difference is one of time
scale—whether the goal is attainable in a reasonably immediate future
or not until the afterlife. This distinction bolsters the Communist
claim of priority in having the true key to history, but it poses no
major practical barriers to alliance in the common cause. The two
parties can join without qualm in pulling down the old order, whether
for its capitalist or un-Christian features. History can decide whose
victory the new order represents, that of the revolutionary priest recon-
structing the City of God or that of the commissar in a classless
society that is shedding its outworn dogma as painlessly as an old skin.

So much for the grand stage, as set for either earthly or heavenly
apocalypse. In the more intimate arena of the Party, the issue seems
to have been resolved in favor of dual membership—open enrollment
of Christian applicants. Although the two doctrines are bound to clash
inevitably at an abstract level, in terms of immediate allegiance they
overlap sufficiently to accommodate that anomaly, a Christian Communist. His position is sheltered by the sheathing of the Party's antireligious sword for the time being, the soft-pedaling of its activist atheism
in pursuit of a surpassingly important goal: seizure of power.

LENIN'S PRAGMATISM AND THE CHURCH

The implications of the Marx-Engels dialectic on religion were not
lost on their assiduous student Lenin. His teen-age enthusiasm for the
shocking truths of atheism battened on the mottoes of the early Marx,
as well as on a revolt against the pious habits of his mother and at least
the letter of church law that his father, a tsarist official, was bound to
observe.[17] His tutor to enlightenment seems to have been his older
brother, Alexander, who introduced him to the opium metaphor in the
Marx critique of Hegel. At fifteen, Lenin is reported to have torn
a crucifix from the wall and flung it on the ground in response to an

official's admonition about his failure to attend services. During his high school days in Simbirsk, he is said to have pointed out the Spassky cloister to a friend, with the comment: "That's where people run from life and hide themselves alive! Good, I suppose, for them if they find solace in this prison."[18] A recent biography comments on the flimsiness of such anecdotes, also pointing out that Lenin's own party questionnaire declares him to have retained his religious beliefs until after the age of sixteen.[19]

In any case, after recounting this promising start and adding to it a number of equally pointed anecdotes, Lenin's atheist editor is forced to admit that "the question of war against religion did not occupy a central place in Lenin's opinions."[20] The mature captain of Russian Bolsheviks had recognized that a fight against crucifix or cloister could bog down his phalanx in a skirmish incidental, perhaps detrimental, to the central struggle for power. In 1909 the chronic problems of an undermanned organization forced him to proclaim: "We must not only admit into the Social-Democratic Party all those workers who still retain faith in God, but we must redouble our efforts to recruit them. We are absolutely opposed to the slightest affront to the religious convictions of these workers. We recruit them in order to educate them and not in order to carry on an active struggle against religion."[21] Even a priest could qualify for his Party card as long as "he conscientiously performs party work and does not oppose the party program."

The young Lenin showed a more personal and hysterical recoil from religion than the early Marx or Engels; but the seasoned Russian leader went further in his willingness to compromise with the forces of the church than did his preceptors. By the turn of the nineteenth century, the clerical Communist or fellow traveler was no longer a hypothetical creature. As an émigré, Lenin had learned of such strange phenomena as special Social-Democratic churches in England in which the congregation sang hymns asking God to lead them from the capitalist wilderness to the promised land of socialism as He had led the Jews out of Egypt.[22] Closer to home he knew of the First and Second Dumas, in which small groups of priests defied the Synod by speeches in behalf of the masses and against the government.[23] In 1908 he was ready to concede that behind such freak examples lay a factor of immense significance for a party that would make revolution in a predominantly rural Russia. To the rhetorical question in the Duma, why do village priests "emerge *more* on the side of the peasant than does the bourgeois liberal," he replied that the priest "lives side by side with the peasant, is tied to him by a thousand circumstances, even at times—through the small landholdings they work on church soil—occupies the same hide as the peasantry." He concluded by embracing the priest-deputy Tikhvinski as a "fearless and resolute defender of the interests of the peasantry and the people."[24]

If Bismarck's *Kulturkampf* stole the thunder from the Marx-Engels campaign against religion, the 1905 revolution can be credited with bringing Lenin down from the heights of atheistic theory to the thickets of Russian political reality. Unprepared as he and his party were for that event, he proved able to distill pragmatic lessons from its failures and to make the painful readjustments in tactics that would assure successful exploitation of revolutionary circumstances the next time around. First of all, he had to come to terms with the living example of a priest, Father Gapon, leading the procession which sparked the revolt to the Winter Palace. This was enough to shatter once and for all the Marxist stereotype of the clerical opium peddler deadening the frustrations of the masses. Lenin did not try to laugh away Gapon's action as a historical accident; instead, he interpreted it as part of a new pattern: "the presence of a liberal reformist movement among some parts of the young Russian clergy," with "exponents at the meetings of religious-philosophical societies and in churchly literature. This movement has even acquired its own name—the 'neo-orthodox' movement."[25] From this premise Lenin jumped to the strange speculation that "it is impossible, therefore, to absolutely rule out the thought that Father Gapon may be secretly a Christian socialist."

Unwarranted as Lenin's conclusions about Gapon's organizational affiliations may be, the revised instructions to the Party are substantiated in any case: don't turn away such a strange bedfellow as a revolutionary priest. Further, abandon the dogmatic antireligious attitude that would obviate such curious collaboration. As a consequence of the 1905 revolution, Lenin admonishes, the fight against religion must take a back seat. Disputes in this area, as in the field of national allegiances, must not be allowed to disrupt the unity of the working class: "The unity of the revolutionary struggle of the oppressed class to build paradise on earth is more important for us than the single-minded opinion of the proletariat about paradise in heaven."[26] Only with this revised order of priorities were the Bolsheviks later able to look the other way while an Orthodox *sobor* was re-establishing the patriarchate and ceremoniously installing an arch-conservative in office

—literally a stone's throw away from their own 1917 revolutionary head-quarters in the same Kremlin.

By that time the Party had had a dozen years to absorb the lessons of 1905 that had "made even some natural friends of autocracy, such as some of the clergy, act against it and help burst the bonds of police bureaucracy." Lenin had lauded Bolshevik flexibility in accommodating these potential allies and scoffed at the rigidity of other groups like the anarchists who refused to cooperate with the clergy in any way. The conditions of 1905 disclosed to him more than one flock of the faithful who, rapt in "the striving for new forms of life," were naturally suited to follow the proletarians' vanguard. They included "Christian socialists and Christian democrats, the indignation of 'the heterodox,' sectarians, etc. . . . whether voluntarily or involuntarily, consciously or unconsciously, growing supporters of the revolution, not only daily but hourly."[27] Once he had dropped his early antichurch stand, Lenin was able to exploit the grass-roots dissatisfactions within the established Church itself. Most of Russia's non-Orthodox and many of her Orthodox had long chafed under the repressive conservatism of Synod and Ober Procurator; to the ears of such groups the revolutionary motto of separation of church and state sounded like a cry of liberation, stripped of its overtones implying liquidation of all religious institutions by the time a ruling party would corner the market on legitimacy.

"Religion is the private affair of each citizen" announced the new Soviet decrees of January 1918,[28] echoing the slogan of the Paris Commune. On the face of it the phrase struck a humanist, libertarian note, especially after centuries of state-supported suppressions of heterodoxy. Once the Party had securely installed itself in power, erstwhile clerical allies would discover the more ominous connotations: curt dismissal, with an aside from the dictatorial state that from then on all private affairs would submit to its censorship. Fellow travelers have a notoriously difficult time collecting on services rendered to a party they have helped into the saddle.

Among the factions of the faithful, the stigmatized sectarians held a special appeal for Lenin as prerevolutionary collaborators. To a veteran in the fine art of "splitting," he saw in them a potent weapon for undercutting the autocratic-orthodox establishment. Even at the 1903 Communist party congress he had urged a resolution for propagandizing them. The following year, in Geneva, he braved the scorn of the Mensheviks and particularly Martov in backing a special journal,

Rassvet (Dawn), for sectarian activities.[29] When conditions improved somewhat for the sectarians with the government's tolerance edict resulting from the 1905 revolution, Lenin withdrew support from these unstable factions on the peripheries of power, to initiate a subversion effort aimed at the body of Orthodoxy itself.

Such a new tack was required in the atmosphere of post-1905 liberalism. The hierarchy was becoming directly involved in politics, defending its budgets in the Duma to unheard-of attacks, and trying to discipline the priests who appeared as deputies of newly legalized parties. Communists had to shed old habits from the underground as they entered the new era of political legality; at first some reverted to type by employing the formulas of dogmatism. One was the Social-Democratic deputy P. I. Surkov, who delivered a fiery antichurch oration written by the veteran atheist V. D. Bonch-Bruevich, replete with the outworn slogan "religion is the opium of the people" and the unregenerate battle cry "not a farthing of the people's money to these bloody enemies of the people who darken popular consciousness!"[30] The Mensheviks, led by N. S. Chkheidze, had tried in vain to make Surkov tone down his tirade and censured him for it afterward, noting that silence should have been in order when encountering this subject close to the hearts of the backward peasantry. Lenin, with apparently mixed emotions, made the best of an embarrassing situation by finding some possible value in the speech as a call to popular revolutionary action. It is worthy of note, however, that no other Social-Democratic deputy was allowed to become intoxicated with the heady heights of the Duma rostrum for further antireligious vituperations.

Lenin's uncertainty in handling the Surkov affair stems from his broader difficulties in refurbishing the Party against the new background of legality. The situation required some ill-fitting adornments for the sake of respectability—but definitely not at the expense of losing revolutionary identity. On the one hand, the Party had to be distinguished from Russian liberals like the Kadets, who had surprisingly also come out for civil control of the Orthodox Church budget; and on the other, from the Social Democrats in Western Europe who, in the wake of Bismarck's repressions and French Republican anticlericalism, were showing a disturbing passivity on the religious question.[31] Lenin was searching for a formula that would guide the actions of his party, of direct relevance to such items as whom to admit as member or ally and whom to attack as formidable foe without scattering one's shot or frightening away the masses. Specifically, the posture he sought had to avoid the reformist leanings or in his terms "opportunism" of some West European comrades. The religious line had to weave in some strain of militance, and in the reactionary Russian Church hierarchy Lenin found a convenient target.

Class enemies abounded in bishops like the Moscow Metropolitan Filaret, whom Lenin could castigate with cause for "prostrating himself before the laws of serfdom,"[32] and in the contingent of leading churchmen in the rabidly anti-Semitic "Union of the Russian People," which spouted obscurantist politics when it was not inciting pogroms.[33] Such primeval horrors were alien to Western Europe; so much the better for the revolutionary cause in Russia. And so much of help to Lenin in trying to solve the dilemma posed by Marx: how to create a revolution in this least likely of countries which had not yet witnessed the full emergence of the bourgeoisie. This theoretical drawback could be turned to good account by an adroit ideologue like Lenin. All he had to do was concede the feudal phase of Russian society, compared with the relatively progressive West, to create for his party the trenchant role of fighting oppression which an enfeebled native bourgeoisie could not possibly undertake. In the West, by contrast, Social Democrats slipped naturally into an "opportunism" unthinkable in Russia because there "the revolutionary bourgeoisie" had fulfilled its "historical task . . . its revolt against feudalism and the Middle Ages." Bourgeois atheism could be traced back to the French encyclopedists; it was nothing new by the time the socialists joined the fray, so it robbed them of a pioneering place in the field. They stood mutely critical while anarchists and Blanquists led the "ultraleft" legions. Secondly, Western "opportunism" derived from another circumstance alien to feudal Russia, true freedom of conscience. Thus a possible communist campaign against the reactionary church was "pushed aside by the fight of bourgeois democracy with socialism, in which the bourgeois regime *consciously* tries to turn the attention of the masses from socialism by setting up a quasi-liberal 'campaign' against clericalism."[34]

The Russian Marxists emerge from the Leninist dialectic capable of making the revolution, their opportunistic colleagues of settling for reforms. Their feudal enemies virtually demand the use of ultimate weapons which would be out of place in the more genteel class struggles of France or Germany. Though not spelled out as such, this is clearly the deduction Lenin wants his adherents to draw, as a way to ward off the occasionally overwhelming doubts about nursing their tiny flame into a conflagration amid the morass of their country's backward social conditions and, further, in the face of the prophetic scorn of Karl Marx. In its small way, the church issue yielded a lot of theoretical mileage for Lenin, as evident from the following two key passages. In the first, he begins by analyzing causes for the softness of the West European Marxist stand on religion, attributing it primarily to the bourgeois anticlerical tradition for the past two centuries. But Russia, he notes, can point to no such pattern, nor is one emerging yet "even among the petty-bourgeois democrats (Narodniki)."[35] The task of battling the established Church, he concludes, is left to the working class of Russia, which, unlike that of the West, must in this sector lead the "bourgeois-democratic revolution" that will sweep away the institutions of feudalism. The "opportunists" in the Party are chided for advocating passivity in the antireligious fight modeled on that of the Western workers; the proper attitude is active involvement, though with all necessary caveats against extremism that might alienate the devout masses.

In the second passage, Lenin develops his characterization of the Russian bourgeoisie. Unlike that of the West, it evinces none of the hostility to the Church that makes an anticlerical effort by communist parties there somewhat redundant. Instead, it is trying to modernize religious practices, implicitly a grave threat to the Party's militance, since a successfully liberalized institution would no longer be the feudal bogey which the reactionary hierarchy conveniently furnishes for Lenin's rhetoric.

> Representatives of the counterrevolutionary bourgeoisie want to strengthen religion, to increase the influence of religion on the masses, feeling the inadequacy, obsolescence, even harm brought on by ruling classes of "officials in cassocks" who *diminish* the authority of the churches. The Octobrists fight against the extremes of clericalism and police surveillers in order *to strengthen* the influence of religion on the masses, to replace at least some means of stupefying the people—the too crude, too obsolete, too dilapidated, unrealizable aims—by more subtle, improved means. A police-run religion isn't adequate for stupefying the masses; give us a religion that's more culture, renovated, cleverer—that's what capital is demanding from the autocracy.

Where Western Marxists might be tempted to settle for reform, the Russian comrades must stop their ears to the siren song which could cause the foundering of their whole revolutionary movement. Lenin is ever concerned with looking after his Party's élan. Thus, Bolsheviks might indeed make common cause with bourgeois anticlericals, but solely for the sake of expedience: "If our general task consists in helping the proletariat to rally as a separate class, able to cut itself off from bourgeois democracy, then part of this task must be the exploitation of all means of propaganda and agitation, which include the Duma's forum, in order to make clear to the masses the distinction between socialist anticlericalism and bourgeois anticlericalism."[36]

In this perspective, Lenin's leniency to Surkov's atheist indiscretions becomes understandable. An isolated display of fireworks could be tolerated; by itself it could do little to further convince the masses that the Bolsheviks were tools of the devil. However, it carried a potent shock for the bourgeois advocates of secularization, keeping them at a respectful distance from Marxist spokesmen who had shown that it was they who called the dialectical tune. It was equally disconcerting for the bourgeois would-be reformers of the Church who saw their compromise position undermined between the two extremes: if a virulent antichurch attack by Surkov seemed to play into the hands of the reactionary hierarchs, relative to their liberal critics, so much the better in terms of the Leninist dialectic. An unregenerate Synod, allied with tsarist autocracy, was a lot easier for the Party to exploit as a target for popular resentment than a liberalized, Westernized church council would have been. The dialectic was predicated on both elements of the Russian religious situation, obscurantist church leadership and frustrated masses of followers, to furnish the explosive mixture that a revolutionary spark might ignite.

Lenin reveals an awareness of both factors beneath the surface of what seems to be his ambivalence toward religion. At one point he uses the early Marx as his text, to blast religion as a "kind of spiritual moonshine in which the slaves of capital drown their human form, their demands for a somehow unique human life."[37] The escape from reality comes dear to "those who work and are in need their whole lives, taught humility and patience during their earthly existence by religion, comforting them with hopes for a heavenly reward. And too, by teaching those living on another's labor to be philanthropic in their earthly existence, providing a very cheap acquittal for all their exploiting life and selling at bargain rates tickets for heavenly well-being." Small wonder, then, that on such a faith we find a citadel of reaction, that the "landowners and merchants . . . are enraptured with how well the little fathers comfort and pacify the muzhiks,"[38] or that secret police Colonel Zubatov in 1901 would scheme to subvert revolutionary organizations by infiltrating them with clerical agents " 'to help' the workers escape the influence of socialist teachings!—but also, however, to help snare unwary workers who snap up the bait."[39]

Yet, in what appears a totally different vein, Lenin relies on late Engels to praise the "democratic-revolutionary" spirit of the early Christians, taking this as evidence that at certain historical periods religion could propagate revolutionary ideas.[40] Even the Orthodox clergy might "awake now to the thunder of the old, medieval order in Russia," and the ordinary priest "who is called 'a servant of God' might join the demand for freedom and protest against red tape and official arbitrariness, against police spies."[41] The Party's red carpet is thus rolled out for the anti-establishment clergy, which is ready to transpose the class struggle to the confines of the Church. And Engels is again vindicated when Lenin charts his party's course of action on religion.

He insists on steering a safe middle passage between the "anarchism" of all-out war against the Church and the "opportunism" of inaction, or a strict laissez-faire attitude to religion. The former seems to be the greater danger in his eyes, as well it might in a country where the bulk of the population still proclaimed their loyalty to the ancestral faith. It is this setting which makes understandable Lenin's endorsement of the moderate stand of Engels on two issues: first, against the atheistic slogans of the 1874 Blanquists, whose misplaced zeal promised to fortify rather than to banish religion because it would produce martyrs around whom the faithful masses would rally; second, against the obdurate Dühring, who, in effect, would have the socialists do Bismarck's dirty work for him, oblivious of the fact that such measures only ended by strengthening the militant clericalism of the church under fire. If a major campaign against the church in France or Germany was likely to boomerang, how much more certain that such a policy would be suicidal in a less enlightened country like Russia, with its unbroken tradition of an established faith. The "war against religion" motto, Lenin concludes, must be shunned as an "anarchist phrase." The revolutionary Party had to resist the temptations of such adventurous politics, relying instead on the laborious education of the proletariat, which, together with liquidation of the exploiters who represented the social roots of religion, would eventually lead to the "dying away of religion."[42]

SOVIET REGIME VERSUS ORTHODOX CHURCH

In a typical anecdote, Lenin is pictured addressing a crowd from Kshesinskaya's balcony in the turbulent summer days of 1917. Suddenly a heckler's voice rings out, "but do you believe in God, anti-Christ?"

Lenin answers mockingly: "Fear God, revere the tsar—isn't that how it goes, *batyushka?* But I don't revere the tsar, nor do I fear God! Listen, *tovarishch,* and I'll tell you why I don't believe . . ." And with a few well-chosen phrases, Lenin vindicates the simple tenets of atheism, causing his audience to howl with laughter as his simple-minded adversary scuttles away in embarrassment. The assembled workers are heard muttering to themselves: "The tsar and God—they're birds of a feather. Both are out to fleece and to enslave us. Down with the religious fraud!"[43]

Apocryphal as they probably are, such stories illustrate two facets of Marxist ideology that are mirrored in Soviet policy toward the Church: cleverness and naiveté. In its Leninist refinement, the theory was sophisticated enough to account for liberal as well as reactionary religious forces and to develop a rationale for exploiting the former, steering clear of the crude atheism of the ultras. At the same time, the communist prophets erred decisively in their forecasts of the withering away of religion once their forces had seized power, as they also misjudged other institutions like the family or the state when it came to their supposedly automatic demise under socialism. Even a few hortatory words of the genius Lenin did not provide the extra push to send religion flying into the evolutionary scrap heap. Obviously, the fault lay in equating the Church with the oppressors' side of the class struggle. Yet it took the Soviet regime nearly twenty-five years to admit the oversimplification inherent in its outlook on religion.

Before the cold dawn of the 1943 reassessment by the Kremlin in which it finally arrived at a modus vivendi with the Church, it conducted a protracted engagement with the forces of religion to make its prophecy of their extinction come true. In some phases of the campaign, the Soviet rulers seemed to accept Leninist ground rules: differentiating between progressive and die-hard factions in the Church, saving their fire for the latter, avoiding an official all-out war and the blows on popular sensibilities that might redound to the benefit of a martyred Church, yet always keeping an activist stance—backing some church groups while checking others—rather than merely turning their backs on the religious sector. When these tactics achieved notably little success, the men in the Kremlin suspended the rules. In their haste to make the historically inevitable transpire within the near future, they at times launched antireligious crusades under the banner of blatant atheism and seemed purposely to confuse the withering of religion with the liquidation of the religious, as evidenced by shuttered churches, jailed priests, and persecuted believers.

A survey of the extensive accounts of Soviet religious policy and practice suggests that these diverse tactics do not form random episodes of
foray and retrenchment. Rather, they follow a distinct pattern spanning
the 1917–1939 period if the following three determinants are hypothesized as having guided Soviet decision-makers. (1) Soviet policy stead-
fastly upholds the ideal of an atheist society, whether to be attained by
foul means or fair, whether in the proximate or the distant future. This
tenet of the communist faith is above question, and it makes any truce
with the Church perforce unstable. The true communist society can be
realized only by a major human transformation, and "the new Soviet
man" can never exhibit such a vital weakness as belief in God. (2) The
antireligious struggle must not preoccupy the Party or distract its
energies from more important engagements. Thus, the godless state can
never be an objective of the first order. This secondary ranking has two
practical consequences for the atheist drive: it can be conducted only
when there are no primary national problems pressing for resolution, and
it has to be put on ice in times of general mobilization or crisis.
(3) Soviet attacks on the Church fall naturally into a cyclical pattern.
We can discern three rounds of battle followed by periods of relative
quiet.[44] At each successive round, the regime steps up the attack against
a progressively exhausted opponent, adds new weapons as it sharpens
the old, closes in from general economic and legal strictures on the
Church to individual jailings and executions of churchmen.

In abstract form, Soviet policy-makers appear to have been tracing
out a sine curve from an origin representing a religious society to a goal
standing for the irreligious state of the future.[45] The oscillations of the
curve swing more widely—surprisingly ending on the downbeat, or relative accord with the Church, rather than on the parapets of the objective
that seemed about to be scaled. A striking feature of the pattern is that
the cycle of antireligious policy describes phases almost directly counter
to those of political crisis. While the latter is touching the nodes of
civil war or the advent of World War II, the assault on the Church shifts
into lower gear. When the crises have been surmounted the anticlerical
attack is stepped up. Only during the regime's onslaught against private
farming does an overlap occur between the targets of churchman and
"kulak" (in effect, any opponent of collectivization); but, then, in the
massacre on the countryside of 1929 the two are hard to tell apart.

In practical terms, Soviet rulers can be viewed as too preoccupied at
generally critical times with what they consider more formidable foes—
White Guard and foreign interventionists, the Germans threatening from

the west—to bother with a clerical adversary. He can be picked off at leisure. His powers of active resistance, puny enough to start with, have been fading fast with each passing round. Once he has ended up on the ropes, it seems pointless for the regime to deliver the knockout punch and much more profitable to assign him some pressing new chores: having him pacify the Orthodox populations of the territories seized in the wake of the Nazi-Soviet pact or letting him do his bit for the war effort, for example.

Such an interpretive model helps put the discrete phases of the policy into perspective. Each fresh tack of the regime—a wave of new repressions, or some special dispensations to the Church—cannot simply be taken at face value as sign of deviation from the basic objective, the withering away of religion in the long term. Conversely, a retreat by the regime, no matter how tenuously staged, cannot be written off as without effect here, as in any other social sphere. The institutions of Soviet society are closely inter-related. Once the rulers have given a respite to the Church, other elements are likely to veer closer to it, lending their weight to a permanent extension of the truce and making it that much harder to resume hostilities later on.[46] Also, the Church itself does not merely lie prone during the intervals but uses them to recoup what strength it can as its leaders grow more adept at using certain techniques to ensure survival. By the time the third round of the conflict was over, they had proved chastened but apt pupils of Soviet conditioning; nearly the entire set of their initial responses to the regime had been discarded in favor of a new range of pliant reactions necessary to seizing the chance at final rapprochement.

ROUND ONE

The revolutionary year 1917 saw the long-delayed convocation of a general council, or *sobor,* of the Russian Orthodox Church that was initially dominated by the liberals who had been pressing for it over one decade. At their first meeting on August 15 at Uspenski Cathedral in the Kremlin, the assembled churchmen postponed parochial business to meet the political challenge already posed by secularization measures of the Kerensky government, especially its nationalization of some thirty-seven thousand parochial schools (one-third of the country's total) and its making religious education in the public schools optional rather than compulsory.[47] The Bolshevik revolution in November tipped the sobor's balance in favor of the clerical conservatives, able to roll up a 141–112 majority in favor of re-establishing one-man rule of the Church in the person of a patriarch who might be better able to face up to the dreaded new regime than would a collegial synod. The dark-horse choice for this post, Tikhon, was installed in a magnificent Kremlin ceremony.

The Moscow Soviet lent its specific permission to this ceremony, maintaining the benevolent neutrality which had been its strict policy toward the uniformly hostile clerics from the outset. Lenin proceeded warily indeed against a church that "until the end" had "remained fettered to a state controlled by a tottering government."[48] Even the three decrees issued by his Petrograd regime in December did little more than confirm the status quo: church and monastery holdings were included in the lands to be nationalized, but this only legalized for the most part the seizures peasants had already conducted on their own;[49] a takeover of church schools merely confirmed the previous actions of the Provisional Government; secularization of birth, death, and marriage registrations remained a dead letter as long as the new regime lacked personnel to open its registry offices. Tikhon hardly required such provocation to pronounce terrible anathema on the Bolsheviks on January 19, 1918, in a message that told Russia's over one hundred million believers: "I adjure all of you who are faithful children of the Orthodox Church of Christ, not to commune with such outcasts of the human race in any manner whatsoever."[50] His rallying call to laity and clergy to defend their church to the point of accepting martyrdom for her sake if necessary was a scarcely veiled call to an anti-Communist crusade. That, except for scattered local incidents, the battle cry of the Patriarch produced no bloodbaths is as much a tribute to Lenin's middle-course tactics as it is an admission of the eroded contacts the Church had with its communicants.

The new Soviet power began a three-pronged counterattack on the Church striving to deprive the institution of its economic base and social status as well as clashing openly with it ideologically, four days after Tikhon's proclamation. (1) The first of its paper bullets was meant to destroy the material and legal basis for organized religion. A decree released January 23, 1918, announcing the separation of church and state and church and school, nationalized all church property. Monasteries were to be broken up and the Church deprived of its legal status as a juridical person eligible for government subsidies. (2) Next, the regime undercut the status of priests to drive them into other occupations and discourage further aspirants to the priesthood; according to the Constitution promulgated on July 10, 1918, they were nonworkers and servants of the bourgeoisie. They were denied the franchise, with a concomitant loss of ration privileges and education rights for their children. Active laymen came under the same ban. (3) Finally, the state moved against the social influence of the Church, especially in the field of education. The 1918 Constitution's famed Article 13 provided illusory equality of free religious and antireligious propaganda. But the protagonists of this handicapped rivalry were to be a church shorn of its material base and a state carrying the loaded punch of a Communist party with a monopoly on political legitimacy. "Actually the formula in the new Constitution was a declaration of war against religion."[51] Religious instruction of children under eighteen was prohibited altogether, that of adults restricted to seminaries of rapidly dwindling number.

These measures indicate Lenin's awareness that oratorical mockery would no longer suffice to blunt the lance of the Patriarch's crusade. Yet the alternate weapon, governmental decrees that could not be enforced through the Civil War years, scarcely served to join the issue. The Patriarch still claimed the initiative as he led protest processions through the streets of Moscow, denounced the decrees and in their turn the Brest-Litovsk treaty and the murder of the Tsar, called for general resistance to deal with sporadic and uncoordinated (by most accounts) harm to priests or church buildings by Red forces, lent his tacit approval to churchmen blessing weapons of the White Guards, and surrounded himself with a round-the-clock bodyguard to await his martyrdom. The governments' devastating response was to ignore his challenge.

The abortive crusade collapsed for lack of cause as no injuries came to Patriarch or the sobor, whose proceedings petered out in September 1918 with empty threats of excommunication against all persons participating in the "blasphemous" seizures of the "property of God." The major immediate damage the regime had inflicted on the Church was measured in rubles and desyatines of land, not in personal casualties. And Lenin's carefully calculated tactic paid off, as "confiscation of the church's land and investments did not arouse the masses to fighting pitch."[52] Tikhon took stock of his losing position and in 1919 called on his clergy to abstain henceforth from political activities—an appeal that was generally heeded.[53]

Having come out victorious in the initial showdown with the forces of religion, the political leadership that had staved off foreign and domestic attack successfully in the Civil War decided, with more vital affairs now out of the way, to step up the pace of its anti-Church campaign. This thrust significantly coincided with the advent of the New

Economic Policy, Lenin's "holiday" for state activities on other fronts. In marked contrast to the regime's retreat to the "commanding heights" of industry and trade, ideological warfare was accelerated. A somewhat chastened Church let itself be provoked into abandoning caution to furnish the precipitating cause of the new clash. It rushed to resist a decree of February 16, 1922, ordering the surrender of all precious metals and jewelry to the state on the fairly specious grounds that they were needed to be turned into relief funds for the sufferers of the 1921–1922 famine. Again the call for resistance by the Patriarch was predicated on the defense of property—this time an assortment of consecrated utensils—and once more it was foredoomed. "The State was able to mobilize vast public resentment against the Church, which found itself in the uncomfortable position of apparently condemning millions of innocents to a cruel death by starvation merely for the sake of a few ancient rules."[54]

Lenin brought the full force of the state's repressive machinery to bear on his discredited, outmaneuvered opponent. Tikhon himself was arrested in May 1922 and eighty-four bishops and over a thousand priests were forced out of office.[55] In the ensuing series of trials of traditional churchmen, Metropolitan Benjamin of Petrograd was condemned to death and it seemed that the same fate might be in store for the Patriarch. Not content with this frontal attack, Lenin also lent his support to a major flanking movement—a faction known as the "Living Church," which advocated a program of Orthodox "renovation" including eligibility of married priests for high office and the recasting of the service in the vernacular, as well as ardent collaboration with communism.[56] The splitters went so far under government auspices as to hold a rump sobor in Moscow in April 1923 that stripped Tikhon of all clerical office and made one of its leaders, Bishop Antonin, "Metropolitan of Moscow and all Russia."[57] What the regime could not storm by direct assault it evidently hoped to capture by means of this Trojan horse.

With the battle all but over at this early stage and tickets being distributed for the forthcoming trial of Tikhon, the government abruptly rang the bell and released him on June 25.[58] His price was a "confession" carried two days later in *Izvestiya* that acknowledged his past political opposition and promised to desist from it henceforth. No doubt the regime put great value on this document as evidence that could discredit church leadership in the eyes of the populace; further, it did not hesitate to pull the rug out from under the Living Churchmen, who had been singularly unsuccessful in winning over a sizable fraction of the faithful; finally, it found expedience in yielding to mounting protests from abroad over the anticlerical purge, which had begun to claim Roman Catholic victims and was causing Britain to threaten withdrawal of her trade mission to the Soviet Union. In any case, the weight of the extorted confession was over-rated, as shown by the immense crowds that flocked to Tikhon's first services after his release and, more important, by the ease with which he voided the acts of the Living Church and reclaimed his organizational primacy.

ROUND TWO

By its sudden cessation of direct conflict with the Church in the summer of 1923, the Politburo acting in stead of the stricken Lenin tacitly conceded that the social roots of religion ran deeper than one might have assumed for a capitalist dope habit. Nevertheless, if they could not be yanked out summarily in one giant effort, the regime still did not have to stand by idly until the distant day when they would wither away by themselves. The period of armed truce with the Church in which the latter had been grudgingly recognized as a bargaining partner could be useful to the regime in continuing to erode the Church's supports and prevent recovery of its lost strength. This extension of its lease on life was clearly meant to be conditional and temporary, and to have no renewal clause.

Among the old harassments that were kept up now was censorship of sermons (instituted December 26, 1922), adherence to a new calendar on which church holidays became working days (July 30, 1923), and a ban on religious instruction even in the churches (June 16, 1924). Material support of the churches was further whittled away by raising taxes on their remaining land and imposing compulsory insurance on their property with the state as beneficiary. The government's decision-makers in the field of church affairs also did their utmost to spread and perpetuate the confusion besetting the hierarchy after the death of Tikhon in 1925.[59] His would-be successor, Sergius, had to defend a second-hand claim: Tikhon had appointed three other bishops to succeed him as locum tenentes and, when they had been sidelined by exile and imprisonment, the number three deputy had in turn named three others.[60] Sergius, last on that list, had to contend with the other five, who could be freed at any moment to assert their precedence, as well as with the leaders of leftist and rightist factions endemically threatening to split the Church over his moderate policies.

The basic terms of the 1923 truce seem still to have been in force in 1926, however, even when Sergius was arrested at the beginning of the year along with many of his clerical supporters.[61] Tenuous as it had become, the Church knew that the short-term lease on its existence had not run out, that its rights to some sort of a bargaining position were still admitted by the Kremlin, where Stalin was now engrossed in liquidating his combined foes. On his release, Sergius evidently thought he had secured validation of his own claim and that of the Church administration to legitimacy at a price no greater than had been paid by Tikhon: a guarantee of political neutrality to the regime.[62] The political supervisors appear to have had second thoughts about their end of the deal—by December Sergius was back in jail and the secret police were putting virtually his whole ecclesiastical contingent behind bars. When he was unexpectedly freed once more on March 30, 1927, he was ready to go the whole way in paying political tribute to the regime in return for its toleration of his administration. By June 14 he was castigating the émigré group of Russian clerics in Yugoslavia who constituted the monarchist Karlovtsi Synod; by July 29, he went whole hog in political submission with a "Declaration" that called on the Church "to recognize the Soviet Union as our civil fatherland whose joys and successes are our joys and successes and whose misfortunes are our misfortunes."[63]

As his quid pro quo, Sergius pointed to a new central administration, a "temporary Holy Synod," he had been allowed to set up two months before, as well as calling for a second sobor to complete his reorganization—although the regime would block its actual convocation for another sixteen years. All blame for delay in securing official recognition of the Church was placed on the conveniently available émigré clergy, thus neatly absolving the Soviets of any antireligious misdeeds and propagating the fiction, nurtured ever since by the Patriarchate's pronouncements, that there has never been such a thing as religious persecution in the Soviet Union. A vital but unwritten part of the deal legitimizing the Sergius-led Church revealed itself in the fate that befell the stunned critics of his declaration, who were speedily silenced by the GPU.[64]

The regime's 1927 skirmish with the Church and the resultant truce, with its benefits for both parties—a clergy politically submissive to the state but headed by a duly legitimated directorate—promised an extended era of coexistence. Yet, only a year later this battlefield became just a secondary sector of the full-scale offensive in the countryside mounted by Stalin,[65] with the twin objectives of outflanking the rightist opposition and herding millions of recalcitrant peasants into collective farms in order to squeeze from them the capital for massive industrialization. The Five Year Plan promulgated in 1928 amounted to programmed civil war. Not unexpectedly, antireligious action was included among the targets for the Plan's "cultural front."[66] The prosperous peasant whose third cow now earned him the title of kulak and thereby his "elimination as a class" was also invariably a pillar of his local congregation.[67] His liquidation by the agents of rural terror also necessarily robbed the Church of its entire local leadership. Some fourteen hundred shuttered churches and uncounted numbers of executed priests bore witness to the 1929 bloodbath which even a hierarchy protected by oaths of loyalty to the state was powerless to stem.[68]

The three-pronged assault on organized religion subjected its victims to cultural and economic isolation, loss of social status, and ideological attack in the following ways. (1) Removal of any cultural services that had remained under Church auspices: a decree of April 8, 1929, barred all social and cultural activities of churches apart from bare services. The constitutional liberty of religious propaganda was annulled by an amendment on May 22, 1929, which provided only "freedom of religious worship and of antireligious propaganda." In autumn 1929 the major trade unions announced that they would have no contact with the Church. Deserted by printers, transport workers, and post and telegraph employees, the Church was plunged into social isolation. On December 27, 1932, priests were forbidden to live in cities and, consequently, urban services became a rarity. (2) Extension of social inferiority to all active lay members of the Church: as opprobrium became automatically attached to church affiliation, overt believers found themselves barred from any administrative, professional, or industrial careers. (3) A switch around 1929 from a-religious to actively antireligious teachings in Soviet schools: a League of Militant Atheists was overfulfilling its own Five Year Plans with a claimed membership of five and a half million by 1937.

Nonetheless, when the dust cleared in the early thirties, the regime once again let its adversary be saved by the bell. It sheathed nearly all weapons of direct attack, although restrictions on cultural activities lingered until the full suspension of hostilities with the Church, which took place from 1934 to 1937. One factor that caused the dampening of open warfare was the mounting foreign protest from Catholic as well as Protestant quarters. An even more efficacious pressure arose once the state had crushed resistance to the collectivization program "when religious leaders often became foci of opposition."[69] Afterward the regime had grounds for coming to terms with the Church, an opponent formidable in the countryside but now neutralized. The tempestuous agricultural episode had subsided, so the Party could well afford to grant the battered Church a temporary respite which would also assuage the feelings of the populace, still raw from the collectivization era's sufferings.

The regime extended this religious truce in the nature of a sop to the people in the "general holiday" proclaimed by Stalin after the domestic successes of 1935.[70] Further, it fitted in nicely with the stabilization of social relations then evident along the broad range of Soviet institutions.[71] Instead of exhausting itself in more all-out attempts to remold social patterns, the Soviet leadership, husbanding its energies for the sustained haul needed to operate a planned economy, now turned to the basic institutions for support. True, the decision-makers tended to view the Church less as a permanent institution than as an ephemeral disturbing feature. To that extent, they would not strengthen it in the sense that they reinforced basic institutions like the family. Yet, provisional benefits could let it linger quietly on the sidelines while essential institutions were being buttressed.

Visions of the withering away of the state, of law, or of the family could be discreetly tucked back into the Marxist hope chest when Stalin found it served his basic aim, "turning the Party into the nation, and the nation into the Party."[72] The withering away of religion, however, was an ideal not so easily put in mothballs. During a period when the Party was attempting to enthrone rationalism at the head of its order of social values, it could brook no claims from ideological pretenders. The doctrine which claimed to submit all phenomena to scientific analysis was incompatible with any faith but a faith in its own infallibility.

Isolated church leaders may envisage an eventual fusion of communism and Orthodoxy. The village priest and his flock might be forced to bow to both, but as manifestations of two disparate realms. The fact that the perfect being of Marx's utopia displayed features not markedly different from those of the ideal Christian would still not reconcile most believers to the realities of Stalinist Russia. Nor did it really alter the regime's dogma of skepticism during the mid-thirties truce. It may, however, have subsequently induced Stalin to see in religion a force for the uplifting of morals, which could be geared into his drive for legality and stability based on "socialist morality." To persons of less political sophistication than the Party elite such concepts as sacred "socialist property" carried less weight than the simple commandments of their priests.

ROUND THREE

The last prewar Soviet onslaught on the Church spanned the years 1937–1939. Shortly before, the 1936 "Stalin Constitution" had lifted the disfranchisement previously imposed on priests as on other "nonworkers." It had also equalized the peasant franchise with the more reliable urban vote. Then, from the suppressed results of the 1937 census, Soviet leaders were appalled to learn that about two-thirds of the village population and one-third of city residents (roughly a total of half of all citizens) still considered themselves adherents of the various churches.[73] With elections to the Supreme Soviet in the offing, the regime sparked a new outburst against religion to keep the churches from influencing the vote. In general, the leadership judged the situation propitious for finally liquidating this endemic focus of opposition and persistent rival for popular allegiance.

The greatest intensity of the new antireligious assault coincided, too, with the all-engulfing purge directed by N. I. Yezhov. Both campaigns showed a like desire of the regime to annihilate once and for all every element of possible internal disloyalty, prerequisite to the tightening of defenses against threats looming from abroad. It is notable that in the case of the church leaders, as in indictments of other groups that fell under the shadow of the *Yezhovshchina,* the purgers linked charges of spying and wrecking of the defense effort to less tangible sins related to the status of the accused as generally undesirable elements in the state. The series of trials during 1937 and 1938 charged churchmen with German and Japanese sabotage and espionage, amid a host of other, equally fantastic charges.[74] During the phase of economic construction, the regime had been content with sidelining ideologically impure elements, encysting them socially; on this day of total mobilization, however, nothing less than one hundred percent loyalty was the standard for permission to exist. Generals, engineers, and other personages instrumental in the establishment of Soviet power were joined in the dock by churchmen who had contributed little beyond extorted oaths of fealty. When Old Bolsheviks in high government posts, and tsarist officers for decades the backbone of the Red Army, went the way of all counterrevolutionary flesh, the purge of the priests came as no great surprise.

The regime still was at a loss about how to deal with the immense number of believers, probably under-rated by the 1937 census, since many citizens had refused to answer the religion question. Rather than provoke them into rebellion by violent repressions, the regime preferred to frighten them into submissiveness through the pointed example of the purge trials. It even added to its image of tolerance at the grass-roots level of religion by issuing bans on direct interference with public worship and on the campaigns of overzealous local Party chieftains shutting down churches in their domains. The body of the faithful was still too extensive for a mass purge. The political leaders could keep it immobilized with their network of controls; as long as the decimated hierarchy was suitable intimidated, the Church was unlikely to have the energy of resources for a fusion with anti-Soviet groups.

The regime's insistence during this period that the Church purge itself of any remaining political affiliations was a necessary prelude to the policy of aligning the "cleansed" institution on the Soviet side at the next juncture. That "New Religious Policy," as Timasheff calls it, was launched right after Yezhov, ringleader of the latest purge, had been removed. Because it did not get fully under way until 1941 and was propelled largely by reaction against the threat of a Nazi "crusade," its consideration is reserved for the concluding chapter.

2

Soviet Believers on the Eve of the War

In their prewar approach to the religious question, Soviet policy-makers called a number of strategic retreats, during which they dispensed concessions to the Church, before resuming the march to a goal they never lost sight of: eventual extirpation of all religious sentiment. The onset of each deviation from the route of direct attack upon the Church came as a surprise to foreign observers, who tended to interpret it as an admission by the Politburo that it was encountering resistance. My analysis of prewar Soviet church policy suggests the contrary conclusion. The men in the Kremlin suspended repressive measures either when a church truce might help advance a new general objective, such as the establishment of foreign trade relations in the early twenties or the consolidation of social controls in the middle thirties, or when a political emergency like the Civil War or mobilization for World War II drew their fire from the church problem. At such times the regime let up in its antireligious attacks, only to resume them under more propitious circumstances.

Whatever concessions were granted the Church prior to World War II, they were little more than straws to clutch at. The regime yielded nothing in the implacability of its atheism. It gave no ground for hope that doles parceled out to believers betokened anything more than the largesse of a Party that felt so secure against Church resurgence that it could afford to be generous to a condemned victim. In this sense its tactics do not constitute retreats, since none was extorted by actual or potential threat from the Church. They can be viewed as retreats only in that the government could not afford to permanently alienate the bulk of its subjects.

At critical times, when major sectors of the Church allied themselves with anti-Soviet forces such as the Whites or the kulaks, they met the same withering fire as all "counter-revolutionaries." The Church enjoyed a breathing spell only when it appeared no longer capable of resuming open resistance, as in the mid-thirties. In the collectivization era, despite protestations of loyalty from the central hierarchy, priests shared the sufferings of peasant parishioners under the brutal excesses that marked the government drive.[1] Their relief came in sight only later, when the regime tried to recoup its losses of public allegiance. The next crest in religious repressions coincided with a turbulent era of Soviet history, the Great Purge, when the Church was again suspect of becoming a focus of resentment. Thus, the New Religious Policy that began to stir in 1939 represents a unique coincidence of national danger and government toleration. It came none too soon.

THE LIMITS OF ENDURING FAITH

Having encountered government attack at any moment for cohesion and united action (and Soviet dispensations when the moment had gone and the Church was obliged to sing praises to the state for such meager rights as the issuance of wedding rings), the Russian Orthodox faithful were demoralized by the end of the 1937–1939 purge. An uncounted number, whose spirits were not yet crushed, practiced their faith sub rosa in what came to be known as the "catacomb church." With cells of believers in collective farms or apartment houses shepherded by a priest who emerged from retirement or from a more mundane daytime job for the occasion, such a religious underground followed the organizational lines of the prerevolutionary Party. Its aim, however, was not to seize power, but merely to keep the guttering candle of faith from being extinguished altogether.[2]

If Soviet policy had not undergone its final démarche toward religious coexistence, there is a likelihood that virtually all believers could have been forced to give up public practice of their religion. With the rise of a new Communist-indoctrinated generation, the number of Russians who would brave the perils of clandestine worship might also have dwindled to insignificance. Harvard Russian Research Center interviews of some three hundred Soviet refugees who made their way to West Germany during the war reveal the limits of endurance of religious faith.[3] Because of the anti-Communist bias of this sample, the group cannot be taken as representative of the general population; but in the absence of any reliable measure of Soviet public opinion, the qualitative validity of the responses makes them a unique source of insight into some aspects of life in the USSR. Use of the Harvard interviews is dictated by lack of any other sizable sample as well as by indications that there was minimal distortion on cultural data, compared with political or social items, in the "life history" protocols.

The younger members of the group generally stumbled over the negative status of keeping the faith. Their teachers and members of their peer groups had brought home to them the rule that religious affiliation would blight their careers.[4] Only a few claim they did not take the consequences. One young man recounts: "Until I entered the Pioneers, I was a believer. I knew my prayers and I went to church regularly with my grandmother. But after a couple of years in the Pioneers and in school, I was a complete atheist." He goes on to describe his conflict with family patterns when he entered the next oldest group of Communist youth, the Komsomols. "My mother was a believer. I once told her to take down the icon which she kept hanging over her bed because it was awkward for my friends to see it."[5]

Another typical case shows what happened when a devout mother would not accede to her son's pleas to save him from the opprobrium of his colleagues, for whom the mere presence of a religious symbol was de facto evidence of hostile propaganda. Soon after his friends have spotted the icon this mother kept on the wall, "at a Komsomol meeting the secretary declared that there was one member present who had in his home an icon on the wall, that he hoped it would not happen in the future. I felt wounded by the remark and was obliged to answer it. I told them I could not separate myself from my family. The next day the director of the school called me into his office and warned me that I was spreading a dangerous form of religious propaganda among the students. 'It will spoil your future,' he said."[6] The blocked-off mobility that awaited young believers proved one of the most potent means by which the regime tarnished the prestige of the Church.

Those who openly practiced their religion were, by the regime's criteria in the thirties, going beyond disrespect to the prevailing ideology. They were slipping backward, flying in the face of the ethos of progress, denying by their example the validity of economic and social gain as a motivational spring. In Alfred Meyer's opinion, the Orthodox mentality clashed down the line with civic responsibilities required by the regime's program of rapid industrialization.

For one thing, religious practices interfere with daily work. Religious holidays constitute a disruption of the citizens' duties. Fasting weakens their efficiency. Religious prayers mean time out from work . . . Religious food taboos and other dietary practices interfere with the regime's food distribution system; any special consideration given to religious believers thus threatens the efficiency of the political and economic bureaucracy . . . Religious law may come into conflict with Soviet law, and must therefore be outlawed. Religious education is opposed to Soviet education. Religious organizations dealing with any problems of secular life compete with bureaucratic agencies and mass organization of Soviet society.[7]

The population group with the least to lose by way of further upward strivings was also the one for whom the political elite had the lowest expectations as subjects for remolding into new Soviet men: the older generation, with a lifetime of religious habit behind it. The Harvard interviewers found that this group constituted the core of the faithful, ever ready to run the perils of secret observance if need be. If the status of older believers was low when their practices were uncovered by the authorities, they were likely to be let off with a reprimand or have their "deviation" passed over as of little consequence. If their social station was high, they might have sufficient vested power to get away with this one idiosyncrasy, especially if their work was not purely ideological. The interviews mention older army officers attending services, with no apparent political ill effects. Such phenomena trace their precedent to the days of the Revolution, when an Old Bolshevik amused the atheist elite by writing at the top of his Party questionnaire, "In the Name of the Father and of the Son and of the Holy Ghost, Amen."[8]

THE SPRINGS OF BELIEF

The tenacious life of the religious flame in spite of all official attempts to extinguish it owes much to its shelter at most Russian hearths. The Harvard interviews are practically unanimous in singling out the family as the source of belief for persons who remained faithful, as well as for those who later became free-thinkers. Typically, the mother or grandmother of the respondent is said to have instilled religious feeling and to have escorted him to church for the first time. The paternal Party soon runs at odds with this maternal transmission belt of Orthodoxy. The child who finds that communist indoctrination clashes with his early teachings is plunged into psychological conflict. For the Church to tip the scales of his divided loyalty, the youth must have shown a high degree of identification of religion with his family—a factor dependent in turn on the strength of his family ties.

The causal chain is described in one interview: "I did not feel the influence of anti-religious propaganda because my religious feelings were closely connected with my family life. Therefore, the attack on religion was an attack against my family. Religion and family existed in my mind as one undivided whole."[9] In this light, the early phases of the regime's attack on religion can be interpreted as only the obverse of the assault on family solidarity—the pro forma civil ceremonies and "postcard divorces" of the revolutionary era, the legitimation of common-law marriage during the twenties. When the retrenchment of the mid-thirties called for restabilizing the family, Soviet cultural policy also had somehow to accommodate the religious feelings anchored at the hearth. Walter Birnbaum notes that the display of basic religious strength in the 1937 census coincided, happily for the future of the Church, with edicts that were meant to reshape the family into a "basic cell of the state": rewards for many children, a ban on abortions, and stiffer divorce laws.[10] Walter Kolarz sets the consolidation of the family into the broader framework of the new "Soviet morality."[11] He quotes Lenin's widow, Krupskaya, as pointing out in 1937 that religion should not be underrated as a source of morality when parents continue to be impressed by the superior behavior of children with religious education; the state should not eradicate religion unless it first proved able to supersede it.

But it must be kept in mind that the family which the regime was striving to reconstitute was not the old-style unit in which religion had played a dominant role. Soviet specifications foresaw a new socialist family stripped of religion so that it could concentrate all energy on work and communal activities of value to the state. The persistence of religion gave the regime pause, perhaps moved it in the mid-thirties "holiday" to admit tacitly that organized belief could not be demolished at one fell swoop. The short duration of that breathing spell, however, suggests that the regime remained unconvinced of the efficacy of its watch-and-wait policy. The petty pace at which religion was receding even in an evidently unfavorable environment caused the dissatisfied political leadership to explode its most violent onslaught on the Church in the late thirties.

Such direct attacks, Lenin had recognized, carried the danger of backfiring. Not only did they create a new gallery of martyrs for the faithful to venerate, but their cruder excrescences rubbed raw on popular sensibilities and made many theretofore uncommitted persons sympathize with the victims. In this connection, it should be noted that the younger Soviet escapees interviewed by the Harvard team repeatedly expressed convictions approving religion on humanistic grounds, although they were devoid of genuine religious fervor. Their broad pleas for toleration are invariably linked to endorsement of a cause their former masters tried so ruthlessly to suppress; they also reflect the situation described by Krupskaya in which the Party offers no adequate surrogate for the moral force of religion. The escapees reveal their indignation at the low level of Soviet morality, which they associate with communism. As one relates: "When I was five or six years old . . . I became an atheist and forgot all about religion. But when the Soviets attacked religion very much, something in me woke up, and I returned to the Orthodox Church."[12] Most other responses of this youthful group do not go so far as actual reconversion. They express a vaguer desire for something the Communist party ethic has not been able to supply. As one Russian defines it, "faith means respect, conscience . . . Even the non-believers must all have some faith."[13] The many Soviet citizens who subscribe to such a formula represent neither doctrinaire believers nor proponents of the vilification employed in the regime's campaigns against the Church. Yet this sizable group could not maintain its natural neutrality when attacks against religion were mounted along the old frontal lines. Their sympathy was drawn to the embattled faithful.

THE ATHEIST COUNTERCRUSADE

Conspicuous among the regime's antireligious tools was the League of the Godless, which turned into a boomerang because of the misguided zeal with which it was wielded against the legions of faithful. It had been formed without fanfare on Easter Sunday 1925 and operated with consummate discretion, in order not to alienate the peasants, until 1929. Then the term "Militant" was inserted into its title, and its coterie of Old Bolshevik and journalist leaders let loose to do nationwide battle with religion as a key feature of Stalin's campaign to smash the barriers against collectivizing and industrializing the country. Sporting its full regalia of central committee, departments, and sections, the League embarked on Five Year Plans to achieve godlessness and to enroll millions of people into a kind of antichurch of materialism triumphant. The discovery was soon made that it was easier to shut down churches and roll up fantastically inflated membership figures overnight than to present atheism as a popular emotional substitute for traditional belief.[14] Soviet citizens did not flock to "Red Weddings" at factories or bring their babies to be dedicated to the Revolution in a ceremony that was supposed to replace baptism; neither did they embrace a calendar in which Sunday and religious festivals were supplanted by assorted communist anniversaries.

Under the unsteady baton of the Old Bolshevik Emelian Yaroslavsky, the League fostered a purge of thousands of Party members who had not severed their ties to the Church—in 1929–1930 and again in 1933—but a distressing number of persons in high places stubbornly refused enlightenment. The Central Purge Commission in 1933 was aghast to find Party members gathering funds to repair churches and, supreme insult, singing hymns while attending meetings of the commission. The so-called "Easter-Cake Communists" (*kulichniye partiitsy*) of revolutionary days, who kept up religious observances out of regard to their families, continued to pop up in Soviet press reports. The comic-opera spectacle of the atheist campaign, with its perennial complaints that its "godless" factory brigades and collective farms were being infiltrated by Orthodox believers who used them as protective cover, carried grim overtones for the Church groups it frightened out of existence. In reaction to the 1937 census results that punctured the naive claims of impending atheistic victory, the inept directors of the League were themselves purged and a new drive brought membership, which in six years had slipped nearly 80 percent from its 5.7-million peak in 1932, back to 3.5 million in 1941, a 50-percent recovery.[15] With a tougher new leadership conducting a more realistic campaign, the League might have come closer than ever before in its history to making good a threat: "another twenty-year period of determined antireligious effort" could succeed in "reducing religion in Russia to a curiosity for museums."[16] To that end, Yaroslavsky proposed in a talk over Radio Moscow at the end of 1939 that the state should take away children from those parents who refused to send them to atheist classes.[17] With the outbreak of World War II, however, the government quietly put the League out of business.

Though not numerous enough to furnish conclusive evidence, references to the League by refugees in the Harvard project lend substance to the foregoing picture of its early failures. Where they attribute any effectiveness at all to atheist propaganda, their impressions date back to grammar school years; not one credits it with a positive influence on his outlook during adulthood. On the contrary, those who were relatively uncommitted in their religious attitudes generally recall the negative effects of League propaganda. One of them relates that his initial coolness to religion was reversed by a godless parade in which people dressed up as priests and nuns were shown in obscene poses. Such crude, irrational tactics (which included the drowning out of church services by "noise demonstrations" of League members gathered outside) bore the stamp of "opium for the masses" too much themselves to lay that charge convincingly at the door of the Church. The man who recoiled at the tasteless parade explains: "Without understanding the substance of religion, I got on the path of belief in God as a means toward the education of the people."[18] His case is noteworthy further because, despite his newfound awareness of the social potential of religion, his education had ingrained the tenets of Marxism so deeply in him that he continued to subscribe to them as well. It is possible that cases of mixed loyalties like this betray receptiveness to the ritualism of both Church and Party observances.

By keeping its ties to the League under cover, the regime maintained freedom of movement in dealing with the Church. Though few citizens were fooled by the supposedly spontaneous nature of the atheist campaign, they did not fully equate the League's policies with those of the government. The fluctuating Party line on the Church further served to strengthen the popular image of the League as a tool that political leadership might employ or discard, as suited its purposes. Again and again the regime underscored the distance that separated its stand from the atheist establishment—now by official reprimands of League goings-on that bordered on vandalism, now by a renewed stress on the withering away of religion as a natural process which could do without puerile efforts to hurry evolution along. The League could quote Marxist chapter and verse to justify condemnation of organized religion, but its manic existence was pointedly not officially endorsed by the administration. By merely condoning the League unofficially the government left the back door always open to the rapprochement with the Church that finally took place in World War II.

Of more immediate consequence, indirect exploitation of the League allowed the Politburo to shrug off foreign protests by blithely denying the campaigns that Soviet citizens were conducting "on their own initiative." The regime could bolster this fabrication by corroborations from Orthodox Church heads like Acting Patriarch Sergius, who in 1930 told a group of foreign correspondents that there was no religious persecution in the Soviet Union.[19] In this make-believe world, the clergy could not expect to improve its existence by recriminations against the government; it had to rely on stoic endurance to keep alive the chance for an extensive truce on the religious front, an option the regime implicitly preserved by its divorce from the League.

PILLARS OF THE CHURCH

Waves of violently repressive measures and constant pressure from political and social elites eroded the religious faith of many Russians. Many others, however, went beyond mere sympathy with the harried flock, or lip service to Orthodox moral values; they continued to count themselves as active Church members and to maintain in some measure the ties that kept their religious communities alive. Their numerous representatives among the group questioned by the Harvard interviewers have recounted the obstacles to practice of their faith. From these accounts the effects can be traced of the three-pronged offensive carried on against them by the regime in what amounted to a war of social isolation on their congregations. The official intent had been to choke off communications among believers and to prevent their crystallization into an autonomous social force.

The government's most direct course was simply to shut down churches. One peasant recalls, "Our children were baptized. We fulfilled all the rites. But there was no church in our village . . . Most of our friends are believers, too."[20] According to a boast of the atheist journal *Antireligioznik* in 1939, 75 percent of the 80,000 Russian Orthodox churches that existed in 1917 had been closed;[21] a foreign expert's more reasonable statistics put the prerevolutionary figure at some 40,000, the pre-World War II total at 4,000.[22] The government replied to recurrent foreign protests by hypocritically claiming that, since there was no law against the existence of churches, the members must have folded up shop for lack of attendance. They did not bother to point out that closings often followed infiltration of congregations by atheist agents, arrests to reduce the membership below the statutory number of twenty, or simply the revocation of building permits.[23] Believers managed to conduct services anyway—illegally, at each other's homes—their religious faith often the only thing that made the economic deprivations of the Stalin era bearable. Many peasants clung to the hope for an afterlife held out by church doctrine as sole escape from the miseries of collectivization. For some, turning their backs on directives from Moscow had become a traditional communal response; others found in religion a spiritual rationalization for a catalogue of seemingly senseless suffering. A former village resident sums it up: "In 1929 things got bad . . . perhaps it's all a curse sent by God . . . the shootings and the hunger."

The second stage of the regime's campaign to impose a quarantine on believers invoked the aid of other institutions to bring home the message that the practice of religion constituted exhibition of a diseased bourgeois frame of mind. Peasants who lit Christmas trees or observed Easter were reported to kolkhoz authorities through the omnipresent informer system and dealt with by reprimands or sterner measures. A similar system of controls pervaded industry and the armed forces. A former Red Army man reports that "it was very hard to be religious in the army. If I tried to sit down and say my prayers, someone came over and cursed me out."

In its third phase, the regime's assault on the Church as a social institution made each individual home a battlefront. Here the essential objective was to disrupt the transmission of religious traditions within the family; at stake was the ideology of the youth to whom the Party entrusted its future. Responses of the Harvard group confirm the virtual impossibility of "enlightening" those devout oldsters who declare, "I would rather die than give up my religion." The regime had to prevent them from passing on their faith to their children, for with prohibitions against religious instruction by priests, the family had become the last outpost of Orthodoxy.

For the young, even the prospect of a blighted career might not suffice to uproot a faith securely implanted by parents. The government had therefore to confront their elders with sanctions for giving religious instruction and thereby undermining the materialist outlook fostered at school. This process is acknowledged by one older Orthodox believer: "I wanted my children to be honest, to be religious . . . They used to pray in the morning and in the afternoon when they returned from school. They never told anyone about their praying. They were afraid. Students used to be suspicious of them. Teachers told the children to investigate and report those who were religious."[24] Another devout couple reports that the ubiquitousness of official sanctions made them decide to drop religious discussions at home. Nonetheless, they were threatened with exile by the authorities when their child blurted out to his teacher that divine vengeance was sure to follow an atheist lecture in class. Only by proving that the child's old nurse was instilling such dangerous thoughts did the parents earn a reprieve.

Under such constricting circumstances there was little for parents to do, especially when the regime's atheist campaign shifted into high gear, except to limit the spiritual care of their offspring to secret baptism. Even this resource was condemned by official propaganda on hygienic grounds. In the baptismal ceremony, according to a Soviet wartime publication, "the weak baby is undressed in the cold church and dipped into cold water. It is also common for the priest to baptize several babies in the same water." And this was but the first step in a series of germ-laden practices: "At mass, dozens—sometimes hundreds—of people approach the priest and receive communion from the same cup, while during the ceremonial kissing of the cross thousands press their lips to the same spot."[25] At the height of the last purge, ingenious believers found ways to avoid microbes and police agents: "in Alma-Ata it is now unnecessary to go to church to baptize an infant, to be married, or to conduct funeral rites. All these ceremonies are conducted by correspondence, or the priest comes on summons."[26] Even members of the elite ignored threats to bring their children to the font. On one occasion, plans to prosecute a Party member for having his children baptized were dropped when it was discovered that all his local comrades had done likewise.[27]

The holy water was hardly dry, however, before children growing up in the Stalinist era were subjected to the pressures of Communist youth groups and Soviet schools. These were forces that a muted Church and its silent adherents could not hope to counter effectively. Reports from Soviet prisoners of war, interviews with émigrés, and data from Nazi occupation authorities all confirm the widespread loss of faith among the youth who had grown up under that system. Even the sons of devout farmers found it convenient to stay away from services, rationalizing their apostasy by citing the scarcity of priests or simply claiming that the rigorous work schedule left them no time for such things.[28] An official of the newly opened Moscow Theological Academy offered the following assessment of the first wartime entering classes: "The instructors saw before them students who were unlike the former ones who had been brought up from their childhood in the spirit of the Church; these were grown men of the present, not seldom only recently converted to religion and having not the least notion of it save the inner impulse to serve God."[29]

If the younger generation had, by and large, lost its faith by World War II, it showed very little enthusiasm for an out-and-out war on

campaign of socially isolating believers had taken it further along the
religion; most people favored toleration of the Church. The regime's
road to atomization of Soviet society. The very arsenal of weapons
employed by the political leadership in molding opinion generated
internal resistances which could not be penetrated by the most potent
propaganda. Utilizing educational mechanisms, like rewarded learning
and simple repetition, the ideological chiefs could make most of the
populace adopt the Stalinist belief system virtually as an implicit,
unquestioned value. But to reach this level, they had to sell the system
to their potential audience in a manner that would leave a modicum of
free choice, at least in the sense that anyone properly "enlightened"
would buy this set of values because of its superior qualities. The young
Communists who endorsed religious toleration were thereby manifesting
concretely their nebulous right of free choice. They were also limiting
their ideological conformity to top-priority goals, not volunteering for
the atheist campaigns conducted by the regime in fits and starts. Finally,
permitting their elders a fairly harmless aberration gave them a chance
to vaunt their own progressive advancement.

By differentially tolerating religion for the masses whenever a new
atheist shock wave had passed, the regime furnished its "vanguard"
another standard by which to claim their title. A second advantage for
the regime in finally retarding this phase of social atomization lay in its
ability to call on believers to unite in "the holy war for the motherland."

3

Nazi Ideology and Administrative Practice on Religion

Nazi ideology was just as adamant as the teachings of Marx and Lenin in denying organized religion a place in the new social order. Taking their cue from Nietzsche, Hitler and Rosenberg rejected the tenets of Christianity as a pap fit only for weaklings and slaves.[1] The master race was to be nurtured on sterner stuff than a commandment against killing or injunctions to turn the other cheek and love one's neighbor. As had the Marxists before them, the Nazis blamed the priesthood for the enfeeblement of the masses and the anointment of the old exploitative classes.[2] Each group expected its new order to bring about a final solution to the religious question as youthful generations stamped out the traditions of their fathers.

The similarity in approach, however, concealed basic divergencies. While the Soviet leaders relied on a syllogism in which the rationalism of communist theory would vanquish the irrational dogma of the church, the Nazi regime evoked the atavistic powers of racism and the *Führerprinzip* to propel their nation on a course for which Christian teachings had no relevance. When it came to offering alternatives to religion, the Soviets looked ahead to the "construction of socialism" and the Nazis backward to a reverence of the Teutonic past that amounted to a new mystique or, as harsher critics termed it, nihilism.[3] A case in point is the difference in Lenin's and Hitler's expressions of their common belief that science would dispel the religious superstition of the masses. For Lenin this meant a program of technological change that would liberate the

49

farmer and worker from the nexus of exploitation. As he put it to a Party congress: "If you procure tractors, you do away with God."[4] For Hitler it meant a civic project centered on an observatory that would attract its share of Sunday pilgrims: "They'll have access to the greatness of our universe . . . It will be our way of giving men a religious spirit, of teaching them humility—but without priests . . . Put a small telescope in a village and you destroy a world of superstitions."[5]

Both efforts foundered. Lenin's naïve prescription produced the notably undesired consequences of priests holding thanksgiving services for the arrival of tractors in their villages and peasants affixing crosses to the machines.[6] Hitler evidently had second thoughts about his rural astronomy program. Further, by 1937 he had shelved plans for a Nazi-dominated Reichskirche to supplant existing churches;[7] during World War II, Protestant and Catholic leaders became more outspoken in their criticism of the regime,[8] but he had to content himself with privately uttered threats to do away with them at a later date.[9]

A second basic difference between Marxist and Nazi ideologies which helps explain their divergent approaches to the church problem stems from the relative weight accorded them by the two sets of leaders. The Soviet leadership seems to show a high regard for ideology as a guide to action and tries to make any shifts in its program appear to fit in the light of consistent theory, although experts disagree on the success with which this has been carried off.[10] Nazi leaders, on the other hand, demonstrated a notable unconcern for congruence in their patterns of belief. They evidenced none of the compulsions of a Lenin making clear in 1921 that the New Economic Policy was no more than a strategic retreat.[11] Neither did they offer a parallel to the Soviet regime's short-run tactics in religious policy, which denied that concessions—from admitting God-fearing candidates to Party membership in prerevolutionary days to intermittently granting breathing space to the Church in response to domestic or foreign pressures—entailed any revision of the long-range program of social transformation, in which the survival of religious belief was not provided for. The Kremlin again and again succumbed to the temptation to give atheist evolution a helping push, to drop any temporary stance of toleration for yet another assault on the Church. Indeed, this stubborn concentration on the regime's ultimate aims was responsible for the harvest of paper successes in the drives for godlessness and for the ever more deeply rooted faith practiced in the "catacombs," beyond the reach of official surveillance.

Nazi leaders hardly bothered to cloak the paradoxes in their ideological potpourri, whether these related to the remarkably un-Aryan physique of its Führer or to weightier matters such as their "socialist workers" party coming to terms with the East Prussian Junkers and the Ruhr industrialists in return for contributions to the party coffers.[12] The one unifying ingredient of contradictory actions was supplied by the leadership's continuous accretion of power. In this quest, expediency was its own excuse. One day Jews could be considered suitable only to fill gas ovens, the next they could be re-evaluated as a fit medium of exchange for trucks.[13] A foreign policy which, on geopolitical and racial grounds, sought to make common cause with Great Britain could be reversed overnight. Lacking any central rationalizing principle approaching the authoritativeness of Marx's and Lenin's dicta for the Soviet regime, the Nazi leadership fell back on the guidance of now one, now another tactical formula spawned by its many contending cliques. The copies of *Mein Kampf* and Rosenberg's *Mythus des 20. Jahrhunderts* that jammed the bookshelves of the Party remained largely unread because of their turgid prose.[14]

The final arbiter on the latest fashion in theories was Hitler, equipped with his notoriously erratic intuition. Once he had taken solitary counsel and announced a new party line, the wary among his lieutenants knew enough to renounce their erstwhile allegiances (for example, Goebbels to the socialism of the Strassers in 1926, Rosenberg to the Russophobia that was out of place in the era of the Nazi-Soviet pact),[15] while the more naïve were left dangling (S.A. chieftains in their bid to supplant the Army High Command in 1933, or Rudolf Hess on his quixotic mission to England in 1941).[16] In such a setting, a "tactical retreat" might be as meaningless as the Munich Agreement or as irrevocable as the scrapping of socialism in the mid-1920's. Consequently, no churchman could be sure whether the Führer's master plan for a Nazi church would remain an empty threat.

EFFORTS AND RESULTS OF CHURCH POLICY

When the Nazi regime encountered traditional social institutions like the church, its standard response was a policy known as *Gleichschaltung* (coordinating, bringing into line). In the lexicon of political expediency this could mean anything from leaving the institution alone, as long as it did not venture into opposition, or radically transforming it with full use of the terror apparatus. In other words, the leaders sought to apply the proper amount of pressure to gear the institution into their hierarchical power complex. Their initial argument for securing a group's subordination tended to be couched in terms of mutual self-interest. Thus, labor leaders were "persuaded" to abandon potentially troublesome independence in return for the promised benefits of full employment in a war economy, while industrialists were sold on guaranteed rates of profit and the exploitation of slave labor. In the same way, the Protestant churches, with their Lutheran doctrine of submission to secular authority, might be bypassed on the road to power; but the Catholic Church, with its supranational ties, called for more direct intervention by a regime that tried to silence it at first through the Concordat of 1933, later through censoring its utterances and closing its parochial schools and theological academies.[17] "Divide and rule" was the tenet of bureaucratic practice in domestic as well as foreign policy, and if the Catholic hierarchy was largely able to maintain its solidarity, the more than two dozen Protestant denominations were natural prospects to be played off against each other by the regime.

Finally, the contrast between Soviet and Nazi ideologies on the church points up a reversal in the political effects generated by each of the two systems. The Soviets more often turned to open repression, although their rationally framed policy forecast attenuation of the antireligious line, once resolution of the "class struggle" had removed the fangs of the churchly enemy. The Nazis, whose dogma was bound to clash head-on with Christian teachings, generally acted with greater restraint; relatively few churchmen were arrested by that regime, which remained circumspect in handling an institution whose sizable popular following it respected. Yet it was the Soviets who managed to achieve a comprehensive accord with the church of their land, granting it official status, coordinating its efforts with the government's wartime and later foreign policies—while the Nazis, more intent on short-run power goals, proved never able to cash in on the potential benefits of turning the churches into active allies of their regime and, on the contrary, drove more and more bishops into vocal opposition. As will be seen later, this hypothesis holds as well for the German-occupied areas of Russia, where the Nazis quickly wore out their initial popular welcome as liberators through their merciless treatment of prisoners of war, general rule of the population as *Untermenschen* (subhumans), forced labor drafts, agricultural requisitions, and many other draconic measures. At the very same time, the Soviet regime was getting the refurbished Patriarchal Church to donate large sums to the war effort, issue a spate of propaganda appeals, and generally lend its moral weight to a national campaign against Hitler as Antichrist.

"POSITIVE CHRISTIANITY" IN ACTION

The complexities of Nazi church policy have only recently been submitted to objective scholarly analysis, notably in the writings of Guenter Lewy and J. S. Conway. There has been no dearth of data, however, to document that Hitler and his chief ideologue in this field, Alfred Rosenberg, shared an equally strong antipathy to Christianity and that Hitler was by far the more cautious of the two when it came to publicly voicing his feelings. Even privately he paid grudging respect to the power of the Catholic Church organization and reined in his restive subordinates when they proposed to tangle with it directly. In this he was not only bowing to the practical problems of dealing with thirty-five million German Catholics, but also applying the lessons of his Austrian and Bavarian experience.

Hitler's youth included a traditional Catholic upbringing, which exerted a lifelong influence on him. Even in March 1942 Goebbels confided in his diary: "the Führer declared that if his mother still lived, she would undoubtedly go to Church today, and he could and would not hinder her . . ."[18] Subsequent years in Vienna taught Hitler the practical rules for success in politics; as he recounted a dozen years later, Georg von Schönerer's Pan-German Nationalist party committed the fundamental tactical mistake of attacking the Catholic Church and thereby splintering its forces.[19] The Christian Socialist leader Karl Lueger, on the other hand, knew enough to tie his mass appeal to the established Church. In Hitler's words, "he was quick to adopt all available means for winning the support of long-established institutions, so as to be able to derive the greatest possible advantage for his movement from those old sources of power."[20] The lesson was not lost on Hitler in Bavaria, the stronghold of German Catholicism: though his 1925 truce with the clerically dominated Bavarian government roused the scorn of his north German nationalist allies, he held fast to the pro-Church line.[21] His new partners, he announced, were more important to him than his old anticlerical supporters.

The way to collaboration with the forces of the Church had been pointed out in the Nazi party program of February 1920, whose Section 24 posited "freedom of all religious confessions in the state, as long as they don't threaten its existence or transgress against the morality of the German race. The Party as such represents the viewpoint of a positive Christianity, without tying itself to any particular confession."[22] Hitler echoed the same sentiments four years later in *Mein Kampf,* coupling praise of both churches for their moral support to the nation with a thinly veiled attack on the Catholic Center party, a formidable roadblock on the Nazi way to power. He maintained his conditional acceptance of religion in public pronouncements following the Nazi takeover, but privately, as in his talks with Rauschning, he revealed an unbending hostility to the values of the Church. Thus, "whether it keeps the jewified Christian faith with its weak morality of compassion, or takes up a strong, heroic belief in God in nature, God in one's own people, God in one's fate, in one's own blood"[23] he deemed decisive for the German people. And, he went on, "a German church, a German Christianity is nonsense. One is either a Christian or a German. One can't be both."

The "positive Christianity" of the 1920 program came to be defined more and more narrowly by the regime. In the 1933 Concordat with the Vatican, Article I liberally decreed: "The German Reich guarantees freedom of conscience and the public exercise of the Catholic religion."[24] But the following year, third-grade pupils were ordered to recite a creed that began, "As Jesus freed mankind from sin and hell, so is Hitler rescuing the German people from destruction. Jesus and Hitler were persecuted but, while Jesus was crucified, Hitler was appointed chancellor" and concluded, "We hope that Hitler will himself be able to complete his work on earth. Jesus was building for heaven, Hitler for the German earth."[25] And in 1935, the journal *Wille und Macht* defined "positive Christianity" as "belief . . . that, in regard to itself and to the state, stays within the appointed limits";[26] that meant not venturing into the political sphere, understood broadly as "anything even of the least relevance to the community of the people," and keeping to a religious sphere restricted to "belief in the supernatural."

Hitler never intended to take any of the Concordat's provisions favorable to the Church literally, as he assured his cabinet in July 1933.[27] The Vatican accord was an undiluted triumph, in his view, because (1) it refuted claims that national socialism was unchristian or antichurch; (2) it represented unconditional recognition of the regime by the Vatican, going so far as to require its bishops in Germany to take an oath to the state; and (3) it spelled the destruction of the Christian labor movement and the Catholic Center party. Less than a year later, the Catholic youth organization was already banned in contravention of the

Concordat and the publications of the Church put under even greater restriction. Soon parochial schools and Catholic welfare activities also fell under the interdict.[28]

If in November 1941 Hitler could conclude that "the Party has been right to steer clear of the Church,"[29] he only meant that the Church had been so effectively emasculated as a potential opponent, there was no point in martyring the few bishops who refused to be silenced. When the Vatican tried to intervene in Church affairs of the occupied territories, Hitler denied the Concordat's applicability beyond the borders of the 1933 Reich.[30] His pique had been aroused by the Vatican's refusal to recognize the legitimacy of Germany's conquests and by its persistence in maintaining relations with East European governments in exile. Foreign Minister Ribbentrop boasted in May 1942 that he could stifle any outcry from Rome in the usual manner: "The Foreign Office has always taken the Führer's inclination to the subject into account in its relations with the Vatican—as the Republic of Venice is supposed to have done for a generation. We have filled an entire registry office with all kinds of unanswered notes from the Vatican!"[31]

OVERCOMING PROTESTANT RESISTANCE

Hitler succeeded in rendering the Catholic Church irrelevant as a political factor, having constricted its scope by a series of decrees against which it could only lodge legalistic protests that were shrugged off by the regime after the Gestapo halted their circulation.[32] The Vatican had trapped itself into this position by its hasty accession to the Concordat, the first of the many foreign accords Hitler signed without any intention of keeping. Still, the Church proved able, after a fashion, to remain master of its own spiritual house. The score of Protestant churches could claim neither a counterpart to the Catholics' unified doctrine and organization nor an international spokesman with the Pope's prestige; in dealing with them, Hitler saw no need for the arms' length treatment appropriate to the Vatican. Instead, he found among them a nationalist sect, the so-called "German Christians," who cheered his assumption of power in 1933 and virtually begged him to assent to their staging a coup d'église of the Evangelical establishment on his behalf.

At the outset these Nazi churchmen had seized control of the Protestant general synod and rammed through the Aryan Paragraph excluding from the priesthood anyone of Jewish ancestry. By November 1933 they were demanding unconditional acceptance of this edict by all denominations. Further, they asked the removal of all "un-German elements in service and confer sion, especially of the Old Testament with its Jewish lenders' morality."[33] No end was in sight for interdenominational strife, they announced, until "the transfer or removal of all priests either unwilling or unable to take a leading part in the religious renewal of our people and in the fulfillment of the German reformation in the spirit of National Socialism." Their later demands included reconstruction of the church according to the *Führerprinzip* and an oath to Hitler to be taken by the clergy as it had been by the state bureaucracy.[34]

Resistance to nazification of the Protestant churches came haltingly at first. A small Pastors' Emergency League rallied around Martin Niemöller in Berlin-Dahlem to argue the legality of the "German Christian" decrees.[35] It did not venture to preach opposition, but only pleaded for a "depoliticized clergy" that would be allowed to plow its spiritual furrow undisturbed. It took a year of state intervention in church affairs before the handful of churchmen, centered in Prussia, was able to expand its program and membership into a national resistance to the demands of totalitarianism. The synod of the new Confessing Church, meeting in Barmen in May 1934, cited Scripture to back its contention that the church could never be reduced to an organ of the state.[36] By then the regime had gone far in filling leading church positions with trusted Nazis and in controlling clerical affairs at strategic points:[37] new elections to church councils had been held under duress, church finances put under state control, commissars installed over the churches of the individual *Länder,* and a former Navy chaplain, Ludwig Müller, placed at the head of the German Evangelical Church as loyal Reichsbishop, complete with bureaucratic apparatus.[38]

By October 1934, the Confessing Church acknowledged that the fight could no longer be carried on within the confines of the regular church organization. From now on it would rely on self-decreed emergency law to reject the nazified church government, with its slogan "One State— One People—One Church" and its papist pretensions exemplified by the Reichsbishop. The intrepid pastors threw all caution to the wind in March 1935, in a message that left no doubt that their quarrel was not with a new creed but with Nazi ideology itself. They specifically denounced the "racist-ethnic Weltanschauung" that was making "blood and race, the nation, honor and freedom into false gods."[39] The regime reacted predictably with the arrest of seven hundred priests who had dared to recite the message.

The surprising thing is that it took so long for the state to gain retribution. Evidently, Nazi leaders had underestimated the lengths to which the recalcitrant parsons were willing to go. This is understandable if one accepts the expert opinion of Karl Barth that German Protestants "almost unanimously welcomed the Hitler regime with real confidence, indeed with the highest hopes."[40] Even if there were some among them whose "Heil Hitler!" later stuck in their throats, they were unlikely to couch their dissent in political terms. After all, they had been brought up on the teachings of Luther, larded with passages admonishing obedience to the ruler no matter how unjust he might be.[41] The regime appears to have overlooked the fact that Luther, while never condoning violent resistance, does prescribe civil disobedience in two special circumstances: if the ruler forces a believer to break the commandments and cause harm to others, or if he tries to pervert church doctrine and claims to "lord it over men's conscience and faith," the subject must disobey.[42] Both grounds furnished the Confessing Church leaders their platform of protest, which attracted enough of a following to convince Hitler, by February 1937, that he could not enforce pro-Nazi uniformity on the refractory Lutherans.[43]

Hitler had from the first shown as much contempt for the Protestant clergy as awe for the Catholic hierarchy. They would be easy to push around, he told a circle of his intimates in April 1933: "They will submit . . . they are insignificant little people, submissive as dogs, and they sweat with embarrassment when you talk to them. They have neither a religion they can take seriously nor a great position to defend like Rome."[44] He dropped them apparently with no regrets when they did stand up to him in their 1935 declaration and, more openly, in a memorandum addressed to him in May of the following year.[45] There the list of grievances went beyond the travails of the churches to the illegality of Gestapo actions and concentration camps and infringements on freedom of speech and press. Hitler's response was to loose a new wave of clerical arrests, shut down resistant theological academies, and proscribe the Confessing Church altogether. He also made sure that Niemöller, arrested in July 1937 and released by the court after seven months' incarceration awaiting trial, was sent to a concentration camp and not freed despite repeated church pleas.[46]

Still, with the clerical opposition decimated, Hitler hesitated to make the strife-torn church into a vehicle for his new order. In 1940, he admitted to Rosenberg that it had been a great mistake to try to build up a unified Evangelical Church as a counterweight to the Roman Church.[47] He recalled a reception he had given for church leaders at which the "true believers" and the "German Christians" had nearly come to blows over questions of precedence. Finally, he parodied an unctuous address by Niemöller spiced with the nautical terms that marked the pastor's speech. For Hitler, such churchmen were objects of derision, not serious contenders for power. If they had not been brought to heel as simply as he had once envisioned, so much the worse for them. In two hundred years, he prophesied to Rosenberg, the people would come to embrace beliefs consonant with Nazi ideology.[48]

ROSENBERG: THE IMPOTENT IDEOLOGIST

Twenty years would suffice for the triumph of the Nazi faith, Rosenberg assured his Führer. Rosenberg's reply deserves extended comment because of his two-fold place in this analysis, here leading ideologist with special responsibilities for Nazi doctrine, later minister in charge of the occupied territories in Russia. In both fields, his grandiose aspirations outran his limited administrative talents—not the least of the reasons Hitler selected him for such posts, buttressing his own role as arbiter of the infighting that was sure to ensue. Throughout all his ups and downs on the Party and Reich political ladders, Rosenberg was driven by his ambitions to shape history as well as by the gratification of an occasional word of praise from Hitler. Yet before long it became plain to him that his advice was not being taken seriously, his orders to nominal subordinates countermanded or ignored. The excerpts from his diary that have been published and even the memoirs composed in his cell at the time of the Nuremberg Trials constitute one long complaint at other members of the Nazi elite who crowded him aside in Hitler's council chambers. He fails to identify a single ally among them in his scramble for power, but he shows no inkling that his record of frustration was due to possible shortcomings in himself.

At the 1940 meeting, Hitler was in effect saying that he was washing his hands of church affairs for the duration and that creation of a substitute Nazi faith would have to await the indefinite future. But Rosenberg refused to take the hint; he was too wrapped up in his early schemes for a new faith, with himself as its prophet, to view the fact that it did not catch on with the people as anything more than a temporary hindrance. Another generation, he explained, would be enough to sever totally the influence of older people on German youth.

When he told Hitler that "surely, sometime someone will lead a new Reformation," it is very likely that he had his own eye on the mantle of Luther. When he later headed the Ministry for the East, he again projected designs on a grand scale, not merely administering subject peoples but building a vast colonial empire of which he would be pro-consul. In neither case did he achieve a decisive say on actual policy or markedly affect operations in the field.

In the early days of the Party, even during Hitler's accession to power, Rosenberg was taken quite seriously by friend and foe alike. He had come to Munich in 1919 as one of the ultranationalist *Volks-deutsche* (Germans born abroad) who were to play leading parts in irredentist Nazi foreign policy.[49] His German ancestry had been a mark of distinction for his petit bourgeois family in the Estonian capital Tallin, formerly the Hansa city of Reval. It recalled him to his defeated fatherland after the Bolshevik Revolution had cut short his architecture studies in Moscow. His first call in Munich was paid to Hetman Paul Skoropadsky, leader of the Russian émigrés, who had headed a reaction-ary government in the Ukraine in 1918 under German aegis.[50] This led to acquaintance with the whole circle of the White Guard whose anti-Semitism drew them into the vortex of disgruntled elements out of which the Nazi party emerged. When Rosenberg became an editor of the party journal, *Völkischer Beobachter*, in 1921, his links with the émigrés provided it with financial support while it furnished them an outlet for their propaganda.

The journalistic post that Rosenberg occupied until 1932 gave him a platform to preach his mystique of racism and Germany's necessary expansion into the *Ostraum* (roughly, eastern space) and also afforded sufficient freedom for forays into other fields. On November 8, 1923, he marched at Hitler's side in the beer-hall *putsch* and, after the Führer's arrest, was named by him to lead the Party in his absence. The rivalries that soon erupted around him seem to confirm the surmise that Hitler had chosen him precisely for the ineptitude that would prevent him from establishing a rival power base.[51] In any case, Rosenberg went against the Führer's advice to embark the Party in the 1924 elections and, probably because of the unexpected success in getting thirty-two deputies into the Reichstag, found himself stripped of the office of deputy leader.[52] Following this rebuff in party administration, Rosen-berg steered his career in a new direction.

He had served as Hitler's foreign policy adviser from the first, so it was only natural that he became the Nazi party delegate to the Reichstag's foreign relations committee after his election to the German Parliament in 1930. From there he moved to leadership of the Party's own Foreign Policy Office and, after the 1933 Nazi assumption of power, appears to have been confident that he was in line for the Foreign Ministry. However, the vacancy caused by ouster of the old Hindenburg appointee von Neurath was filled by Ribbentrop. To compound Rosenberg's frustration, directives from his party office were ignored by the diplomatic staff.[53]

The choice official assignment seemed always to elude Rosenberg's grasp. By 1940 he felt he had reached an utter impasse: another apparently sure thing, a job as Minister of Education, fell through.[54] This time he rationalized Hitler's broken promise as giving in to the sensibilities of Mussolini for the Catholic Church, which Rosenberg had been attacking without pause. But this unsatisfying explanation could not salve the indignity of the chore Hitler did saddle upon him, that of heading a special staff to salvage archives and art treasures in Nazi-occupied areas for possible use by the *Hohe Schule*, the super-university that was to be built after the war.[55] From the near-obscurity of this, his first state post, Rosenberg was plucked by Hitler in April 1941 to become governor of the vast Russian reaches the regime planned to occupy following its surprise attack set for June 22.

The unexpected elevation to office, a shock even to Rosenberg himself, brought in its wake the familiar administrative muddles that dogged his career. Events in the occupied areas seemed to transpire virtually independently of the directives he issued from the Ostministerium headquarters in Berlin. His memoirs tell the usual tale: he was being outmaneuvered by rivals, primarily Gestapo chief Himmler, the Führer's deputy Bormann, and Marshal Göring, super-tsar of the economy; he was stuck with hostile subordinates, particularly in the Ukraine, where Reichskommissar Erich Koch went his own merry way; he was being given the run-around by Hitler, who saw him less and less frequently and cut off his complaints with markedly greater impatience.[56] This was a predictable fate for an ideologist who in 1942 was still clinging to his schemes for a new Nazi religion that would replace the Bible entirely by *Mein Kampf*.[57]

ROSENBERG: THE ENEMY OF ROME

The great stream of articles, pamphlets, and books Rosenberg had been producing since 1921 was less notable for the originality of their ideas than for the scurrillousness of their attacks on Christian doctrines, notably Catholicism. Justice Robert H. Jackson, chief United States counsel at the Nuremberg Trials, surveyed the monumental Rosenberg opus and concluded wryly that it amounted to a "wooly philosophy" which "added boredom to the long list of Nazi atrocities."[58] At the other end of the critical scale, Hitler, though time and again rescuing Rosenberg from official oblivion, privately admitted that he wouldn't waste time actually reading his protégé's masterpiece, *Der Mythus des 20. Jahrhunderts.*[59] No doubt Rosenberg himself perceived that the work, which had sold three-quarter million copies since its publication in 1930, owed its success more to notoriety than to the clarity and persuasiveness of its argument.[60]

In July 1939 Rosenberg finally acceded to perennial requests to present the ideas of the *Mythus* in abbreviated, comprehensible form.[61] The resulting "Theses on Weltanschauung" echo the earlier work's scorn for existing religions but are equally devoid of concreteness in their description of the *Volksreligion* that is supposed to replace them.[62] In the *Mythus* his offer of tolerance for the prevailing churches had been predicated on curious conditions: that they do nothing to interfere with the "supremacy of national honor"; that they substitute Nordic sagas for the "cattle-trading tales" of the Old Testament; that they delete "superstitious passages" from the New Testament; that they make sure Jesus is portrayed blond and slim, a "spear-carrying" God instead of the subject of a "perverted crucifixion"; and that the gallery of martyrs be refurbished with the fallen heroes of World War I. In the "Theses," he peremptorily dismisses the "Oriental, Jewish-Syrian" teachings of the Bible. In their stead he sees the "unity and will power personified by the Führer animating a new Germanic community which has renounced all foreign influence to receive guidance from its "racial soul.""

For all its obfuscation, the Rosenberg mystique did play a part in the regime's religious policy. As far as the Catholic Church was concerned, Rosenberg's gospel represented a mortal danger. Rosenberg recognized tha his *Mythus* was a liability to Hitler in the policy of neutralizing the forces of the Vatican; he bowed to considerations that kept Hitler from proclaiming the work as an official document and even went so far as to offer to resign from the Party if it would ease matters for the Führer. The proposal was rejected, but the attacks from Catholic quarters mounted. By 1935, Cardinal Faulhaber of Munich had spoken out against the *Mythus*, but Rosenberg conceded that "it would be politically inadvisable" to proceed against him; however, he departed from the realities of the Church-political situation by thinking he could simply have the Cardinal "jailed according to the 1934 law

against attacks on Party and state."[63] If Rosenberg consistently under-
rated the forces of the Church, the Church committed no like error
of judgment in regard to him. Pope Pius XI apparently even took the
pains of wading through the *Mythus,* and in January 1936 he protested
to Hitler "the poison of libel and detraction of the Church, its history
and its institutes, its servants and its leaders, that trickles daily from
this source." Rosenberg was at the core of the Church's problems in
Germany. It is the "writings of this influential official of the leading
party in the state that have truculently presented the anti-Church and
anti-Christian spirit which is now permeating the entire educational
system, under official and semiofficial auspices."[64]

The regime evaded the Pope's protest by claiming that Rosenberg
was only speaking for himself, but its repressions of Catholic social
and cultural organizations betrayed its sympathies. Pius pursued the
issue, summing up his outrage most openly in the message *Mit brennen-
der Sorge* (With Burning Sorrow), published in March 1937, which
refuted the Nazis' deification of race, nation, and state as counter to
Christian doctrine. But the grounds for this protest were still legalistic
—infringement of the Concordat's provisions—and thus proved ineffectual in moderating anti-Church policy. The regime's lawyers prepared
denials and countercharges, while its police stopped distribution of the
papal message within Germany.[65] Soon the kid gloves were removed
entirely with a propaganda attack on alleged immorality in the monasteries that produced not only a spate of sensationalist news stories
to titillate the readers of Sunday supplements, but also a series of
show trials of monks and priests accused of assorted currency manipulation and morals charges. The aim, as a secret Gestapo directive of
1938 makes clear, was the destruction of Catholic religious orders.[66]

Throughout this period Rosenberg was chafing at the bit, impatient
for Hitler to signal total warfare with the Church, and marshaling his
forces for the showdown he expected momentarily. In 1935 he instructed the Party Reichsleiter and Gauleiter (national and provincial
chiefs) to screen their staffs for anyone who might side with the
Church rather than the Party when the hour struck. Later in the year
he lamented that "it is still too soon to let the Hitler Youth loose." His
ire was especially aroused by civil servants of the pre-Nazi era who
quietly blunted the edge of anti-Church measures "and encourage
the bishops to continue their sabotage."[67] In the army he railed against
the officer corps, "a religiously conditioned group" that passed over
young Nazis for promotion if they did not attend church on Sundays.

Even after he had succeeded in getting an official ban on compulsory attendance, he heard that soldiers who shunned services were made to scrub barrack floors.[68]

At every turn Rosenberg met resistance: from Hitler, who continued dousing his anticlerical ardor and shelving his plans for all-out spiritual war; from the other Nazi leaders, who left him eating the dust in the race for power and for whom his preoccupation with ideology was at best a nuisance; from Catholic clerics, who had the temerity not to succumb gracefully to his announcements of their immediate demise. Rosenberg's chronic frustration at the petering out of his grand efforts was relieved at times by the conviction that history was on his side, a belief that was reinforced whenever he surveyed the cheering masses from the rostrum at Nazi meetings. This was particularly gratifying in "black Münster, the ancient citadel of the Vatican" and headquarters of his archenemy, Bishop Clemens August Count von Galen, where he basked in a "seemingly endless ovation" from a rally of twelve thousand. He concluded that it showed "the great breakthrough is continuing and we only have to take care there is no deluge."[69]

In the same year, 1939, Rosenberg mounted a new ideological barrage against the Church. In his "Theses" he declared: "The habit of a Roman Priest is the uniform of the mortal enemy of German rebirth, the opponent of a united German Reich."[70] In November he persuaded Hitler to give him a new assignment: to bring about "the unification of National-Socialist philosophy."[71] What might be thought an unenviable task would, he hoped, finally give him the chance to vanquish Church sympathizers in the army. His new duties entailed setting up "an educational center for selected officers to instill in them historical consciousness of our struggle, to extend it to the barracks and camps, and to assure National Socialism the leadership in the spiritual war."[72]

But hardly a week after this rare gesture of Hitler's encouragement, a chagrined Rosenberg faced up to the vitality still shown by the supposedly stricken Church. As he noted in his diary: "The clerical printers are working overtime—tracts, sermons, and psalm books inundate the front. There are now some churches in which sermons are held that represent deliberate sabotage." He had at hand reports from Party leaders all across Germany attesting the resurgence of the Church enemy. From some pulpits "the war is being portrayed as God's punishment on National Socialism." Certain theologians even had the temerity to petition the government to have the educational system put into the hands of "the professionals of the churches." At the end of the passage Rosenberg makes the startling admission that the exigencies of World War II may have made his whole ideological effort redundant: "It has been proven that, as a Nazi, one can fight against Marxism and democracy without knowing the least bit of Weltanschauung of the new age."[73] That is a curious confession for the certified philosopher of the Nazi party.

Rosenberg's alternate project, to supplant the Protestant churches with a new faith that would involve his filling Martin Luther's shoes, had also been checkmated by this time. The configuration of forces that defeated it differed somewhat from that which scuttled his anti-Catholic campaign. In this sector there was none of the regime's concern for the international resources of the Vatican, for not pushing a unified church beyond the point of no return to the anti-Communist rationale of the Concordat. But beneath the surface Nazi leaders perceived the same dangers in the scattered Evangelical denominations as in their centralized Roman counterpart. An attempt to infiltrate either institution could backfire and result in conversion of the would-be quislings. In the end the safest policy for both churches was an armed truce, on the assumption that they would continue to lose ground under the emergency conditions of World War II and that they could be totally suppressed after its victorious end.[74]

In fulminating against the "sabotage" of isolated church leaders, Rosenberg had never grasped that for Hitler even an unyielding bishop could have his positive uses. As long as he addressed his protests to the proper authorities, he in effect "stayed within the bounds of allegiance to the legitimate, God-willed authorities, within the bounds of allegiance to Führer and Chancellor. In spite of everything, the masses of believing people were put at Hitler's disposal for his crusade against Bolshevism and were led into battle by the army chaplains of both religious confessions."[75] The isolated priest whom Rosenberg accused of drawing anti-Nazi lessons out of the horrors of war was far outnumbered by his brethren, who offered solace untainted by recriminations in their churches. This was also fully appreciated by Hitler; as he told Himmler in 1942, "if filled churches help me keep the German people quiet, then in view of the burden of war there can be no objection to them."[76]

Secret police chief Reinhard Heydrich had recruited former priests for an intelligence network that stretched as far as the Vatican, but his scheme to infiltrate the Catholic clergy with Hitler Youth as under-cover seminarians, who would attain leading positions in twenty years from which they would subvert that Church—and Protestant ones in the same way—was vetoed by Hitler, apparently out of fear that their religious immersion would leave lasting effects.[77] Rosenberg had pinned his hopes on Reichsbishop Müller, whose nazified Evangelical Church was to present him with a forum for his *Volksreligion*. Amid the dissensions of German Protestantism, that project never got off the ground either. At first the regime tried to salvage what was possible by two contradictory tactics: denying any rift in the Protestant establishment, yet setting up a Ministry of Church Affairs under the Prussian bureaucrat Hanns Kerrl to force the warring factions together.[78] Later, during the war, Nazi leaders circulated secret directives which admitted that neither tactic had worked—if anything, the interdenominational struggle had been exacerbated. Therefore, the regime was to reverse its strategy: from now on it would promote, rather than stifle, dissension in Protestant ranks. Instead of backing a Trojan-horse group to seize control of the clerical establishment, it would make life equally difficult for all church factions.[79] Their internecine struggles were sure to reduce their hold on individual believers, creating a gap that the Party would rush in to fill with its credo.

Amid the twists and turns of Nazi church policy, all dictated by expediency, Rosenberg saw the progressive frustration of his plans for a new Nazi faith and the decline of his powers to influence the course of events. In August 1934 he recorded his growing disenchantment with Reichsbishop Müller, who, even through his loyal *Reichskirche,* still insisted on going through the motions of a religious leader. What irked Rosenberg particularly was that Müller had stripped one of his officials of all church offices for attacking the Bible at a Party rally in Berlin the previous November. After all, notes Rosenberg, the offending Dr. Krause "was merely repeating my *Mythus!*" If Müller's sect looked none too promising as a vehicle for Rosenberg's ideology, it might be better just to have "the churches dry up" and to wait for a new medium to emerge out of the Hitler Youth. That would not take too long, according to Rosenberg: "In ten years the time may be ripe for a Reformer who will remodel the churches and give them the heroic lines of our time."[80] This is the role to which he aspired.

Rosenberg was generally too preoccupied with the attacks being directed at him from Catholic quarters, and with Hitler's failure to order an official counterattack on his behalf, to pay much heed to sniping from the Protestants. It came as a shock to him to find out in early 1935 that even they "have issued half a dozen brochures against me." They were distinctly the lesser clerical evil, their critiques "decent in form, boring in content." Still, Rosenberg was disturbed by their display of "common convictions" with the Vatican, and he asked sarcastically "why they don't return to Rome, into the big sheep-pen out of which they have strayed, to now stand around shivering."[81] Whatever relief he may have felt at the dumping of the Reichsbishop was soon dissipated by the appointment of the Church Minister in 1935. Müller at least had been an apostle of the *Mythus* though, according to its author, an imperceptive one; Kerrl was too close to the old-line Protestant leaders with whom he sought to make the regime's peace, too disinterested in ideology to suit Rosenberg's purposes.[82]

When Rosenberg notes the fact that Kerrl is Göring's protégé, he also implies resentment that others of the Nazi elite surpassed him in influencing religious policy. Yet 1935 marked only the first stage of that process, capped in 1940 by Bormann's clear pre-eminence. In one of the ironies of Nazi history, Bormann's guidelines call for the "withering" of all Christian denominations, coming as close as official policy ever did to realizing the first phase of Rosenberg's earlier plans.[83] But the second phase, erection of a nazified church, was no longer under serious consideration by the leaders who had shouldered Rosenberg aside—although he remained true to his quixotic pattern by offering yet another proposal for a National Reich Church in January 1942, in more radical form than anything he had suggested in the *Mythus*.[84] If occasionally his memoirs betray an awareness of how low his status as ideologist had sunk, that does not seem to have discouraged him from the single-minded pursuit of his counter-religious objectives. For instance, he shrugged off the news that Bormann, since 1941 in sole charge of Party policy on the churches, scrawled on the margin of the latest Rosenberg memo, "I am not accustomed to deal with idiots."[85]

Before Bormann stepped into the Deputy Führer's post vacated by Hess in 1941, Rosenberg was trying to win the bureaucratic infighting that could have raised him on the reformer's pedestal by three means: collaborating with Müller to resurrect the *Reichskirche* scheme, shaming or coercing the other denominations into falling in line behind it, and checking the "unideological" policies of Church Minister Kerrl. First, he rushed to the defense of Müller, despite the low esteem he had earlier expressed for his abilities, to protest the "shabby treatment" of the Reichsbishop at the hands of the new Ministry.[86] Second, he kept up a steady sniper's fire at the Protestant establishment for its lack of fervor in supporting the Nazi cause. A typical passage from a speech to a Party congress at Nuremberg in 1937 reads: "The churches had the grand opportunity of putting their work at the disposal of Adolf Hitler, when the new state was being built, and of marching with him. They let the opportunity slip, and when one does not, or will not, recognize such chances of world history, one has oneself spoken the verdict of destiny."[87] Third, he fulminated against the compromise course of Kerrl, a "subaltern type," whom he held responsible for the resurgence in church strength by 1939.[88]

While Hess was still at Hitler's side, Rosenberg turned to him for a sympathetic hearing of charges against Kerrl's competence. He attacked the Church Minister, both for his imprudence in discussing the Party's anti-Christian stand in a church journal, and for his disobedience of Hitler's instructions by continuing attempts to weld the denominations together in a church union. His sharpest shaft, however, was directed at Kerrl's explanation that it would be pointless to cut off subsidies to the churches since there was no positive substitute to take their place; this betrayed his utter ignorance of the proper Weltanschauung, according to Rosenberg. Furthermore, restricting Nazism to the guidance of scientific research or governmental affairs, as Kerrl had suggested, would take no account of the new belief Rosenberg had been propounding in the past fifteen years. It would amount to leaving the field "to the warmed-over Protestant confessions, which are crumbling apart today," and, in the wake of their certain failure, to letting the Catholic Church reassert its leading role.[89]

BORMANN'S DOCTRINE OF EXPEDIENCY

By the time Bormann was in the ascendancy, Rosenberg had lost his audience in the inner circles of the regime, and it was now his turn to come under fire.[90] Bormann first took him to task for approving Müller's project of writing "Guidelines for Religious Instruction," a draft of Party orders to the schools. Surely Rosenberg should understand that the Party couldn't involve itself in Christian teachings—"Christianity and National Socialism are phenomena due to totally different basic causes. They differ so radically from each other, it's impossible to develop a Christian teaching that can be approved on the basis of the National Socialist Weltanschauung, just as the Christian denominations can never agree fully to embrace the Weltanschauung of National Socialism." In short, it was futile to talk of a synthesis of the two faiths, in Bormann's opinion, if only because Christian teachings had no place for "the racial question, the question of preventing or destroying worthless life, and the [Party's] position on marriage, as is evident from priestly celibacy as well as the orders of monks and nuns, the dogma of the immaculate conception of Mary, which contradicts the Germanic spirit, etc." By this time, Rosenberg must have been aware that his dream of a nazified church lay in shambles. The Party would refrain from the remodeling of the churches he had been demanding with himself as the would-be architect of a new Reformation.

Indeed, Bormann went on to put the Party's religious policy in such basic terms of expediency that it reduced the functions of the ideological niche Rosenberg had carved out for himself to the menial task of a scribe. The policy could not deal with church affairs in the broad fashion of Müller's "Guidelines," since that "would just transfer the confessional fight to the arena of the Party." Admittedly, as Rosenberg had pointed out before Hess, Christian teachings would have to be replaced with something better. But, as Bormann turned this argument around, it meant either not doing anything to the churches until the appearance of the new faith Rosenberg had constantly predicted or adding a few special Nazi commandments to the biblical ten. The Decalogue itself must not be tampered with, as Rosenberg had earlier demanded, because "for most comrades today it represents the only guideline for their moral conduct and for an orderly social life in the national community"—quite an admission for a Nazi leader with no use for organized religion, and one which Rosenberg could never have been expected to agree with. But for Bormann even a despised faith could have its uses, if only it helped maintain a pacified population. Here he gave a more mundane reason to Rosenberg for tolerating religious instruction: if the Party did not do so, it would likely be blamed for the current rise in juvenile delinquency. The only job left was the writing of some extra commandments, for example, for bravery, against cowardice, for the love of all animate nature, and to keep the blood pure. Should Rosenberg accept the challenge (he never did), he could presumably busy himself with the preparation of such a Nazi catechism to be imparted to all German youth.

By June 1941, a month after the departure of Hess, Bormann felt securely enough entrenched to spell out the Party's opposition to the churches without reservation, in a top-secret decree to all Gauleiter entitled "The Relation of National Socialism to Christianity."[91] It opens with the thesis that "National Socialism and Christian concepts are irreconcilable." The scientific truths of the former are contrasted with the false dogmas of the latter. From this it follows that the Party must "refuse to strengthen existing denominations or to promote emergent ones. No distinction can be drawn here among the various Christian confessions. For the same reason, the proposal to erect an Evangelical *Reichskirche* through a union of Evangelical churches has been irrevocably cancelled, because the Evangelical church faces us with the same hostility as the Catholic. Any strengthening of the Evangelical church would merely work out to our detriment."

At this juncture of World War II, on the eve of the German invasion of Russia, Bormann felt that the Party not only could dispense with the services of denominations it had once sought to exploit, but also that it no longer needed biblical injunctions to regulate a populace mobilized for war. His decree goes on to announce:

> For the first time in German history the Führer consciously and completely has the leadership of the people in his own hand. With the Party, its components and attached units, the Führer has created for himself and thereby the German Reich leadership an instrument which makes him independent of the Church. All influences which might impair or damage the leadership of the people exercised by the Führer with the help of the NSDAP, must be eliminated. More and more the people must be separated from the churches and their organs, the pastors . . . Just as the deleterious influence of astrologers, seers and other fakers are eliminated and suppressed by the State, so must the possibility of Church influence also be totally removed. Not until this has happened does the State leadership have influence on the individual citizens. Not until then are people and Reich secure in their existence for all the future.

He concludes with an admonition drawn from the "divide and rule" principle, which symbolizes the way in which Nazi church policy had come full circle: "The interests of the Reich do not lie in the surmounting of factionalism in the Church, but rather in maintaining and strengthening it."[92]

CONTINUITIES OF DOMESTIC AND OCCUPATION POLICIES

The regime's tactics toward the Protestant churches thus ran the gamut from a fifth-column attempt to seize control, to a state-sponsored scheme to impose unity on the denominations, to interventions of the terror apparatus to suppress the church factions that refused to be "co-ordinated," finally to a negative neutrality toward all factions while dissension among them was fostered behind the scenes. When the same leadership had to address itself to the task of developing a policy to govern Church affairs in Russian areas under Nazi occupation, it resorted to a virtually identical arsenal of measures. Instead of following a somewhat logical sequence, however, as it had domestically, the regime mixed its weapons arbitrarily and in a self-contradictory fashion in dealing with the Russian Orthodox Church. In both spheres, it seemed to force the pattern of events into confirming the expectations of its ideology, beginning with a situation that appeared promising for exploitation but ending up with one in which most church groups had, indeed, become the opponents they were all along suspected of being.

In one sense, then, Nazi policy toward the Russian church groups represents a set of reflex actions that proved inappropriate for a range of conditions radically different from those of the domestic setting. In another sense, the course was predetermined for the German occupation authorities, since any departure from it, either in the direction of total war on religion or in the form of genuine tolerance, would have upset the balance achieved back home. Especially when it came to considering official support of church groups, Nazi governors have indicated that they were aware that such a move would be misconstrued as a shift in the basic Party position, hence they shrank back. It was unthinkable, in Bormann's view, to have the antireligious ideologue Rosenberg—by then Minister for the East—proclaim religious freedom in the occupied areas in May 1942.[93] He apparently persuaded Hitler to reject the idea because of the storm of protest that might have been expected from German churches not getting the benefits proffered by Rosenberg to his Russian subjects.

The preceding survey of Nazi domestic religious policy indicates the palette of options available to occupation authorities in the Russian territories; two other factors that determined the particular policy mix selected for the areas under their separate jurisdictions must also be considered. First, each German official to some degree was guided by the overall goals of occupation policy, of which the regulation of religious life was only a minor part. Second, of much more direct relevance to his administrative behavior in this field, he had to accommodate the interests of the Party or special state agency that he served. These had a two-fold bearing on his decisions of church questions: he had to consider whether each decision could be rendered in a way that would facilitate his fulfillment of key assignments, and he was drawn to adopt a positive course of action which was most likely to enhance the power of his office and agency vis-à-vis that of his rivals.

The fluid conditions of the occupation were even more conducive than those of the domestic setting had been to the development of informal lines of authority and the clash of bureaucracies arrayed about rival leaders. Each subordinate official quickly became attuned to this constant competition for pre-eminence, playing for progressively higher stakes the closer his status to the inner circles of Party and state. He soon learned to discount ideology and the theoretical bases of policy as crucial factors in the resolution of problems and instead, to invoke them in order to secure a tactical advantage for the position of his office at the expense of others. To some extent the contradictions in policy were an inevitable consequence of the pervasive power struggle among the occupation agencies. Frequently they were also deliberately staged as tests of strength between bureaucracies with intersecting fields of authority, of which there were at least seven involved in the administration of Russian Church affairs.

4

German Policy Toward the Orthodox Church: The Minister versus the Commissar

If German policies toward the Church in the occupied Russian territories were beset by inconsistency, contradiction, and petty bureaucratic bickering, they only reflected in microcosm the conflicting aims of the Nazi drive eastward. Grandiose dreams of the past decade had envisioned an empire in which millions of bovine Slavic subjects existed for the greater glory of the Third Reich. The native population proved of no practical use to military and civil administrators, for whom they were at best a mass to be squeezed dry of labor and foodstuffs and at worst a rabble to be ruled at gunpoint. Local officials, as members of agencies with overlapping areas of jurisdiction, also found themselves caught up in the feuds of their chiefs. Any long-range political objectives were soon lost sight of as each satrap competed for quick successes that could aid his scramble for advancement and the enlargement of his prerogatives.

On the ideological level, Nazi leadership never came to terms with the realities of Soviet Russia. The daily life of the people and their problems had little relevance for the rhetoric of Hitler and the man he selected in April 1941 to be Commissar for Questions on the East European Space, Alfred Rosenberg.[1] Considerations at that airy level centered on the mystical concept of the *Ostraum*. This term carried much more than the connotation of a strategic factor; it also connoted an ambivalence in which fear of the Russian hordes mingled with longing to turn their vast resources to German advantage: the borderlands to be a giant buffer zone against Asiatic invasion, the inhabitants shifted like pawns to facilitate their submission, their labors to bear trains of luxuries to the tables of the master race.

In the books of the Nazi planners, German domination of Russia rested on the circular logic of racism and the inexorable demands of national destiny. If this was cloaked in the language of eighteenth-century colonialism, there was, nevertheless, no complementary understanding that civil servants would have to be trained for their administrative posts in the East, nor any recognition of responsibilities toward the future subjects in something like a "white man's burden." Simple application of Teutonic force would suffice to yield one-way benefits. In *Mein Kampf* Hitler had already pointed at the course of German expansion eastward as the means to satisfy Germany's need for enough *Lebensraum* to provide permanent security.[2] Shortly after the invasion of Russia, he translated his plans into the terms of classic imperialism. "What India was for England, that the Ostraum will be for us," he declared, specifying Russia's future functions to consist of supplying the Reich with food and other "useful articles."[3]

In the context of Nazi colonialism, a faithful party Gauleiter became ipso facto qualified as a Generalkommissar administering the entire Ukraine or Belorussia, and an ideologist like Rosenberg qualified to take complete charge of the Ministry for the Occupied Eastern Territories or *Ostministerium*, in July 1941.[4] This was a rationale conducive to fanciful estimates of Russian social forces. When it came to religious policy, for example, the preconceptions of German officials led them to assume that they would be dealing with some sort of primitive tribal rite. As Rosenberg assured Hitler, it did not have to be taken seriously, this "oriental custom with nice songs," which amounted to little more than "fetishism."[5] German administrators could afford to be indulgent about such practices; they might even be fostered as a means of keeping Slavic subjects tractable. The pattern of cynicism had been established by Hitler for Poland in his 1940 strategy sessions: "Polish priests will receive food from us and will, for that very reason, direct their little sheep along the path we favor . . . If any priest acts differently, we shall make short work of him. The task of the priest is to keep the Poles quiet, stupid, and dull-witted. This is entirely to our interests."[6]

The colonialist analogy soon proved irrelevant to day-to-day administrative tasks of the occupation. The oversimplified guidelines based on it were of little use to an official deciding which one of several rival religious associations to license or whether to grant subventions to a pro-German church. Prewar Nazi planning had set up a model in which superior force shuffled inert groups of subjects at will. When the dust had settled behind the first wave of German panzers, however, there were neither sufficient staffs of administrators available to pursue policies except at critical points in the rear areas, nor did the population take readily to its preordained status of subservience. The early master plans of Rosenberg had foreseen an empire of small dependent states carved out of Russia, with "depopulated Slavs" displaced in key regions by German settlers.[7] Once the occupation was under way, publication of such partitioning schemes would only serve to stiffen the resistance of a population already antagonized by economic extortion and political repression, as the Wehrmacht's propaganda branch pointed out.[8]

The empire builders shelved their projects for the duration when the requisitioning agents and SS squad leaders took command of the occupied Russian territories. The subtlety of long-range designs was lost on administrators pressing immediate aims under conditions of total mobilization. If their operations required theoretical justification, it was provided by the pragmatic rule: any measure has to yield the maximum gain to the Reich's military-economic power for the minimum expenditure of human and material resources. In the Russian case this amounted to instant exploitation, as suggested by Rafael Lemkin's classification of European territories under Nazi rule: (1) the so-called "German lands" like Austria were absorbed under the pretext that "we're only taking back what belongs to us"; (2) in relatively nonstrategic countries such as Denmark, cooperation was "forced" through existing social institutions with German supervision in crucial areas; (3) "despoliation" was applied to territories like Poland, where little collaboration could be expected; (4) the Ukraine and other parts of Russia were unmitigatedly exploited as *Interessengebiete* (interest areas), where "the main task of the occupying power is to draw . . . raw materials, food and labor," since no indigenous elements were deemed fit to participate in the organization of central governments.[9] The propinquity of the former Soviet areas to the front and their links to a nation whose government kept transmitting calls for resistance furnished added reasons for an ironclad set of Nazi controls. For the population the system amounted to a virtually unrelieved state of siege.

Whatever small part Orthodox Church leaders had hoped to play in the imperialist script of Rosenberg's ministry was gradually trimmed off by the regional and district commissars who directed the local occupation dramas. In Berlin the order of priorities had reserved a low but positive function for churchmen; among the daily pressures of the field there was less and less concern for such factors bearing on popular morale. It was of little import to Nazi commissars whether laborers were loaded onto cattlecars bound for Germany willingly or not, or whether farmers yielded up their produce to armed squads with a smile. Within a few months of the invasion, the authorities increasingly relied on force, rather than persuasion, as the instrument of rule. Russian clerics, like the nationalist leaders of the Ukraine and Belorussia, found themselves no longer singled out for special treatment but lumped with the population at large, randomly suspect of potential rebellion. Both groups thus found themselves deprived of the middle ground they needed to survive, because by official standards any neutral force was an enemy in disguise. They were left with the dismal choice of collaborating with a despised regime that had no use for them, and losing their following in the process, or taking up with the partisans and leaving their flocks leaderless.

The majority of the cultural elite appear to have circumvented the dilemma by combining lip-service collaboration with inner resistance, as will be seen in Chapter 6. They temporized in the hope that rendering the smallest possible service required by the authorities for survival would not compromise them in the people's eyes. At times they did so in the desperate belief that Nazis and Soviets would mutually annihilate each other and that in the ensuing anarchy, like that of the post-World War I period, a third force might prevail.[10] Even so, churchmen and nationalists were left with the problem of searching among the myriad agencies of the German occupation to find one willing to purchase their token support. None seemed notably eager on any terms, at least until the waning months of the war, when Nazi leaders were re-evaluating their forces in the light of disastrous defeats. Still, there were degrees to this unwillingness; on closer examination, German bureaucratic hierarchies disclose a spectrum with varying intensities of anti-Russian attitude. Some of the less intransigent, though they were also the most impotent, offered half-hearted collaborators terms they could live with. As they became aware of the rivalries that existed among these competing structures, priests and nationalists could become adept at playing one off against another—though admittedly their leverage was minimal—

and gain a toehold for survival in the spaces left by conflicting directives.

German policy in the occupation of Russia was mainly refracted through the following structures. The first, led by Hitler, Bormann, and Erich Koch, Reichskommissar for the Ukraine, barred the Russian people from participation in the "New Order," since such *Untermenschen* were not fit to assert any rights; this attitude was largely shared by Himmler's SS, especially its *Einsatzgruppen* (breach troops), charged with exterminating Jews and certain other categories of the population, though it did permit a select few collaborators to don its black shirts. Next were the economic agencies, like those in charge of farming and forced labor, intent on little beyond the most efficient exploitation of their subjects. Then came the Ostministerium, which saw the enemy as the Kremlin and the Great Russian people and, therefore, was ready to enlist the support of other Soviet nationalities; this was generally consonant with the approach of the Propaganda Ministry, trying to win popular acclaim for its anti-Communist message. Further along this continuum of diminishing anti-Russian outlook stood the military commanders seeking to secure their rear through sporadic gestures of accommodation; most favorably inclined was the Foreign Office, whose influence evaporated as the war progressed.[11]

Instead of a single German policy, then, there were some seven approaches to the administration of Russian lands. Investigation of the specific decisions in the religious field can be pursued along these lines, but none of them constitutes a policy—a reasoned and consistent course of action—so much as it does a shorthand account of directives that served as afterthoughts of the staffs and factions within them intent on advancing their statuses. Organization tables of the occupation hierarchy introduce a false note of bureaucratic rationality into the picture. The fundamental layer consisted of medieval fiefs which the retinues of Nazi officials claimed for themselves, where staff and line authority stood for little. What mattered was the personal connection each could trace to the camarilla surrounding the Führer. By the arbitrary favor of this court, subordinate could dictate to chief, a government minister be consigned to the futile job of issuing unanswered memoranda. In an attempt to gain that favor, an isolated overlord like Rosenberg could and did reverse positions repeatedly—a foredoomed quest, since military-economic necessities had overtaken political considerations in the first year of the occupation.

RUSSIAN ORTHODOXY IN THE THIRD REICH

Political factors had played a role in the schemes that attracted the Nazi leadership three or four years before the invasion of Russia. Even then, however, the projects did not allow for the future expression of popular aspirations. The reading of social realities drew on the wishful counsels of 1918 vintage émigrés, the die-hard variety that had embraced Hitler in his fledgling days in Munich. Typical was the plan to build up an organization of Orthodox clerics in Germany for eventual use as a fifth column to take over the Church within Russia. By 1938, the regime had gone so far as to erect in Berlin a fine new Russian cathedral, which "was becoming a beacon for all the Orthodox in Europe, especially for Soviet refugees."[12] In addition, nineteen other Orthodox churches in the Reich had recieved government funds for repairs.

The man chosen by the psychological warfare strategists to captain this project was a figure of curious antecedents and abilities, equally fluent in German and Russian: Archbishop Seraphim, also known by his German name, Lade. According to a Swiss source, Seraphim had been converted to Orthodoxy in Russia and, after his deportation by the Soviets, had surfaced in Germany as an anti-Bolshevik propagandist.[13] He owed his investiture in the "Living Church of the Ukrainian Renovators" to a Russian émigré newspaper in Paris, *Poslednye Novosti*, but had yet to find a legitimate Orthodox Church body to certify his episcopal rank. Undeterred by his checkered past, the Nazis named him "Leader" of all Orthodox in the Third Reich and in all the territories it controlled. His authority as Bishop of Berlin and Germany was eventually confirmed by the Karlotvtsi Synod, the monarchist émigré church center in Yugoslavia.[14]

The advent of Operation Barbarossa found Seraphim ready to repay his German sponsors. In an "Appeal to All Russian Believers" on June 22, 1941, Seraphim exhorted the faithful of his homeland to join Hitler's "crusade against the enslavers of Russia" and to do away with "the Red devils."[15] The singular lack of response to his appeal was matched by the reluctance of churchmen in areas quickly overrun by German arms to put themselves under his jurisdiction. The German seizure of western Poland two years before had marked the apogee of his power, for he had then been able to pressure the Orthodox metropolitan of Warsaw, Dionisius (Valedinski), into submission.[16] It had proved a short-lived victory, however, because in September 1940 the German governor of

Poland, Hans Frank, buttressed his own power base by restoring ecclesiastical sovereignty to Dionisius in return for a pledge of civil obedience, thus effectively pushing Seraphim out of the picture.[17]

Back in Berlin, Seraphim seems to have channeled his reduced influence to shaping developments in the occupied Russian territories through the Cultural Ministry representative on the Eastern Church[18]—a frail reed on which to anchor his great ambitions. From time to time in the first years of the war, a bishop of right-Ukrainian persuasion would declare his allegiance to Seraphim, overestimating the latter's abilities to intervene in diocesan Church feuds.[19] Seraphim had to pass up such opportunities because the regional commissars kept him out of their fiefs, preferring to work with local churchmen whom they could manipulate more directly. Toward the war's end he had become a somewhat chastened figure, conducting services for the *Ostarbeiter* (forced laborers) and prisoners of war at their camps in the Berlin area.[20]

The inglorious end of Seraphim stands in marked contrast to the grand future that appeared to lie in store for émigré clerics in prewar Nazi councils. When the influx of Austrian and Czech believers in 1938 into the Berlin diocese had outdistanced its available supply of priests, for example, a German-sponsored Orthodox theological faculty was set up in Breslau (Wroclaw) the following year. Its director had also come by a circuitous route: Archimandrite Vassily Pavlovski, from the seminary in Harbin, Manchuria, elevated to bishop by the Serbian Patriarch Gavrilo. Thus the apparatus of a pro-Nazi church movement was primed for subversion of Orthodoxy in the East, its prestige gilded by the reactionary wing of émigré Church leadership. It had been endorsed by no less than Metropolitan Anastasius, head of the Karlovtsi Synod, "the most respected Russian cleric in the Balkans" at the time.[21] For all its resources and backing, however, the movement depended on a summons by German administrators in the field that never came.

The occupation authorities passed up the devious schemes of the fifth-column advocates for functional and personal reasons. They were caught up in a succession of immediate local crises for which more direct, cruder methods seemed appropriate. They found little practical use in the projects of émigrés, out of touch with a new generation of Soviet social realities. When Hitler learned in May 1942 that former Russian princes and politicians had assembled at the Hotel Adlon in Berlin to press their views on some sympathetic officials from the Foreign Office, he ordered an abrupt halt to the proceedings.[22] Less impotent quarters than the diplomatic were made impervious to the temptations of such gatherings by their anti-Russian bias. If they did not subscribe entirely to the *Untermensch* formula and stressed the utilization rather than the extermination of their Eastern subjects, German policy-makers still looked only to non-Russian nationals for a modicum of collaboration. They tended to make an oversimple equation of Russians with Communists and therefore deferred the employment of anti-Soviet forces under their own leaders, like General Andrei Vlasov, until the desperate final months of the war.[23]

ROSENBERG'S DREAM OF EMPIRE

It was hardly accidental for most German civil administrators in Russia to despise their subjects—if only because the rulers included a disproportionately high number of *Volksdeutsche*, naturally predisposed to such an attitude. Hitler showed some understanding of the subconscious self-hatred which motivated that group when he asked: "Have you noticed that Germans who have lived a long time in Russia can never again be Germans?" His answer was: "The huge spaces have fascinated them. After all, Rosenberg is rabid against the Russians only because they would not allow him to be a Russian."[24] Yet it was the same Alfred Rosenberg whom Hitler chose to head the Ostministerium, theoretically the command post for Nazi rule of the occupied territories. Choice of a minister afflicted, not only with psychological blind spots to his assignment, but with a twenty-year record of ineffectual administration, would seem perverse unless it is concluded that those were the very qualities for which Rosenberg was picked. He would command only a staff of counsellors in Berlin, drawing a veil of legality over the brutal political and economic actions of the field forces who did the actual ruling.

But Rosenberg had something more than incompetence to recommend him. He had also authored the grand plans for transforming the Soviet state into a conglomeration of dependencies that could be manipulated from Berlin. This dream of empire echoed Hitler's own and furnished an ideological justification for the undertaking in Russia, which was not supposed to meet with any native resistance. From the first, Rosenberg had been convinced that a host of "friendly nationalities" waited to do the Germans' bidding because of its hatred of the Great Russians. As far back as 1934 he had reported to the Führer (whom he worshipped) on "the centrifugal forces at work in Russia," volunteering to follow such events closely, since "one has to be ready when things have developed far enough."[25] The repressive measures of Nazi commissars severed such schemes at the root, though that did not prevent Rosenberg's aides from trying to revive the idea by showers of memoranda.

It had become virtually a reflex for the grand strategists to advocate their devious projects by the time the pressures of the invasion calendar had made them obsolete. Relevant only to the embittered hopes of pro-Nazi émigrés, such briefs were couched in terms to appeal to the pragmatists, promising to advance the German war effort at minimal cost. In this vein, Arno Schickedanz, an assistant to Rosenberg who later became his overseer for the Caucasus, in 1939 addressed a memorandum on future policy for *Osteuropa* to Hans-Heinrich Lammers, chief of the Reich Chancellery. He argued that military as well as political plans for "the future solution of East European questions" must focus on "the politico-psychological preparation of the population of these areas, on the one hand to facilitate purely military action, on the other eventually to exploit broadly the various nationalities for German interests, which will be decisive for the future order of the entire Ostraum." He held out high hope that Ukrainians and Belorussians would be ready "to welcome a power that will protect them from Moscow—at the same time, helping to secure German *Lebensraum* far into the East, and with their own, not with German, blood." This was the shortcut to the "extensive destruction of Russia, as unsuccessfully pursued by Charles XII . . . The collapse of the Soviet paradise will come with the revival of all the national-political forces suppressed by the Soviet regime . . . that would also be the right moment for using both these peoples in the service of German interests to push back Muscovy."[26]

The characteristics that had cast Rosenberg into the role of an *idéologue manqué* before the opening curtain of the occupation drama later made him into a natural loser to rivals heading other agencies out for quick exploitation. He sensed the defeats ahead of him in a note of April 2, 1941, on the "aims and methods of the future occupation of the Soviet Union."[27] In order to establish a reason for the existence of his ministry, however, he was driven to insist on the priority of its "political" mission and to decry a policy determined solely by "military-economic necessities." Here he admitted the importance of economic goals but contended that only long-term ones would assure a steady flow of materiel from Russia for use on the Western front. The unspoken implication is that, if stripping and pillage were to yield to more sophisticated forms of exploitation, the Ostministerium, as the only available center for political coordination, would have earned for itself a leading part.

When it comes to religion, Rosenberg was moved by the same con-figuration of motives to paint great opportunities in strokes of extreme caution. The policy was framed in a way that provided full employment of Ostministerium officials, since they were only to support select denominations that intensive screening had indicated would be the aptest vehicles for anti-Russian exploitation. The complications are emphasized in Rosenberg's memorandum of April 29, 1941: "Church questions throughout the East are of varying nature and require careful treatment in regard to their history, present legal condition, and the relations we desire to achieve in the future."[28]

The following month, Rosenberg lectured his future Reich commissars on the federative empire of puppet states he planned to carve out of Russia. "In the field of church policy," he stated in a section deleted from the final draft, "tolerance edicts may guarantee freedom of purely religious belief, although without any assumption of governmental responsibility for it. Here, too, we will have to take measures that reflect the varied conditions of each Reichskommissariat."[29] Rosenberg may have retracted these sentences because he had second thoughts about the domestic repercussions of issuing even semiofficial declarations of tolerance for occupied areas when the regime had never admitted such rights at home.[30] It was over a year before such an edict finally appeared —and then it was in the hands of the regional commissars—to enhance their powers rather than Rosenberg's. But before discussing this further, it would be well to summarize the position in which the Ostminister saw himself progressively isolated at his headquarters, the former Yugo-slavian Embassy on the Rauchstrasse in Berlin.

A thumbnail sketch of Rosenberg during the occupation period would have to begin with the judgments of postwar commentators that this was a minor figure with "ambitions and hopes out of proportion to his talents."[31] Though it is quite true that he suffered from "too much thinking, too little commanding,"[32] this is only half the story. The two men whom Hitler selected to do the actual governing—Erich Koch in the Ukraine, Hinrich Lohse in the remaining areas lumped together as the *Ostland*—had been party Gauleiter in their own right. With the Führer's tacit consent, they lorded it over their private empires, for-bidding their subordinates to receive the Ostministerium's deputies and not bothering to call on their nominal chief during rare visits to Berlin. Under such circumstances it is small wonder that Rosenberg hardly ever ventured into the occupied area and that his field trips were brief, cere-monial affairs.[33] Rather than risk being snubbed by underlings who outstripped him in power because of their entree to Hitler and Bormann, Rosenberg nursed his injured pride behind his Berlin desk.

From his paper throne, Rosenberg could for a time console himself with a twin set of delusions: first, if Hitler would only listen to his proposals, he would be convinced of their excellence, succumb to the cameraderie of the old Munich days, and put the Ostminister into his deserved place of precedence; second, if he tacked the course of his policy to draw alongside that of the other agencies involved in the occupation, he could form a combination formidable enough to bring his subordinates to heel. At the end of two years, both hopes lay shattered. The intervals between visits to the Führer lengthened. Rosenberg saw him three times after the invasion in 1941, three more times in 1942, and then at a disastrous final session on May 19, 1943.[34] With each conference, it became more evident that Hitler had no patience for Rosenberg's grand schemes; he turned the occasions into schoolboy lectures on the need to learn from the "practical experiences" of brutal commissars like Koch instead of criticizing them. Temperamentally incapable of accepting this rejection from his leader, Rosenberg blamed his troubles on Himmler and Bormann for having turned Hitler against him.[35]

In his second vain endeavor, the search for bureaucratic allies, Rosenberg showed that, persistent as he might be in his loyalties, he was inconsistent in his policies. Time and again he sought to make common cause with rival officials, ready to trade key parts of his program for their support. Even his nemesis, Himmler, was pursued as a possible tool to put Koch in his place. The desperate bid included an offer to have SS Obergruppenführer Gottlob Berger head a "political guidance staff" in the Ostministerium in summer 1943.[36] Like the other abortive coalitions this one crumbled, leaving Rosenberg shorn of yet another sector of his shrunken jurisdiction. Such trades were bound to work out to his disadvantage, since his opponents in Party, state, and secret police apparatus held all the trumps: power, entree to Hitler's inner circle, and an undeviating line of total exploitation of subject peoples without any of the niceties Rosenberg wished to observe.

The man who had begun his ministerial career with a policy premised on winning the allegiance of his Russian subjects had shifted his ground so much by July 1944 that he endorsed the so-called "Hay Action," an abortive SS plan for "reducing the biological potential" of the Slavs by abducting all children between the ages of ten and fourteen.[37] Even this kind of reversal could not change Hitler's rejection of him as a "sentimentalist" nor persuade the hard-line officials that they had any need of him. By October 1944, self-delusion had finally given way to despair, and Rosenberg tendered his resignation to the Führer.[38] The last act was as anticlimactic as those foregoing: there was no acknowledgment of the resignation letter, and Rosenberg stayed on till the end, surrounded by stacks of his unanswered memoranda.

EVOLUTION OF THE "TOLERANCE EDICT"

A typical excursion by Rosenberg, the paper warrior, is described in his attempts to produce a workable system to regulate religion in the occupied Russian territories. This labyrinthine quest occupied the better part of a year, during which his staff labored over sixteen draft proposals and endless revisions, only to accede to Bormann's pressure and have authority under the final "Tolerance Edict" of June 1942 end up in the hands of local commissars.[39] It had begun as a fairly simple idea: to incidentally stake out an area for the Ostministerium's jurisdiction. It ended up as a cumbersome legal document erecting a licensing procedure to keep church associations geographically limited and politically impotent. To Russian believers under German rule, this meant another set of Nazi restrictions—and, over an activity conducted freely for the past year, cause for resentment rather than the gratitude expected in Berlin.

The initial call for religious toleration might be thought to have stuck in the throat of a man like Rosenberg, who had inveighed so long and loudly against the organized religions of Germany. He appears to have made up his mind, however, that such negative attitudes would be out of place in his new position as would-be lord of empire in the East. Indeed, he seems to have convinced himself that he had actually issued "a special 'church tolerance' edict" in 1941, though he could produce no evidence to substantiate this claim at his Nuremberg trial.[40] At the outset, the project was overlaid with wishful thinking. A simple expression of the Reich's benevolence was expected to bring churchmen to the Nazi cause, as Hitler's first speeches had once persuaded right-wing émigrés to subsidize the *Völkischer Beobachter* under Rosenberg's editorial guidance. In this spirit, an early draft of the edict confined itself to the following three provisions: "1. All residents of the occupied eastern territories are guaranteed freedom of religious belief. 2. Persons who share the same religious belief are given the right to form religious associations. 3. Implementing orders will be issued by the Reich Minister for the Occupied Eastern Territories."[41]

A universalistic declaration on this order might have led to a propaganda victory for the German administration if it had been issued early enough; but before it could be launched it was scuttled from four directions. First came Rosenberg's own reservations toward the Catholic and pro-Russian Orthodox denominations, for whom intolerance and repression were in store. Next, the scheme was punctured by objections of the Ostministerium departments heads, who became embroiled in controversies over such details as appropriate forms for registering each church, how the political reliability of its membership could be ascertained, and what civil code provisions were relevant to its property holdings.[42] Third, Bormann took the opportunity on April 3, 1942, to hurl a missile at the now legalistically embellished draft in the shape of a ten-page critique that proved he could beat Rosenberg's bureaucracy at its own game. After seizing on a number of oversights in the draft, such as its lack of guidance on how to dispose of the property of a church which had been denied a license, Bormann twitted Rosenberg with the question: was it right for a Reich Ministry in the midst of war to occupy itself with registering the tiniest sect and scrutinizing each of its budgets? Finally, the stillbirth of the project was being assured by the ongoing programs of the secret police and the other agencies engaged in the occupation, whose inhuman approach was driving the potential quislings Rosenberg's scheme had counted on into isolation or determined opposition to the Germans.

In regard to the first factor, Rosenberg had made clear all along that he had no intention of suspending his anti-Catholic and anti-Russian biases in formulating a tolerance edict. Its positive features were exclusively intended to benefit churches hostile to the Moscow Patriarchate—mainly nationalist factions in the Ukraine and, to a lesser degree, in Belorussia. But each of these two major provinces under occupation also contained sizable groups of Catholics—concentrated in the western regions, and in the Ukraine predominantly affiliated with Uniate churches that combined Slavonic rites with allegiance to the Pope. In them Rosenberg recognized his natural enemies. Any extension of their influence would encroach on his sphere for manipulation.

These considerations already dominated the policies Rosenberg sketched out on May 7, 1941, before he had any Russian territories to administer.[43] He begins by referring with trepidation to a "large instruction center for Ukrainians in the Vatican, trying to strengthen Catholic influence in the Ukraine." Then he takes note of the traditional bonds to the Kremlin that have made the Orthodox churches in the Ukraine "an immensely strong tie for Russian imperialism." Both of these elements, he cautions, should be borne in mind by his future commissars to avoid supporting any church that might turn out to be a two-edged sword in their hands. Their first step must be to survey thoroughly "how much churchdom has been stamped out" in their domain. Then, they are to tread a narrow middle road, "neither reactivating the repressed church-dom nor continuing the Bolshevik stand on religious extermination." The paramount aim of the officials is to maintain the upper hand, not to set in motion forces they will be unable to control. Rosenberg rec-ommends permitting "confessional associations . . . but without govern-mental support" to prevent churches from growing to the stature of national political centers, while leaving German officials free to switch their backing to rival groups who might prove more pliable. Finally, it is axiomatic for him that "church possessions are the property of the state" and that "the German Reich . . . will have to decide whether and when new confessional arrangements are to be allowed."

As Soviet experience had shown, a social institution with latent political force, such as the church, had first to be depoliticized—purged of its traditional web of associations—before it could be converted into a tool of the regime. For Rosenberg, drafting a policy for the occupation, the lesson translated itself into a de-Russification program for the Ukrainian Church: "The basic rule must be that the language of all asso-ciations be exclusively Ukrainian and that all priests belong to the Ukrainian populace." While that church, like the one in Belorussia and in the Baltic states, could be cut down to size by ethnic-denominational barriers, churches in the "parts inhabited by the Russians" were to be fragmented horizontally, along geographical lines. They were to be restricted to local associations, severed from the upper layers of their hierarchies.

A year later, in May 1942, Rosenberg submitted Draft Number 16 of the Tolerance Edict to Lohse and Koch, his commissars for the Ostland and the Ukraine, and in the letter of transmittal showed a bland assump-tion that he could still put into effect his multifaceted religious policy to the last particular.[44] The letter's imperious tone betrays no doubt that the Ostministerium lacked vital data on any of the myriad sects in the occupied territories, as well as any awareness that it had insufficient power to implement its schemes in every locality. Rosenberg announces:

"We have been acting from the viewpoint that there must be no religious associations in the occupied territories which might somehow, by means of pastoral action, build up political configurations directed against the German administration." The "eastern peoples" would have only priests who belonged to their nationality and not to "universalistically inclined churches and religious associations." Specifically, this meant fragmenting the Baltic Protestants along ethnic lines and Belorussian believers by denomination, and keeping Catholic and Russian Orthodox churches in check.

Rosenberg goes on to provide for every eventuality in the case of the Ukraine, where German policy is to plumb the depths of deviousness by countering "the domination of the Russian Orthodox Church" with an insurgent nationalist wing, the Autocephalous Church, but to guard against pitfalls in the process. As he puts it: "We expect the Autocephalous Church to become a rallying point of many Ukrainian nationalists. I don't see any danger in that, since that would give us the best opportunity to keep an eye on them. It might even be advisable to include them on the church councils, so that they can in this way work off their energies on churchly matters."[45] For the project not to backfire, German officials would have to render their support surreptitiously. And in order to undercut the position of the metropolitan who headed the Autocephalists they were backing, the commissars had to circumvent him and deal directly with his bishops. Any religious strife that follows such machinations was of no great concern to Rosenberg, "as long as the commissars do not let it be expressed in ways that are harmful to the economy." His conclusion, couched in the naive terms that equate his pronouncements with accomplished fact, declares: "The new order in agricultural relations and the granting of religious freedom are the basis for popular leadership in the East."

What Rosenberg had not foreseen was that when German promises to remove Soviet controls in key fields such as agriculture and religion merely brought in their wake new sets of repressions, the popular mood of frustrated optimism would turn to vengeful bitterness. Thus Rosenberg had stirred the hopes of Latvian cultural leaders in a speech of May 15, 1942, by declaring: "It will be the task of German leadership in the future to create the prerequisites for popular cultural activities in the course of time. If, for example, the Reichskommissar for the Ostland soon issues an order to regulate the question of the legal rights of religious organizations, thereby religious toleration will be restored as the natural basis for the internal life of the liberated people by an action of the German administration against the antireligious Soviet system."[46] The actual text of the Tolerance Edict issued on June 19 showed that, in the practice of German officials, regulation was to outweigh toleration. All religious organizations were required to register at the office of the district commissar, who could remove any member on their roster if there were "doubts of a general political nature about him." Further, "religious organizations and their local and higher organs" were admonished "to restrict their activities to the execution of religious tasks," under penalty of fines or dissolution if they were to stray from this path or "endanger public order and safety."[47]

In the final analysis, the debacle of the Ostministerium's religious policy was due not so much to its hesitancies and miscalculations as to the fact that its implementation was entrusted to two Reich commissars who had little use for it. Lohse, in charge of Belorussia and the Baltic states, was too intent on pursuing his feudalistic pretensions—requisitioning suitably furnished castles for himself and his staff—to concern himself with the needs of his subjects.[48] The much more formidable Koch, whose Ukrainian domain embraced the bulk of the population, industry, and natural resources in the occupied Russian areas, displayed contemptuous indifference to social institutions like the church, which might detract from his prime aims: economic exploitation and political repression. When a Ukrainian Autocephalous Church did develop, as Rosenberg had anticipated, Koch's reflex was to suppress it because it might grow too powerful to dominate; he had his staff give desultory aid to rival religious organizations as part of his standard "divide and rule" response.[49] Rosenberg protested to higher headquarters such sacrifices of long-range policy for the sake of immediate results but, time after time, in vain. In his Nuremberg cell, he refused to concede that his quest had been hopeless—if only Hitler had lent a sympathetic ear to his "proposals regarding the political and cultural autonomy of all the peoples of Eastern Europe."[50]

POLITICAL PRESSURES AND CULTURAL FORCES

Of course, Rosenberg was indulging in a self-serving exercise when, in retrospect, he made it appear that he had lost valiantly in an attempt to promulgate a more enlightened and humane cultural policy than that of his rivals in the occupation hierarchy. During his term of office, he had been ready to endorse brutal measures in principle. He had distinguished himself only by questioning whether the desired effects could not be achieved with greater subtlety. It was small wonder that such fine distinctions were lost on officials in the field, who were carried away by the destructive spirit of the invasion and the Nazi racism Rosenberg himself had fostered. One of his typical memoranda sums up the priorities for administering the "Eastern Occupied Territories" in the following terms: "The attitude of the German offices to the native population is determined on the one hand by political and economic goals and on the other by the attitude of the population to the Germans."[51] With reference to the second aim, he adds the caveat: "Groundless strict measures are not desirable and are, therefore, not to be taken." There is no evidence that such vague afterthoughts led to any perceptible easing of the desperate conditions imposed on the subject peoples.

The local German commissars who dispensed life and death were hardly ever of the opinion that their arbitrariness was "groundless." Their own Ostminister had explained to them two days before the invasion that they should feel no obligation to feed the Russian people from the granary of the Ukraine. This was "a hard necessity that lies outside any feelings," because German needs dictated that "the future will hold very hard years in store for the Russians."[52] A year later, Rosenberg had lectured: "that thousands are badly cared for or are badly treated is taken for granted"—followed by the cavalier assurance, "You don't have to grow gray hairs over that."[53] If he balked at the prevalent strong-arm methods, it was not for reasons of policy, but of expediency: "We have to find the psychological points where we can dominate them with less strength and get the same results as though we had a hundred police battalions."

It was to safeguard a paper empire dependent upon long-range political tactics that Rosenberg repeatedly wrung his hands over the other occupation agencies that refused to see beyond "military-economic" aims or to refine the techniques of terror he decried later at Nuremberg as "Heydrich's methods."[54] The letters he wrote in 1942 to Fritz Sauckel, the plenipotentiary general for labor mobilization who was in charge of the universally hated labor draft, read like the protests of a Western humanitarian until it is realized that they merely express the indignation of a satrap resisting encroachments on his domain. Rosenberg is dismayed at the brutal seizures of men and women and even "youngsters from fifteen years on up . . . allegedly picked up on the street, from the market places and village festivals, and carried off." At the same time, the Political Department of the Ostministerium was piously exclaiming, "In the prevailing limitless abuse of Slavic humanity, recruiting methods are used which probably have their origin in the blackest period of the slave trade."[55]

Secure in a niche protected by the camarilla around the Führer, Sauckel could scoff at such "atrocity reports." After all, he had always fed the foreign workers, twenty-seven million of whom he boasted of having carted off from all Nazi-occupied territories by spring 1943; no one need remind him that "a machine runs only as long as there is fuel."[56] If anyone were at fault here, Sauckel maintained in his rejoinder, it had to be the Ostministerium officials not cooperating sufficiently with his staff. The criticisms leveled by Rosenberg could hardly be expected to bring about change, since they offered so little by way of alternative. He had objected to labor draft methods as "not thought out and unjust," only to commend the "cleverness" of some commissars who had seen to it that "workers were brought to the railroad station to the accompaniment of music as they departed for their assignments in Germany."[57]

The same quibbling over details and an overriding concern for his ministry's prerogatives characterize Rosenberg's pleas to Army Commander General Wilhelm Keitel for better treatment of Russian prisoners of war, some three million of whom are estimated to have starved to death in the German camps.[58] To Rosenberg's mind, the whole affair amounts to little more than a botched-up job of public relations: "The camp commanders have forbidden the civilian population to put food at the disposal of prisoners, and they have rather let them starve to death. In many cases, when prisoners of war could no longer keep on the march because of hunger and exhaustion, they were shot before the eyes of the horrified civilian population, and the corpses were left."[59] Once he had gone through such perfunctory motions and seen his remonstrances tossed aside, Rosenberg invariably fell into line, passed the offending orders along to his staff, and, more surprisingly, even discovered rationalizations for the kind of crude exploitation he had resisted earlier. Thus he finally did approve the proposed deportation of youth from occupied territories on the grounds that "a desired weakening of the biological force of the conquered people is being achieved."[60]

The superficiality of Rosenberg's divergence from the more vicious makers of occupation policy also conceals an underlying conformity regarding the church question. Rosenberg might have looked askance at the rounding up of worshipers leaving churches he had intended to exploit or, on the occasion of a priest's visit to a prisoner camp, bemoaned the bad local publicity that leaked out.[61] But, while he would later claim in his war crimes defense to have been put off by it, he was not at the time essentially at odds with Bormann's crass position as expressed in 1942: "The Slavs are to work for us. Insofar as we don't need them, they may die . . . Religion we must leave them as a means of diversion."[62] This also amounts to "toleration" of sorts. In delving through other layers of the German administration, the "leaving" of religion is a recurrent theme. Crucial distinctions crop up, however, in regard to what religion should be left *for*—what the social context of the church was to have been. "Religion left to the people" held a different meaning for Rosenberg's Russians, given permits to build churches if they manifested the proper anti-Soviet spirit, and to Bormann's Russians, allowed to mumble prayers while being dragged off to slave-labor camps.

Hans Koch, a former German intelligence officer whose work with Ukrainian nationalists involved him in church affairs during the occupation, later recalled to a Harvard interviewer that "the official, Bormann-sponsored view was that 'there is no church question.' "[63] In contrast to such a negative attitude toward indigenous institutions—letting anything that was of no immediate use perish—Rosenberg addressed the following words to a meeting of army commanders: "the position of the Church in the north and middle occupation districts is absolutely positive [potentially pro-German]—till now there has been little use made of it."[64] This was said in January 1943; but nine more months passed before the fading German fortunes of war combined with the news of Stalin's September reception of Metropolitan Sergius in the Kremlin to erode the adamant stand of Nazi leaders opposed to open collaboration with the Orthodox churches. They now permitted the convocation in Vienna of a special conference of eight Orthodox bishops led by that faded white hope of the fifth-column advocates, Seraphim of Berlin.

The reaction among churchmen in the occupied territories to such belated attempts to revive the appeals of the Karlovtsi Synod was exemplified by the Orthodox head in the Baltic, Metropolitan Sergius the Younger. He thought the proposed alliance between Church, monarchist councils, and Nazis would be disastrous because "the Bolsheviks would depict it as if the émigré bishops were utterly subservient tools of Germany policy."[65] The same circumstances that had produced the Vienna conference were yet to cause eleventh-hour reversals of German policy in the two major provinces under occupation. The spring of 1944 witnessed church councils of Belorussian as well as Ukrainian Autocephalous clerics, or at least of the handful that could be hurriedly assembled by the retreating Germans to make meaningless declarations of unity in the anti-Soviet cause. The Belorussian council in Minsk was held after three years of consistent repression by the Ostland Commissariat of nationalists who had steered the movement for church autonomy.[66] A similar air of unreality pervaded the council in Warsaw, where fleeing representatives of the two main Ukrainian Church factions that the German Commissariat had deliberately kept at loggerheads till then were exhorted to unite.[67] Even at this low point in their fortunes, they were kept apart by disputes over precedence.

The Ostministerium was behind these last-ditch attempts to salvage whatever possible of its earlier plans for non-Russian, anti-Soviet institutions on which to erect a German puppet empire in the occupied territories. But the end had been lost sight of in the face of the Red Army advance, and the means came to hand only because the Gestapo had dropped its disdain of them. Nationalists in churches and elsewhere, rejected as untrustworthy and unnecessary partners in the power of the occupation authorities, suddenly looked attractive as a rear guard that might help stave off defeat. The re-evaluation was based on expediency, as a letter from the SS liaison to Rosenberg makes clear: "We should establish closer relations to use the Church for our ends. Since the Orthodox religion is alien to Germany, it will have no bad results here [unlike Bormann's and Rosenberg's initial fears]. We should encourage a union of the [Ukrainian] churches, as this would lead to a depolitization of religion, whereas now the conflicting groups use the religious conflict as a screen. Religion is *per se* a pacifying factor."[68] Such unanimity between security police and Ostministerium views might have drastically altered the course of German church policy if achieved at the onset of the occupation. Coming as it did in June 1944, it was too little and too late to have any practical consequence.

KOCH'S UKRAINIAN DOMINION

Erich Koch, Reichskommissar for the Ukraine, was technically subordinate to Rosenberg, whose ministry had been charged by Hitler with administering all the "eastern territories." But in effect, the power of the lieutenant outclassed that of his chief. The informal lines of organization that Koch would use to construct his well-nigh invulnerable position in the occupation hierarchy were already forged at the meeting in which Hitler decided his appointment.

As recorded with evident satisfaction by Bormann, the session of July 16, 1941, began with a lecture by Hitler directed at Rosenberg,

Göring, General Keitel, and State Chancellery head Hans-Heinrich Lammers on the secret aims of German policy in Russia.[69] Strategic areas, such as Galicia and the Crimea, were to be "Germanized," the population to be displaced by Aryan settlers, and the remaining Russians to be impressed into a permanent slave empire. In the Führer's voracious figure of speech, "the basic problem is to split up the giant cake into bite-size portions, so we can first dominate, second administer, third exploit it."

Rosenberg rose in alarm to defend the political mission of his ministry, with its positive assignment for non-Russian people, the worthiest of whom would be chosen to serve as aides of their German masters. Each Reichskommissariat, he contended, had to treat its subjects differently. In the Ukraine, particularly, this meant that the Germans had "to appear as protectors of culture," found a university in Kiev, reawaken the people's "historical consciousness," and even "promote certain strivings for independence." The coldness of the other Nazi leaders to such projects was expressed in the curt rebuttal of Göring, not in his capacity as air force chief but as director of the Four-Year Plan for the Economy. Our immediate aim, he reminded Rosenberg, is "to secure our food supply"; everything else on the occupation agenda would have to be deferred indefinitely. Then he turned aside Rosenberg's nominee for the Ukrainian post and submitted Koch as the man with "the best drive and preparation for the job." Hitler's perfunctory approval of Koch sealed the issue.

The new commissar of the richest agricultural and industrial province of the occupied territories launched a campaign of gross repression in the Ukraine, with his flanks fully protected. When he curtly informed his staff, "I will draw the very last out of this country. I did not come to spread bliss,"[70] he was justifying the faith of his sponsor, Göring. When he lumped his subjects indiscriminately with other Slavic peoples as fit for nothing but enslavement, he could call on an even more potent protector, Martin Bormann, who proved always ready to intercede with Hitler on Koch's behalf. By the time Rosenberg managed to see the Führer to argue preferential treatment for Ukrainians, he met only rebukes for his own "softness."[71]

In addition to his personal tie to Bormann, Koch could maintain a direct line to his superiors in the party hierarchy by retaining the post of East Prussian Gauleiter (provincial Party chief) that he had occupied since 1928. This offered him two opportunities: first, easy access to Hitler's wartime headquarters; second, a convenient source for like-minded staff members to replace the relatively "liberal" specialists furnished him by the Ostministerium.[72] Koch's ruthless rule also earned the admiration and support of the security forces under Himmler, as well as of the agents conducting the labor draft and agricultural requisitions. While Rosenberg could only dream of empire, Koch earned the epithet Grossherzog (Grandduke) Erich by lording a realm from the Baltic to the Black Sea.[73]

If Rosenberg was to obtain a modicum of implementation for his decrees on the occupied territories it would have to come from Lohse, his own nominee to govern the Ostland, that is, the Baltic and Belorussian areas—not that this Reich commissar had greater respect than Koch for his impotent chief, but just that he also looked on his subjects as possible collaborators rather than as mindless slaves. Lohse, however, had none of Koch's contacts, executive abilities, or unyielding determination. In the minor part he did play, there was, furthermore, none of Rosenberg's hatred for the Russians and for institutions carried over from the Soviet era. "It doesn't matter whether we use the old Bolshevik or the new Nazi economic forms," he told his staff. "What counts is which ones deliver the most."[74]

When both Reich commissars published an Ostministerium order, Lohse might accept its intent but observe only the sections that suited his pragmatic purposes; Koch tended to disregard it altogether. Thus, both men had issued virtually identical decrees in June 1942, governing the registration of religious groups.[75] In the Ostland, some measure of "toleration" did indeed ensue, as described in Chapter 6. The religious revival was permitted to extend to the Russian Orthodox dioceses, although a directive from Rosenberg's staff had earmarked them for "opposition and eventual extinction" as "major carriers of Russian influence" in the Baltic.[76] In the Ukraine, the entire spirit of the order was negated: Koch's staff at first dismissed the issue as another of Rosenberg's ridiculous attempts to enhance the image of the German administration, then frustrated the efforts of any church that showed signs of developing into a genuine popular force. Such a response ran true to form for an officialdom that had nothing but contempt for its subjects, and for a man like Koch, who could hurl away the traditional bread and salt offered by a village delegation with the snarl that it was an insult to dare to offer gifts to a German dignitary.[77]

UNTERMENSCHEN AND THEIR BELIEFS

Rosenberg had promoted the deliberate, though often covert, subvention of non-Russian cultural institutions because he intended them to form vital links in an anti-Muscovite federation. These appeared as dangerous vagaries in Koch's eyes: Ostministerium plans to establish a four-year Ukrainian school system, for example, were only inviting trouble; they would have to be sabotaged in order to keep the population in impotent ignorance.[78] Koch tackled the religious question in the same spirit, the common denominator being his conception of all Slavic nationals as brutish *Untermenschen*. This is evident from his remarks to a staff meeting at his headquarters in August 1942: "The attitude of the Germans in the Reichskommissariat must be governed by the fact that we deal with a people which is inferior in every respect . . . From a cultural point of view, we have given the Ukrainians both churches. Further cultural work is out of the question."[79] Religious organizations could be "given" when no expenditure was entailed and because Koch regarded them as harmless conclaves furthering the stupefaction of his subjects.

Dependent for the implementation of his religious policy on Nazi cadres that shared Koch's prejudices, Rosenberg could expect his most strenuous efforts to produce at best a hollow victory. For the first year of the occupation, he had labored to budge Hitler from snap judgment "that church activity is entirely out of the question."[80] A toleration decree had become essential in early 1942, Rosenberg argued to the Führer, because a spontaneous religious revival had transpired in the meantime, and by further ignoring the issue the Germans risked being confronted with the fait accompli of strongly entrenched church organizations. In the logic of expediency Rosenberg used to marshall his case, "various large church groups were organizing, but such a development could not be allowed to proceed unsupervised; it had to be guided, so that the proposed instructions, or orders, were meant to prevent our being faced with undesired surprises." Hitler was persuaded to lift his veto, but not before Bormann had revised the proposed decrees to leave their promulgation to the Reich commissars, so that any new control functions would enhance their powers instead of Rosenberg's. In the hands of a man like Koch, Hitler and Bormann could safely assume, the Toleration Edict would be a mere bone to toss his subjects to make them more docile. As a postwar German account sums it up: "The Tolerance Edict could be passed more easily since Koch didn't interest himself in this problem and offered less resistance to its solution. It met an enthusiastic response from the population, especially the Orthodox clergy of the Ukraine . . . Not the Tolerance Edict but its good results enraged Erich Koch."[81]

Koch may indeed have been irate at the relish with which his bare-bones toleration was snapped up by the Ukrainians, particularly by the nationalists among them who extracted from it what they could to nourish their ailing cause. But it would be naïve to assume that his off-hand gesture had not been directed by ulterior motives from the start. It seems much more likely that he found it congruent with the rationale, stemming from the *Untermenschen* stereotype, that Hitler had expounded at his headquarters on April 11, 1942: "In any event . . . the creation of uniform churches for larger Russian areas is to be prevented. It would simply be in our interest if each village had its own sect, which developed its own conception of God. Even if, in this way, scattered villages form magic cults like the Negroes and Indians, we would only welcome it, because we would only be increasing the divisive elements in the Russian space."[82]

Nazi leaders who fixed the aim of the occupation in terms of maximum exploitation at minimal cost were prone to view obstacles to its realization in an oversimplified manner, within narrow time limits. The predominant concern of the Hitler-Bormann-Koch clique was the steamrolling of any resistance offered by their subjects and the discounting of any political complications that might ensue. "Divide and rule" had been Hitler's trusty formula for the extension of power, domestically and internationally. Transposed to the occupied territories, the device became the "divisive elements" formula, an attempt to disrupt all forms of social cohesion. The toleration Hitler was finally moved to authorize was of a specious variety to confound a Russia he had called "the most God-obsessed state ever. Everything is accompanied by religious ceremonies."[83]

Hitler's prescription, as dispensed by Koch, called for the calculated confusion of religious life to engender a proliferation of local sects whose squabbles would make them an easy mark for German domination. It is in this context that Koch spoke of giving "both churches" to the Ukrainians—if there had been only one, it would not have merited his charity. Actually, his domain embraced three major churches, the first two prevailing among the peasantry: (1) the Ukrainian Autocephalous Orthodox Church (known by its Russian initials as UAPTs), which sought total independence from Moscow church authorities, use of Ukrainian liturgy, and collaboration with radical Ukrainian nationalists; (2) the Autonomous Ukrainian Church (or AUTs), permitting local substitution of Ukrainian vernacular for the Slavonic liturgy it generally preferred and favoring loose ties with the Patriarchy after it had gained its rights by mutual consent rather than revolution; (3) a group maintaining its allegiance to the patriarchal hierarchy, concentrated in russified cities like Kiev and Kharkov, continuing Church Slavonic services, recognizing Moscow's ecclesiastical authority but demanding autonomy in some areas, and, unlike the other groups, not objecting to Russians holding high church office in the Ukraine.[84] There were also some half-dozen minor groups, the most sizable including remnants of the so-called Living Church and the Renovators, driven underground because of their pro-Soviet views, as well as some surviving congregations of "Old Believers" among the Great Russian population.[85]

The resulting religious complexion of Koch's domain was so splintered by factionalism, without even taking non-Orthodox groups like the Uniates into account, that an effort by German officials to keep the churches from coalescing was hardly required. The following picture emerges from the expert testimony of Dr. Hans Koch: "[In the Ukraine] there was no German over-all policy towards the Church. In effect, each district commissar decided for himself. Often, perhaps too systematically to be an accident, neighboring areas adopted contrary policies; this seemed to be an implementation of the '*divide et impera*' pattern. There was thus an artificial effort to keep the different trends in balance so as to prevent the unification of the population around any one of them."[86] The experiences of regional church bodies, described in Chapter 6, bear out the surmise that the contradictions of German religious policy were indeed deliberate: invariably, official recognition was given to a church faction that did *not* represent the consensus of the area.

As long as grass-roots dissension persisted, Koch did not have to intervene personally in the affairs of fragmented church organizations. He could generally rely on his aide, Joachim Paltzo, head of the Political Section, to maintain developments at a stage of controlled unrest.[87] Paltzo's simple device was to foist unpopular bishops on recalcitrant congregations, for such hierarchs would naturally be most pliant in the hands of his staff. When the heads of the Autonomous and Autocephalous Churches tried to reconcile their differences behind German backs, the Reichskommissariat summarily vetoed their tentative agreement in October 1942.[88] Most of the time, the clash of personalities within the churches kept them out of negotiating distance. Koch's officials not only managed to stay on top of a chaotic situation they had helped to foster; they also exploited the confusion that made Ukrainian believers the most helpless victims of draconic measures such as the labor draft, seizure of produce, or extermination of Communists, partisans, and Jews.

Rosenberg, in his cautious way, raised "no objection to occasionally contributing supplies for the reconstruction of churches,"[89] though he would stop short of officially backing religious organizations to avoid identifying the Germans with a group whose prestige was an incalculable factor. Koch did not even permit fund-raising which might promote church interests beyond the local level. On February 19, 1942, he ordered that "no taxation for religious purposes is to be imposed. Religion is the private affair of everyone. The cost of private matters must be borne by the individual. Therefore, the care of Orthodox priests must be financed by voluntary donations from those who enjoy their services."[90] On May 4, he informed Autonomous and Autocephalous Church leaders at his head-quarters that they would have to stay out of parish policies, that churches were not allowed to own land, and that religious instruction would be prohibited in schools.[91] Koch found it anathema to enter into paternal relations with the *Untermenschen* or to expend German aid on their churches.

Subsequent regulations by the Reichskommissariat Ukraine further narrowed the scope of religious activity. The Toleration Edict of June 1942 was followed the next month by an order restricting ecclesiastical organizations to individual districts.[92] Four months later an edict offi-cially dissolved the sobors, or governing councils, of both Autonomous and Autocephalous Churches. On November 18, Koch criticized the frequent closing of local administrative offices on weekdays that were Orthodox holidays. He considered this "not admissible when German holidays have been moved to Sunday to eliminate stoppages in the labor process. The only Greek Orthodox holidays allowed are Christmas, New Year's, and Easter."[93] On November 29, the order was extended to indus-trial and agricultural establishments. Any potential lowering of work-man's morale and loss of productivity caused by such measures did not concern a commissar obsessed with the day-to-day exploitation of his subjects.

In vain did Rosenberg's office protest the "manhunt without regard to health or age" that was being conducted with particular savagery in the Ukraine by the labor recruiters, as well as other brutal actions of Koch's staff which "fly in the face of all political knowledge."[94] The secret memorandum of October 25, 1942, containing these charges, also lamented the lapses of church policy: "The religious freedom was . . . supposed to evoke a propagandistic shock wave. However, after months of negotiations, it was decided not to announce religious freedom offi-cially, instead to let it occur without causing a ripple. Thus the propa-ganda effect was generally lost." It concluded with a plea to reverse "a policy of treating the occupied population as second-class whites, whom providence supposedly gave as its sole task the provision of slave labor for Germany," and called for the ouster of Koch. Hitler and Bormann turned a deaf ear to such indictments, since their man in the Ukraine was merely embodying their own views on the occupation. If anything, the attack of the Ostministerium heightened the stature of Koch. It made him appear as a "realistic" administrator in the eyes of the Nazi leaders to whom Rosenberg's men were addled "romantics." In 1943, Alfred Fiedler, the SS officer whom Koch had made his deputy for labor conscription, could still compose a public pamphlet characterizing the Ukrainians as typical *Untermenschen* whose primitive mentality called for the use of clubs.[95]

TWO BRANDS OF UNREALISM

It is interesting to note how the internal strains of the Nazi administration pushed Rosenberg and Koch into positions on church policy that ran counter to their earlier inclinations. Rosenberg's antireligious bent shaped his criteria in selecting officials for his new ministry. "The whole Christian outlook makes one incapable of carrying on work in the East, for the community of the hymnbook is put ahead of the needs of the Reich," he wrote in July 1941.[96] By May of the next year, however, he was promoting the cause of selected church groups, such as the Autocephalists in the Ukraine, as cultural barriers to Russian influence. He went to the overoptimistic lengths of informing Hitler that "it was easily possible that the Ukrainian church leaders would get together to elect a Patriarch. I pointed out that this had virtually been done . . ."[97] Of course, these forecasts were wrecked by Koch's manipulation, but even without that intervention it is hardly likely that the atheist staff of the Ostministerium could have effectively come to terms with the native church leadership.

Erich Koch, on the other hand, prided himself on his Protestant upbringing as well on his efforts to bring about a union of Evangelical denominations in Germany. His memoirs, though no doubt colored by having been composed in the Polish prison where he was undergoing a war crimes trial, recount his nascent Marxist sympathies as a young railroad worker in the Rhineland and his conversion in the early 1920's to the Nazi party because of the toleration plank in its platform.[98] Identified with the left wing of the party led by the Strasser brothers, Koch claimed to have kept both his socialist and Christian sympathies intact during his tenure as East Prussian Gauleiter. He had a curious way of expressing the socialist sympathy, for in fifteen years he had turned the stock manipulations of his personal "foundation," the Erich Koch Stiftung, into a fortune of four hundred million marks. His proletarian antecedents stood him in good stead in the spring of 1945, when he refused Hitler's order to stay at his post.[99] They enabled him to melt into the refugee stream that escaped the Red Army's advance into East Prussia, and to assume the identity of the worker Rolf Berger in a Hamburg suburb until war crimes investigators tracked him down and handed him over to the Poles for a long deferred trial.[100]

Hitler's assignment of Koch to the Ukraine in 1941 seems to have caught him unawares, uncertain at first of what course to pursue. He attributed his selection to his successful record in pig production for the Four-Year Plan, and maintained later that he had shown his socialist faith by promoting sovkhoz-type agriculture in his commissariat. Again a note of skepticism is called for, because the collective farms that were kept in operation by the Germans, despite popular demands to dismantle them, conveniently suited the conclusion of Göring that "to avoid, as far as possible, halts in production and interruptions in the delivery of agricultural products, the present kolkhoz system will have to be maintained."[101] Koch put it the following way in August 1942: "The only contribution which the indigenous population can make to its liberation is to repay Germany by labor and food deliveries for a small part of what Germany has sacrificed in the blood of its best sons . . . And if we are faced with the choice of whether our fellow nationals in Germany or the Ukrainians should starve, we certainly know which choice to make."[102]

Socialism to Koch meant little beyond an extension of Stalinist methods to subjects he still considered in 1943 "too inferior to be compared with the Germans,"[103] since "the least German worker is racially and biologically a thousand times more valuable than the population around here."[104] In such a perspective, religious toleration, too, could be translated only into a cycle of repression against pro-Russian and pro-Ukrainian church groups, as each in turn was deemed a greater threat to total dominance by the occupation authorities. Whatever Koch's motives when he worked for unity among the Protestant denominations of Germany, his repressive regime in the Ukraine, grafted onto his stereotyped view of the people, led him to reverse his tactics when dealing with the native church factions. As late as June 1943, a secret report of the German Propaganda Ministry confirmed that Koch "insists on having clashes between the Autonomous and Autocephalous Ukrainian Churches to prevent a unitary movement."[105]

Rosenberg's *idée fixe* was that a derussified Soviet Union, split into national units, would welcome the hegemony of the Third Reich. This proposition assigned an important role to popular reaction, although it reserved for the Germans a monopoly of political initiative; its missing middle term was the position of the Great Russians, from whom the other nationalities were to be "liberated." Even they might not be entirely excluded from cultural activities, as indicated by Rosenberg's vague assertion that "Russia proper must put her own house in order."[106] Attention to psychological factors disposed the Ostministerium to attempt a grand gesture regarding religious liberty and, while that was in abeyance, to milk the most propaganda value possible from whatever gains the churches were making on their own by "circulating pictures and stories of services showing believers, who had been brutally persecuted by Bolshevism," in their refurbished quarters.[107] The morale of a people fit only for servitude was irrelevant for the clique around Hitler, Bormann, and Koch, whose sole standard was the maximum exploitation of labor in which only the length of the workday and the stripes of the taskmaster's whip were admitted as determining factors. The one mental attribute of slaves that might be of concern was their impulse to revolt, and the Reichskommissariat's prophylaxis for this was a divide and rule formula based on the masters' preponderance of force.

Rosenberg's and Koch's conceptions of their subjects represent two variants of unrealism. The Russians, treated according to the former as feudal serfs for a future Germanic empire of the East who were to display devotion in gratitude for circumscribed dispensations, or impressed as slaves into the service of the latter, were in neither circumstance permitted to emerge as human beings with a right to private aspirations. Thus genuine cooperation on their part was precluded by the Germans, who thereby failed to pick up what might have been a decisive advantage in their Eastern campaign. Resentments of the population against their former Soviet rulers, auguring a friendly or at least hopeful reception of the Germans at the onset of the occupation, were left largely untapped. Soon the people had good reason to be overcome by hatred for their new masters, who not only treated them as pawns but did so with a ruthlessness surpassing Stalinist methods. The initial popular consensus had been that German policy had brought significant improvement at least in the life of the repressed churches. In the course of the occupation, enthusiasm in this sphere wilted, as it had in the political and economic areas, when news of the Kremlin's amelioration of the Church's plight trickled through to a population disillusioned by the arbitrariness and negativism of German policy.

5

German Policy Toward
the Orthodox Church:
The Ancillary Agencies

While the primary struggle over occupation policies was pitting Reichs-minister Rosenberg against Reichskommissar Koch, five other German agencies were also engaged in the competition for primacy in making decisions in this area. Unlike the main contestants in the battle, these ancillary agencies were preoccupied with missions outside the con-quered Russian territories. But, like the protagonists, they improvised policies to advance their status in the Nazi hierarchy, though their posi-tions tended to array them with either the "hard-line" or "soft-line" advocates in approaching the subject peoples. As might be expected, the latter camp lost—just as Rosenberg had been stymied in his efforts to upgrade the priority of cultural-political as against military-economic goals.

To an even greater degree than it had for the Berlin Ministry or the Ukrainian Commissariat, the religious question played a marginal role for these agencies, hence they did not assign special staff sections to handle it. They had not expected to encounter the problem but found it thrust upon them. As Orthodox congregations attempted to reorganize themselves and as church factions contended for diocesan authority, the German official on the spot—whether commander of a security squad or an army unit, propagandist or economic administrator—had to decide how to steer developments in the most advantageous manner for the accomplishment of his primary mission. In Berlin, diplomats of the Foreign Office were also trying to have their say on this issue, since it bore on the conduct of policy toward neutral states and the Vatican. The official reactions to the Church ranged from cynical manipulation of Gestapo detachments to the substantial help rendered by some regular army units. These contradictory approaches allowed a resurgence of religious life to take place, but their inconsistency and the clear edge of the "hard-liners" in determining the course of German policy left the population with no general feelings of gratitude for the authorities.

THE TERROR APPARATUS

One inherent characteristic of "security organizations" in a totalitarian state is a striving to expand their sphere of operations and prevent intrusions from competing agencies. Such organizations force more and more groups into the category of "enemies of the people," for without victims the apparatus would grind to a standstill. The political police inject the suspicion of danger into every situation facing the regime so that its services will be required. This overemphasis of and hypersensitivity to political danger runs through reports of the *Einsatzgruppen,* the special extermination squads of the SS and SD that Himmler assembled to liquidate Jews, Gypsies, and other "undesirables" in the occupied territories. Divided into four units of some five hundred to one thousand men each, they were to sweep the rear areas—Gruppe A in the Baltic states, B in Belorussia, C and D in the Ukraine—murdering untold millions.[1]

One such report contains a section on religious activities during the period from July to September 1941 which reads: "The Orthodox Church is trying to gain ground again, especially in areas always part of Russia. The danger exists that it may exploit the readiness to cooperate of the population, which till now has been suppressed in all spheres, by giving it a nationalist shape. Clergy of all denominations are, therefore, permitted to exercise their spiritual functions only after a political examination." A curious admission after this diagnosis of dangers that lurk in the church picture follows: "However, the religious need of the population is so spontaneous and primitive that they do not care in what liturgical form services are held."[2] It is difficult to find an adequate explanation of that sentence. It could be a bow to Hitler's conception of the *Untermensch,* with his many strange sects requiring German provocation to erupt in strife. It could, as well, imply that there are sinister forces at work giving a reprehensible twist to the fundamentally simple popular sentiments. The security police would then assume the practicable task of ferreting out a few nationalist church leaders, rather than having to repress all believers.

Himmler's files contain a memorandum stating that his discussion with Rosenberg on November 15, 1941, to propose an SS liaison on the church question ended in an "uncompleted conversation."[3] The abortive arrangement would no doubt have foundered on the insistence of Himmler that distinctions could not be made among that "entire East European-Central Asiatic horde" into which he lumped all the Slavs. In dealing with them, he proclaimed on October 14, 1943, "we must renounce false comradeship, misunderstood generosity, false weakness, and false apologies to ourselves. In these things we must recapture the courage of brutal truthfulness and frankness."[4]

Of all the policies fashioned by Nazi occupation authorities regarding the churches, that of the SS-SD-Einsatzgruppen is extreme in the degree to which it is shot through with inconsistencies. In part, these may represent the deliberate working out of the divisive formula fashioned by Erich Koch in the Ukraine. Yet, where Koch tended to dismiss the religious question as nonexistent, the Einsatzgruppen generally rated it as a crucial factor. Some of their contradictory practices may have been a function of the varying conditions encountered in their field work; administrators like Koch and Rosenberg remained tied to preconceptions about their subjects and changed their policies notably little in response to reports from their sparse staffs.

In a file of Einsatzgruppen reports, the summary statement "church attendance heavy" echoes from widely scattered parts of the occupied area. Isolated instances of drastic measures against churchmen are reported, such as the notation of December 5, 1941: "Occasionally a religious meeting in Kiev. Archbishop Alexei Gromadski was taken prisoner. Two priests were executed because they were considered Communist agents."[5] Gromadski of Volhynia, foe of Ukrainian autocephaly, was released in short order only to be eventually assassinated by either Germans or nationalists on May 7, 1943. The most credible versions of the incident blame his murder on Melnyk's or Bandera's bands of partisans, whether by design or in a flurry of gunfire directed at the official German vehicle.[6] In any case, there are no doubts about the SS killing of the two priests as NKVD agents because one was found with a leaflet from the Metropolitan of Moscow calling for resistance against the Germans. In this, as in other cases, the terror apparatus displayed few qualms about shooting priests on any weightier pretext than served it in the execution of secular suspects. In 1942, for example, another typical entry reports that "a

Russian priest was shot in Tossno for resistance to the Germans," with a similar unconcern for detailing any evidence.

The priests tolerated by the Einsatzgruppen, according to their reports, were forced either to stay out of politics altogether or to toe the Nazi line without deviation. One of the SS units reported the issuance on July 5, 1941, of a "nonpolitical and supraparty national Ukrainian newspaper whose first copy contains greetings of the Uniate Metropolitan Szepticky." This church head was also "to read a 'Hitler letter' on July 6, thanking the Germans for the liberation, with text agreed upon by us."[7] The venerable bishop, scion of the Polish aristocracy, with a lifetime of service to Greek Catholicism and Ukrainian nationalism behind him, delivered his Nazi-edited sermon the day after the SS had crushed an attempt by Iaroslav Stetsko, lieutenant of Stephen Bandera, to take advantage of the chaos in Lvov, the capital of Eastern Galicia, to proclaim the formation of a "Ukrainian State" there. Once the coup he had backed was in shambles, Szepticky could do little for his cause, except render the required homage to Germany, if he were to escape the arrests in store for the ringleaders.[8] From his see in the General-Gouvernement administered by Frank, Szepticky kept trying to influence church developments in the Reichskommissariat run by the much more intolerant Koch. An attempt to increase his leverage in August 1941 by linking up with the Uniates of the Reich was vetoed by the Gestapo because it portended "an undesirable strengthening" of that church.[9] At the same time, his assurances to the Germans that Uniates would help promote popular cooperation better than other church groups were discounted as self-serving.[10] So were his declarations against Banderovites and other anti-German Ukrainian nationalists.[11] The continual frustration of his efforts and a growing awareness that the only use the SS had for Ukrainians was as accessories to Einsatzgruppen mass murders made him more skeptical about the benefits of collaboration.

A secret report of the German Foreign Office concluded "that the Metropolitan was adamantly opposed to the Nazi anti-Semitic outrages and that by late 1943 he had come to regard Nazism as even a greater evil than Communism."[12] For the SS, however, even a reluctant ally could have his uses. Although Himmler knew that Szepticky had protested the Nazi-organized pogroms, he was still able to obtain from the bishop an endorsement of the new volunteer-staffed unit of the Waffen-SS, the so-called "SS Division Galicia," thirty thousand strong. What's more, he got Szepticky to help furnish chaplains for each of the division's detachments and even to supply Father Laba, of his own staff, to be chief chaplain.

That the Church received the short end of this bargain is indicated by a letter from SS Obergruppenführer Gottlob Berger, Himmler's liaison with the Ostministerium, on July 22, 1943, transmitting a copy of Laba's sermon asking all Galicians to help "Hitler and the German people destroy Bolshevism." Berger notes that the sermon contains "dangerous expressions," a reference to its nationalistic overtones, but that "we will soon pull this tooth."[13] He goes on to comment that although Himmler was willing to use the clergy's influence in the division, if they began to "agitate" they would be thrown out and the Metropolitan himself "would have to bear part of the consequences." There is no further record of failure by the bishop or his aides to abide by their code of conduct as laid down by the SS. The Germans kept deferring use of the Galician division until their desperate military straits of summer 1944. Szepticky's death later in the year at least spared him the harsh wave of repression that engulfed his Uniate brethren when the Soviets retook the area.

Where the SS had found it profitable to manipulate Uniates in the Ukraine, it had no qualms about assuming the anomalous position of a protector of Orthodoxy in Belorussia, at least against domination by any outside force but itself. An Einsatzgruppen report of July 28, 1941, outlines the following countermeasures to be taken against attempts of Roman Catholic clergy to infiltrate the area from Poland for missionary work: "(1) Prohibiting the influx of Roman Catholic clergy into White Russia; (2) returning those already there to their places of origin under any pretext; (3) restricting Roman Catholic clergy resident in White Russia to their places of residence and not allowing them to take any trips, ostensibly for security reasons; (4) checking émigrés returning to White Russia on their Catholicism and treating them accordingly; (5) rapidly activating and supporting the work of the Greek Orthodox Church."[14] A dual motivation for the surprising fifth point is supplied later by the same report. To cap an account of overflow services in the Orthodox cemetery chapel at Minsk, during which two thousand believers assembled and forty-five children were baptized, it is stated that "the sermon was delivered in the form of thanks to the Führer." Catholic priests, on the other hand, were suspected of using their proselytizing to win Belorussian converts to Polish nationalism.

Part of the contradiction between sporadic repression and encouragement of church activities by the Einsatzgruppen is resolved in view of their primary role. As a field force, they were under constant pressure to act toward any native institution in some fashion, to edify their Berlin superiors with reports of ever new successes. Of course, they had to justify such actions in term of their mission: the elimination of political opposition. Wherever they stumbled upon strong religious sentiment, they were prone to adapt it into their policy in an ad hoc fashion, notably by making priests tractable mouthpieces of German propaganda even while disparaging such pliant clerics as "primitive folk."[15] They were also aware that accomplishment of their routine tasks, especially detection and destruction of partisan bands, would be greatly facilitated by popular cooperation secured by the clergy in general as well as intelligence obtained by select priestly agents of the SD.[16] Thus, although just as adamant in their Untermensch views of the Russians as Koch or Bormann, and lacking in any respect for the clergy, the security police units "activated" religion whenever it seemed expedient to serve their short-run interests.

The unrealized promises of the approach to church groups by the Einsatzgruppen is aptly illustrated by one of their reports, dated July 26, 1941, from the Baltic. It observes that Latvian peasants, particularly older ones, have acted in a friendly fashion to German troops, in contrast to the hostility shown by the urban population. In an illuminating aside, it refers to the "religious question" as "perhaps decisive in determining the attitude of the rural population in the future as well. A clever propaganda could find the crack here for an open break with the Soviet regime."[17] That conclusion represents the most explicit acknowledgment by any occupation agency of the inherent anti-Soviet quality in the release of religious feeling suppressed under Communist rule. It is echoed in a report from the Ukraine pointing to religion among the peasantry as a key "to ruling this people easily."[18] Exploitation of this potential force was, however, once again nullified by the Einsatzgruppen tactic of pressing too fast, too hard. Preoccupied by their repressive tasks, they could not rest content to develop a slow but perhaps lasting friendly spirit within the population toward its Nazi rulers. By purging independent-minded priests and dictating the texts of sermons to be cast into paeans of praise to Hitler, they only conjured up the image of former Soviet methods, which was bound to chill any popular illusions regarding German tolerance. The persuasiveness of such extorted homilies, lacking genuine conviction on the priests' part, must have been largely lost on the believers.

The Einsatzgruppen reports salted magnified appraisals of pro-German sentiment with terse comments on threats from certain churches such as Orthodox Renovators and Old Believers, but above all Catholics. Some of this slanted reportage may have been intended to impress higher-ups.

In addition, it may reflect the self-delusions entailed by subjective methods of investigating popular attitudes. A typical report, dated August 31, 1941, describes "clerics who have so far been encountered outside large cities" as "primitive people. They are praying in their churches for the victory of German arms and calling upon the population to fight together with the Germans against the Partisans."[19] This stands in direct contradiction to laconic notices of priests shot for anti-German activities including the harboring of partisans. Sermons that the security troops heard were arranged by them or performed for their benefits. Yet, through an echo effect, they are interpreted as signs of either the "primitive" nature of the clergy (the ease with which they could be turned into German tools) or a genuine desire for collaboration.

The Einsatzgruppen fathomed the complex nature of the church problem when they declared the "fundamental question" to be "whether it will be possible to re-erect the God who has been deposed and made ridiculous—and to give him an authority which will transcend outer ceremonials and lend him moral significance."[20] Such an assessment jibed with the private aims of Hitler: "The Russians will be allowed to turn against their priestlings but not to turn that into a struggle against authority."[21] The difficulty in moving from such judgments in 1941 to an effective policy in the central years of the occupation can be traced to official inability to come face to face with the actual conditions pervading Russian church life.

For one thing, the Germans lacked a reliable index to gauge native religious strength. The preconceptions and the conflicting criteria they did employ inevitably led to a potpourri of policies. Besides the review of sermons already mentioned, and the more realistic estimates of church attendance—even though they were often listed only in general terms such as "light" or "heavy"—the Einsatzgruppen had no standard for ordering their scattered sampling of active, church-going religious feeling. Official reports only occasionally guessed at the sentiment of the bulk of the populace, which was not to be found attending officially sanctioned sermons. One of the security squads arrived at the conclusion that "religion is an important factor," on the surprising grounds that "even Old Bolsheviks prayed before their execution."[22] Another group generalized from what it took to be the typical "first question of a local Ukrainian, 'When can we go to church again?' "[23] In contradiction to the repeated finding of other reports from all occupied areas that religion was the sole preserve of elderly female peasants, a third squad in the Zhitomir area asserted categorically: "The opinion that the youth is indifferent to religion is incorrect for the countryside and only partly applies to the cities."[24] This analysis then touches on another factor overlooked by previous reports: "It is apparent that Orthodox self-expression is markedly weakened; there exists a catacomb religiosity like that of ancient Christianity."

The security police in a totalitarian regime maintains notably close ties to the leadership, to which it presents an endemic danger of running amuck and inflicting irreparable damage to the economy or of aspiring, itself, to the supreme power. The blind obedience which it is called upon to exhibit by a regime that seeks to guard against such eventualities often saps its initiative; it is appropriately termed an apparatus or a machine. The confusion of the Einsatzgruppen when plunged into independent decision-making on religious issues can be regarded as a minor but typical symptom. The church question fell outside the beaten path of security problems, so that responses tended to be ineffectual, even grotesque. As the final hour was striking for the Third Reich in April 1945, Himmler is seen by one dramatist in the characteristic act of contemplating "the colonization of the Ukraine with a new religious sect recommended by his masseur."[25]

The very introduction of the church item into the security agenda illustrates the aforementioned propensity of the apparatus to stake out ever new claims. If it found such an area virtually bare of politically dangerous elements, it was at a loss as to how to proceed. This tactical ambivalence helps account for the paradox that the Gestapo could at the same time represent the branch of occupation administration with the greatest potential and opportunity for action, yet be the one least active in religious affairs in any consistent way. It called for a "quick decision of the church question" but expended its energies, not on concrete proposals, but on schemes to make army commanders grant it political screening rights over church elders and priests who could be forced into "closest dependence" to its offices no matter what the policy was to be.[26] The agency which alone was able to glimpse the chance of using the church as the wedge to sever all popular ties with the Soviet system will be remembered only for its shooting of "leftist" priests, hampering of Catholic expansion, and censorship of sermons.

THE PROPAGANDISTS

The Propaganda Ministry of Joseph Goebbels could claim its full share of ideological contradictions and interagency rivalries when it undertook its assignment: broadcasting the Nazi message to the peoples of the occupied areas. Thus, Goebbels had to resolve the dilemma of making a successful presentation of the German case to an audience of Russians whom he, no less than Bormann or Koch, regarded as Untermenschen.[27] He also had to come to terms with the nominal head of all political work in the East, Alfred Rosenberg, for whose administrative abilities he had nothing but contempt, as well as effecting some sort of liaison with the commissar of the Ukraine, Erich Koch, whose strong-arm methods hardly softened audience resistance to a sales pitch by the propagandists.[28] The Goebbels staff, however, never admitted to the temptation of dismantling its information mills aimed at subjects of such inferior status as to be unworthy of the trouble involved in their enlightenment. On the contrary, it sought continually to step up the efforts of its Eastern section, headed by Eberhard Taubert, who had given proof of his limited abilities in 1933 when he helped assemble the flimsy evidence against those accused of setting the Reichstag fire.[29]

Where internal policy contradictions might have vitiated any achievements by an activist or administrative agency, for the Propaganda Ministry they could be turned into an opportunity to modulate its message for different groups of listeners. In the cynical exercise of his function, Goebbels had as little use for consistency as he had for truth. These were dispensable qualities when communicating to various audiences; they only mattered in formulating the confidential reports on public morale which were meant to guide other agencies in selecting the proper arms for winning their subjects' allegiance. A directive, circulated "strictly for official use" toward the end of the occupation era, exemplifies the insidious approach that the "highest government offices concerned" had sanctioned toward the Russian Orthodox Church: "Propaganda in the area of church questions is to be aimed so that the churches can be harnessed to the support of our cause, but not so that we have to identify ourselves with the churches, if merely for the reason that only the older generation still adheres to them."[30] The directive does not spell out how German officials are supposed to "harness" religious feeling yet do it so inconspicuously that they could not be "identified" with the churches.

Harnessing implies going beyond the censorship of sermons, and indeed, there is evidence that propaganda workers often scoured former godless museums to procure religious books and implements for services. The population could not help noticing such interventions and, consequently, "identifying" the Germans with the churches to some extent.

The Goebbels staff might have salvaged some measure of the neutrality demanded in the directive by making it appear that it was granting dispensations only in response to the insistent wishes of the people. It was also aware that it had to parcel out these subsidies in order to prevent the objects of support from developing a strength and independent spirit that might make them spurn the Nazi harness. The achievement of docility was the principle needed to justify any action on behalf of the churches. It lay behind the top-secret evaluation by the Propaganda Ministry of the so-called toleration decrees in June 1942, which it saw "preventing the occurrence of religious strife and, while fully assuring freedom of religious belief, eliminating the political influence of religious organizations—especially of the Russian Orthodox Church."[31]

The harnessing theme of Goebbels strikes a markedly different note from the harsher tones of brutal exploitation, such as Koch's, and those of repression by Himmler's security forces. It should logically have harmonized with the approach of the Ostministerium, since in the reports of both there is a like regard for popular support, a regret for the lost opportunities in securing it, and a dismay at the gratuitous use of terror that makes "political work" well-nigh impossible. The discord that actually sprang up between the ministries of Goebbels and Rosenberg can be attributed primarily to "personal and departmental jealousy."[32] Superimposed on the mutual hatred of these two chief intellectuals of the Nazi elite was an extended strife over jurisdiction of propaganda work in the occupied territories, which came to a head in May 1943 with an appeal by Goebbels to the Führer against Rosenberg's attempts to stake out a monopoly in the field that went so far as to request that the Finance Ministry stop payments to propagandists in the occupied territories.[33] Hitler's decision in August 1943 seemed to settle the issue, with policy set by the Ostministerium and field work to be done by branches of the Propaganda Ministry.[34] This apparent victory of the propagandists caused Rosenberg to protest that they were interpreting it too broadly, trying to take over control of the entire press in the occupied territories.[35] The final entry in Goebbels' diary shows that the wrangle was far from over four months later:

> How badly we are doing our political job in the East can be seen from the fact that Rosenberg has still not carried out the Führer's order to transfer the propaganda there to us. He is doing everything he can to sabotage and torpedo it. I don't understand how the

Führer can leave such an obstreperous nincompoop in his job. If I were in his place, I would clear the boards in a hurry. Rosenberg has done more harm than good, not only in the East but also in the realm of politics generally. It is high time for a showdown.[36]

Behind the clash of personalities and bureaucracies, the Goebbels-Rosenberg discord also revolves around a difference in strategies. Both insisted that political aims should take precedence over immediate economic extortion and the rule of terror; but Rosenberg took German promises to the population seriously, whereas for Goebbels they were just a cheap method of winning instant acclaim. Where Rosenberg kept in sight his vision of an anti-Russian empire under the swastika while he drafted directives to foster such indigenous forces as the Ukrainian nationalists, Goebbels focused only on the short-run objectives of psychological warfare. The propaganda chief's concern was with appearances rather than with the content of policy. He was repelled by measures of crude exploitation only because they were crude, not because they were exploitative. His penchant for the refined twist is shown by his endorsement of the toleration decrees, not in the pronationalist spirit in which Rosenberg had conceived them, but as a distraction of the people from the stringent features of the control system:

> We have finally had the good sense to issue a decree which guarantees absolute religious tolerance in the eastern [occupied] areas . . . Personally, I believe we must change our policies essentially as regards the peoples of the East. We could reduce the danger of the partisans considerably if we succeeded in at least winning a certain measure of confidence with these peoples. A clear peasant and church policy would work wonders there. It might also be useful to set up sham governments in the various sectors which would then have to be responsible for unpleasant and unpopular measures. Undoubtedly it would be easy to set up such sham governments, and we would then always have a façade behind which to camouflage our policies.[37]

Goebbels' cynicism puts him at a greater remove from the naïveté of Rosenberg than from the barbarism of Koch. In May 1942 he received a briefing from Koch's aide, Joachim Paltzo, which included complaints against the ineptitudes of the Ostministerium that were music in Goebbels' ears. He concluded afterwards that "Rosenberg himself is by nature a theoretician, and it is quite evident that he must have constant conflicts with so pronounced a man of action and brute force as Koch."[38] That the comparison was intended to be invidiously applied to Rosenberg is confirmed by Goebbels' subsequent self-satisfied note: "Koch asked me to give him substantial support in matters of propaganda and stated that our work alone had thus far been of assistance in his difficult tasks in the Ukraine."

An appreciation of Koch's aims was likewise mixed with a disdain for the "suicidal" methods through which they were pursued in a September 1942 report on an extensive survey of the occupied territories by Dr. Taubert and Eugen Hadamowsky, director of Radio Berlin.[39] These two top propagandists saw nothing wrong with the forced labor program and even asked for wider use of beatings by the security police to replace softer punishment of the resisters among the population. Koch's fault lay not in his employment of the stick but in his disregard for the efficacy of the carrot: "The Eastern peoples must be given a program, though none of its promises are carried out before victory is achieved. Instead, this program must be held out as a goal for which the Eastern peoples think it worth investing their labor and risking their blood."

The manipulation of religious feeling was to play a central part in such a strategy, according to Taubert and Hadamowsky:

> Above all, the person of the Führer must be presented—in a way that might seem mystical by German standards—as bringer of light, liberator, and bearer of joy who is to lead the way to a heavenly future. Our current posters "Hitler, the Liberator" have become sacred possessions in all peasant and worker shacks throughout the East. The Greek Orthodox Church, at least in part, prayed on the Führer's birthday. All means of the churches, mysticism, religion, and propaganda must henceforth be employed to this end: "Hitler against Stalin!"—or "God against the Devil!"[40]

The prime mistake of Koch and administrators of his ilk consisted in flaunting their contempt for the cultural institutions and beliefs of their subjects: "If our own people do not understand this theory but continue to speak cynically about the 'natives,' 'half-monkeys,' 'colonial policy,' 'exploitation,' 'liquidation of the intelligentsia,' a limitation of education, closing of universities, suppression of artistic and cultural life, sabotage of churches, etc.—then our propaganda will ultimately appear cynical and backfire." The implication of the report is that not the doing, but the indiscreet speaking of such things was to be avoided. If churches were to be sabotaged, for instance, this intention was to be shielded behind the secrecy of internal German memoranda. In the words of the report: "We must, therefore, speak two tongues."

Goebbels over-reached himself when in the beginning of 1943, after the German reversals at Stalingrad, he tried to persuade Hitler to issue "A Proclamation for the East"—the ultimate in high-flown promises to the people of the Soviet Union, which its proponents had not the least intention of keeping.[41] The draft prepared by Goebbels indicates the continued high estimate he put on the potential strength of the population's frustrated strivings for an unfettered church: "Fight on with us against hated Bolshevism, bloody Stalin, and his Jewish clique; for freedom of the individual, for freedom of religion and of conscience, for the abolition of slave labor, for property and possessions, for a free peasantry on its own land . . . for everything of which Bolshevism has deprived you."[42] It is highly unlikely that anyone would have put great stock in such pledges once two years of German occupation practices had given them the lie. Apparently Hitler, in rejecting the proposal, did not think so either.

The Propaganda Ministry thus had to fall back on its meager resources, rendering sporadic and furtive aid to churches it remained convinced could be turned into tools of the German war effort despite the misgivings of higher-ups and the countervailing attitudes of other occupation agencies. Its major energies were expended on interoffice memoranda in Berlin, for until early 1944 its workers were effectively kept out of the field, and by then estrangement of the Russians from their overlords in the occupied areas had probably reached a point of no return. The inclination of the propagandists to put the Church to "positive" use, for all their distorted understanding of it and their limited means of action, resembled the approach of the security troops. The prime task of both was the elimination of political opposition. The tactics of the two forces diverged, however. Where the Einsatzgruppen resorted to prophylactic or retaliatory measures against outbreaks of resistance, the Goebbels staff concentrated on changing attitudes. The obsession of the security forces with political dissidence let them utilize the Church positively only in isolated instances; on the whole, they were more attuned to the potential dangers it represented. In their reports, clergymen appear as something akin to witch doctors, perhaps useful "in the inner pacification of the Russian space" but whose simple rituals would merely be unsettled by a Kraft durch Freude (strength through joy) campaign.[43] Only the exceptional priest was of interest, to be charged as a Soviet spy or hired as a Nazi agent. The propagandists could adopt a more consistently constructive approach, in line with their attempt to engender friendly feelings for the Third Reich among the occupied peoples, rather than rely on fear alone.

But a strange air of unreality pervaded the efforts of the Goebbels staff to find a common ground for collaboration with the forces of religion. The spiritual nature of the Church constituted an extraneous element for them. The security police had fumbled with this problem, largely peripheral for their mission, having spent most of their time trying to estimate its strength and direction. The "enlighteners" saw in it little more than fallow ground for ideological exploitation. They had no use for all the precise distinctions applied by the Einsatzgruppen. Whether the religious stratum was old or young, rural or urban, whether it favored autonomy or autocephaly, whether it expressed its beliefs openly or in "catacomb" services—as a popular force with no essential ties to the Bolsheviks it was to be encouraged and, in turn, forced to express gratitude for its "liberation." In this simple proposition, the Germans retained an escape clause by acting only behind the scenes. With their puppet strings to the Church adequately concealed, the Propaganda Ministry's men had no reservations about eliciting the Church's identification with them; their only caveat was to prevent a possible liaison between the Church and those nationalist groups they deemed "politically unreliable."

The foregoing policy determinants are reflected in a report entitled *Probleme des Ostraumes* (Problems of the Eastern Space), by Herr Oberführer Scheidt, director of the "head office for church-political tasks in the occupied Eastern territories," part of the Ostministerium's political department. First, Scheidt comments on the widespread religious revival evident by 1942, interpreting it as a protest against Bolshevism rather than as a symptom of deep faith. Then he declares: "We don't have the intention, derived from German preconceptions, of determining the religious life in the occupied Eastern territories. We confirm the religious impulse and do not interfere with the form in which it is expressed. What we demand of followers of the religious life is a loyal attitude to the institutions created by the Reich, and the complete separation of religious and political matters; the Church has to limit itself to exclusively spiritual affairs."[44] Though this passage emanates from Rosenberg's rather than Goebbels' ministry, it covers virtually all the bases in the evolution of a propaganda line on the church question. Another propaganda directive from the same source in March 1942 recommends the circulation of pictures and stories of services showing "believers who had been brutally persecuted by Bolshevism" in their renovated churches.[45] It notes that such publicity would help break down popular misconceptions that German occupation authorities were merely following domestic religious policy.

The psychological warfare legions simplified their audience problem in the occupied areas by consolidating targets, lumping together all subgroups reached by the religious appeal. They found in packed churches alone a sufficient gauge of the depth of religious feeling; still, they hesitated to link the German administration to what might be an obsolescent feature of the cultural scene. Although the Rosenberg and Goebbels ministries tended to disregard this qualification in practice, its persistence in their thinking calls for added comment. In essence, these officials did not want to hitch their propaganda line to a sinking ship. If religion was only the preserve of the older generation, its support would evoke the scorn of irreligious youth. The compromise lay in a policy of backstage liaison. If the Germans had the priests praise them and laud Hitler as a saviour, a substantial part of the population, the churchgoers, might become Nazi sympathizers or at least immunized against the charge that Hitler was an antichrist. Yet, by not committing German administrators publicly to the restoration of Orthodoxy, the Nazis might appear to the freethinking groups not as backers of religion but merely as protectors of freedom of conscience. By such a surreptitious approach, then, the propagandists stood to gain all around.

The benefits of relaying favorable religious bulletins from the occupied areas to German publications represented a bonus for the propaganda experts in their exercise of distilling maximum profit from a minimal investment. Domestic religious bodies had long been a thorn in Hitler's side. Congregations of pastors like Niemöller constituted one of the few "Aryan" groups that dared openly defy the leadership. Portraits of the Führer on altars may have found favor with the masses, but they clashed with the sensibilities of the strongly devout. By depicting the Wehrmacht as liberators of religious Russians from Soviet persecution, the propagandists tried to dramatize the compatibility of Nazism and Christianity. Their frequent references to Soviet "atrocities" against believers were designed to make Nazi church administrators look like crusaders in comparison.

A special edition on the Western front by the Berlin illustrated magazine *Signal* (December 1943) transmits a message in this vein. Prominently featured is a picture of a crowded church service in which nearly all the worshipers appear to be women, with the following caption:

It doesn't require great fantasy to imagine what the people of the East, who for centuries have been counted among the especially religious people of the Christian world, suffered under such a regime. Today, in the free Eastern territories the churches have been reopened and are packed for every service . . . Believers queue up the street, finally liberated from the terrible pressures of not being able to practice their religion. High up on the steeple the bells sound their eternal bronze speech . . . Thus it once was in Russian churches . . . but the Soviets destroyed churches or turned them into storehouses, stables, or godless museums.[46]

Another photograph, depicting an Orthodox baptismal ceremony, is captioned: "Like the old, the youth again goes the way of belief. Parents can baptize their children once more." From such a text it is possible to infer the Propaganda Ministry's unsureness regarding the religious response of the younger Russian generation. Whether or not deducing from a single baptism that "youth again goes the way of belief" constitutes wishful thinking, it is certainly stretching a point when none of the photos in German wartime publications shows adolescents or young adults attending Orthodox services.

Always in the back of the minds of the Goebbels staff, in working in the occupied territories, was its primary ideological assignment in Germany. It was fully cognizant of the problem of tailoring news from the East to suit a domestic audience that, in the religious sphere as in many others, had long chafed under a rigid control system. Nazi leadership could hardly be made to appear more intolerant to the master race than to the Untermenschen. Thus, the Propaganda Ministry announcement of the tolerance decrees by the Ostland and Ukraine commissariats in June 1942 bore the footnote that these measures were "too administrative in character for publicizing."[47] The intent of the notation is borne out by a highly classified directive of the same date providing that "news about church conditions in the Eastern occupied territories, which was released there, is not to be received by the German press."

How, then, account for items on the order of the above-mentioned Signal issue? The answer lies in characterizing the religious revival as entirely spontaneous in nature. Christians back home are thereby given a living example of churches that are content to simply express gratitude to their Nazi supervisors without making any demands in return. Only news of this sort was passed by the censors. The blackout covered bulletins that might show active involvement of German administrators in

Orthodox Church life, as well as reports of negative developments, such as the interdenominational strife of the Ukraine. The noninvolvement precept of the propagandists thus yielded domestic fruit besides its uses by fieldworkers. In the occupied territories, their pose of benevolent neutrality had been meant to leave them sufficient distance to exert leverage behind the scenes. The inherent limitation of such arm's-length treatment lay in the inability of the Goebbels staff to keep control of their subjects, as churches slipped the Nazi grasp to pursue their own ends often in opposition to the increasingly stringent measures of the authorities. Once priests found praises to Hitler sticking in their throats, there was little the Propaganda Ministry could do to reverse developments.

THE ARMY

Although individual Wehrmacht units and commanders rendered more direct aid to Russian religious groups than any other German agency, it would be overstating the case to say that this amounted to a conscious policy on their part. Without any deliberate plan, officers of advancing units would accede in an off-hand way to petitions from the people of a newly overrun town for the reopening of churches. At times chaplains accompanying the regiments would help organize the first services, or some sympathetic soldiers during a lull in the fighting would personally take part in restoring church buildings that had fallen into disuse. Occasionally, a local religious renaissance in the East Ukraine was supervised by a Galician or West Volhynian churchman who had tagged along with the Germans. But against this record must be considered the evidence of perhaps the bulk of the military, obeying orders from the High Command to stay out of church affairs altogether until civil administrators took over—not to mention instances of vandalism and desecration of churches by German soldiers.[48]

Still, the Wehrmacht in the field compiled an impressive list of acts of assistance to native religious organizations, on the whole. Attempts were also made by the military governors of certain rear areas and by some *Abwehr* (counterintelligence) officers to translate such uncoordinated efforts into a consistent German occupation policy of support for religious freedom. But these efforts failed for at least three reasons: Rosenberg and other civilian officials resisted the potential encroachment of the army on their preserve; the security troops, whose authority superseded that of military governors, were opposed to the ad hoc handling of the church question by army commanders; the High Command pressed its demands for noninvolvement by the army in indigenous church affairs, in accord with the Nazi party line.

Field-Marshal Maximilian von Weichs painted the following picture for an American interrogator after the war:

> German soldiers entering the Ukraine wasted no time removing the disgraceful decorations of local churches. They cleaned the buildings and prepared them for services. No move could have helped German propaganda more than the first religious service held in such a church. It resulted in a rapid improvement of morale among the local populace and a great willingness to make donations to the church. Ignoring this fact completely, the German High Command [in Berlin] issued an order shortly after the beginning of the Russian campaign forbidding soldiers all participation in the rebuilding of churches and prohibiting the conduct of army church services in Ukrainian buildings . . . Any open-minded German could recognize the deeply religious leanings of the Russian population, prevalent mainly among the older people. Yet we frequently chose to ignore the fact that large segments of the population which had remained in the occupied territories were composed of children and old men who had lived in pre-Bolshevik Russia. There were many instances when German officials publicly expressed the view that their task was to control a mass of beastlike Bolsheviks.[49]

The recollections of von Weichs, like those of innumerable other retired Wehrmacht generals, do not disguise their self-serving features, their common refrain of "we would have won if it hadn't been for" Hitler's madness or the stupidity of certain Party officials or the blindness of the High Command. They are also typical of the postwar military memoir in depicting the author as a humanitarian, hailed by his conquered foes. It was in the same vein that Panzer General Heinz Guderian recounted the taking of Glukhov, a town near Briansk, where "the population asked our permission to use their church as a place of worship once again. We willingly handed it over to them."[50] Guderian, who became army chief-of-staff in the final year of the war, likewise commented on the changed mood of his subjects from the open-arms welcome given the Wehrmacht to the coldness evoked by civilian administrators.[51]

Wartime reports of German soldiers buttress the benign pose of the memorialists, at least for the first few weeks of the Russian campaign.

One correspondent describes the "first church services in Smolensk in twenty years," held in August 1941 at the cathedral, which had been reopened with Wehrmacht help.[52] He tells of "people coming through a desert of destruction in their joyously bright clothes with Sunday bouquets" and expressing their thanks to the German infantrymen who stand by. The ancient priest conducting the worship is found hidden out in the cathedral cellar, having survived Soviet repressions by working on farms and in road gangs. What the reporter is evidently ignorant of is that the very success of the Smolensk services led to the "Führer Order of August 6, 1941," prohibiting further army assistance to the churches, that von Weichs had fulminated against. Reinhard Heydrich, chief of the security police, had been infuriated to hear of Germans going out of their way to "revive religion in the East," the habitat of the Untermensch.[53] The pressure of the SS, added to the protests of the Ostministerium, made the High Command yield, thereafter barring army chaplains "from participating in the religious life of the civilian population."

The particular ire of the Einsatzgruppen was directed at the Catholic chaplains of the Wehrmacht and to some officers who countenanced their crusading efforts. Reports from Belorussia—Baranovitse, Minsk, Vitebsk, as well as the Smolensk area—speak in alarmed tones of army services open to local civilians.[54] As a result, some native Catholic priests—automatic suspects of the Gestapo—won a favored position and were occasionally assigned a vacant chapel by the local commander. Of even greater concern to the security troops was a Catholic revival being exploited by "Polish nationalists."[55] Orthodox religious forces were not viewed as a threat of the same order: the SS was content to press for High Command agreement to allow security screenings of priests and to prohibit church organizations above the district level, both of which had been obtained by December 1941.[56] A year later, German commanders in Ukrainian front-line areas helped reopen churches, with soldiers even serving as godfathers at baptisms; but the Einsatzgruppen merely noted that such events could "strongly influence the population in a pro-German sense and extend pacification of the area."[57]

This kind of Wehrmacht support to the churches was perforce given unofficially, by local commanders who dared to defy the hands-off policy of Berlin. Even where they chose merely to observe the letter of the nonintervention order, however, they recognized the fait accompli of the religious revival that had transpired before the August interdict. Friedrich Heyer, who later became a scholar on Ukrainian church affairs, was a soldier in front-line units that witnessed the resurgence of congregations "in nearly every Ukrainian town . . . [Invariably] the German Kommandatura orders the reopening of the church."[58] Sometimes, as in Zhitomir, the army chaplain helped organize the initial service; sometimes, as in Proskurov, this was done by a priest who had accompanied the Wehrmacht from Galicia. The first military edicts, according to Heyer, also provided for the return of former church properties.

Emigré testimony, from a former director of a refugee relief committee in the occupied territories, confirms that in northern Russia, too, "the German military authorities gave encouragement and support to the Church." But he makes the further point that such aid had to be provided outside official channels: "In some instances they restored to the Church the property which it had owned before the October Revolution (though they did not restore the legal title of the Church to the property)."[59] With direct subsidies or other administrative support of the churches ruled out, local commanders followed their personal inclinations in ruling on religious matters. The resulting picture is marked by the same inconsistency that the military had shown in deciding whether to keep schools in their command open or to shut them down.[60] Positive army contributions to the churches over an extended area often amount to little more than historical accident. Thus, a number of Ukrainian congregations benefited from the decision of General Karl Rudolf Gerd von Rundstedt, in charge of Army Group South, to leave church questions to a staff member who happened to be a Protestant theologian, well versed in and favorably disposed toward Orthodoxy.[61]

It is the same staff officer to whom Heyer attributes the sympathies to Ukrainian nationalism and the Autocephalous Church which led to the first direct German support of that denomination.[62] The stage for such intervention had, however, already been set by the decision of Admiral Canaris' counterintelligence branch in 1940 to help the West Ukrainian nationalists organize units for military service in the approaching Russian campaign, as well to establish puppet local governments.[63] In both operations the separatist church groups whom the nationalists favored became the indirect beneficiaries. But this link also exposed them to the SS crackdown on nationalists who overstepped their quisling assignments by proclaiming their autonomy. Entry of the Einsatzgruppen on the scene marked the end of effective military authority.

The temporary check to the fortunes of the Autocephalous Church was made permanent by the regime of Erich Koch. His "divide and rule" tactics against the churches formed but one facet of a strategy of riding roughshod over native aspirations and institutions. With his lines to the Führer intact, Koch had nothing to fear from the protests of Generals Hallstein and Heusinger that his actions were "sabotaging" the German war effort.[64] As long as the Untermensch outlook he epitomized reigned supreme at Hitler's headquarters, military commanders were only wasting their breath urging a psychological warfare campaign in which Russian churches would play a central role. The two most notable such proposals were proffered by General Friedrich von Unruh in November 1941 and by General von Schenkendorff in March 1942. Both these commanders of rear areas of Army Group Center concluded that in trying to win the Russian people over, "religious freedom" would have to be granted right away.[65] Their conclusion may also reflect an attempt to outflank the pressure of the Gestapo, which had focused on their command in its protests against joint military-civilian services.[66]

The possibilities glimpsed by the generals were effectively, if unofficially, put into practice by various of the front-line units. They helped churches, generally on the pragmatic grounds that such actions engendered a friendly response from the population, facilitating their supplies, communications, and social relations and protecting their rear. No doubt, a special effort to help was made by the strongly devout who could still be found among the rank and file and, as Rosenberg had noted, particularly in the officers' corps.[67] In their grappling with the realities of Russia, many soldiers discarded the stereotype of the subhuman native, as shown by their books and articles from the Eastern front. They looked on the persons they encountered not as future slaves, but as representatives of a new order to replace Soviet domination. They explained any objectionable traits of the native population as due solely to the evil traces of Bolshevism: after these superficialities had been swept away by German enlightenment (usually a brief conversation in sign language with the soldier writing the book) the Russians of course realized all errors of their previous Communist ways and became fervent disciples of Nazism. The Russian people, especially the peasantry, was seen as basically good; Communist delusions were attributed entirely to the threat of the Kremlin—and once that pressure was removed they could be easily discarded.

Typical of this genre is August Haussleiter's *An der mittleren Ostfront* (On the Middle Russian Front), published in 1942, which describes the many churches of Kaluga whose "decorations had long crumbled away." In the only chapel still fit to function, "candlelight yet flickers in front of the darkly varnished icons, and old people bend their knee at the altar." Haussleiter feels himself in a land where "churches have been turned into stables, ceremonious old Christmas pictures painted over with whitewash, and feeding troughs set up where once the altar stood."[68] Another account by Paul Werner, *Ein schweizer Journalist sieht Russland* (A Swiss Journalist Sees Russia)—though hardly through neutral eyes—tells what happened when German soldiers moved beyond observation to participate in the native religious rebirth. The scene is Kiev, the Ukrainian capital that had been occupied on September 19, 1941, and where a nationalist unit under the command of Andrew Melnyk had arrived three days later to set up a new local administration.[69] "The Germans cleared the mines from St. Andrew's Church in Kiev. Five days after the occupation, they received and sanctioned the request of a Ukrainian delegation to hold services there. Daily masses were organized after utensils had been obtained from a museum, and huge crowds attended services."[70] The photographs documenting Werner's report are notable for showing several young people, mainly peasant girls, taking part in the services.

A secret dispatch by Major O. W. Müller describes burgeoning religious life in the occupied territories as encompassing all groups except urban youth.[71] As a result, he notes that, by autumn 1942, there was an acute need in the central areas for church equipment, religious pictures, books, and so on, which he asked the Propaganda Division to supply. In addition to a shortage of younger priests, there was an opening for a bishop in the "Army Group Center" sector that he "urgently requests" be filled. Evidently, Orthodox organizations were still directing requests to occupation authorities, as they had a year before, to distribute the limited supply of priests more evenly through the countryside.[72] An interesting sidelight on Müller is that he served as Ostministerium representative to his army group, indicating the liaison that existed between Rosenberg's staff and the military.

Indeed, there were common grounds to motivate joint action by officials of the Ostministerium and army commanders. Rosenberg's policies of religious toleration and cultural development jibed with the attitudes of the more liberal generals. By the second year of the occupation, their jurisdictional disputes were being transcended by a shared revulsion against the terrorist methods of the Einsatzgruppen, the Ukrainian commissariat, and agents of the labor draft and agricultural requisition —all of whom were fueling popular hostility and a formidable force of partisans. On December 18, 1942, the Rosenberg ministry hosted a prominent assembly of army officers and, at this unique gathering, agreed to work out a platform stressing positive political aims to meet the requirement for "a radical change of Germany policy."[73] The incipient breakthrough in civilian-military cooperation was squashed peremptorily by Hitler. When the Führer learned of the conference, he admonished Rosenberg not to meddle in military affairs and the army representatives not to venture into political matters without express approval from the High Command. Thenceforth, decision-making powers over the occupied territories swung back to the forces of repression and terror. In the sphere of religion this spelled the undoing of the military measures that had been promoting local church activities. Among the population it engendered yet another wave of disillusionment, as religious rights granted by the advance guard of the conquerors were abruptly circumscribed or denied altogether.

THE ECONOMIC AGENCIES

A welter of German bureaucracies concerned itself with the economy of the occupied territories; Göring, as head of the Four-Year Plan, was nominally in charge, laying down overall policy through the *Wirtschaftsführungsstab Ost* (Economic Directorate for the East) and trying to coordinate parallel functions of the Ministry for Economics, the Ministry for Food and Agriculture, the Ostministerium, and the High Command's Office for Armament Economy. The common denominator of all these agencies was an insistence on squeezing the last drop of work and supplies out of the subject population. As Göring had expressed it when he cut short Rosenberg's dissertation on Russian cultural values at the meeting with Hitler on July 16, 1941, the immediate aim was to secure the food supply; everything else would have to wait a long time.[74]

The Agricultural Administration, under the direction of State Secretary (later Minister for Food and Agriculture) Herbert Backe, employed the simple yardstick of food deliveries to the Wehrmacht and the Third Reich to gauge its achievements in the occupied territories. To obtain maximum leverage from its limited staff, it latched onto the existing kolkhoz and sovkhoz systems as furnishing readymade machines for exploiting the Russian peasant. The universal hope of the farmers for the dismantling of collectivized agriculture was cruelly frustrated.[75] In a policy that one analyst has termed a mixture of compromise and deceit, German "reforms" changed little in the old system except the name of the despised kolkhoz (to *Gemeinwirtschaft*).[76] The upshot was that a motley crew of *Landwirtschaftsführer* (agricultural leaders) supervised the fulfillment of quotas now determined in Berlin instead of Moscow. The Orthodox congregations who had dedicated services to the Germans in April 1942 for the promised abolition of collectivized agriculture found that their thanks had been rendered prematurely.[77]

German reluctance to tamper with institutions that had already proved their value as political controls extended to the Agricultural Administration's approach to the churches. The tenth of "Twelve Commandments" which were to guide the activities of agricultural district leaders proclaimed: "We do not want to give the Russians a new religion. But the Russian is in his way a religiously superstitious person—that you should take cognizance of. However, dealing with religious questions is not part of your task."[78] This fitted into the framework regarding ideological issues in general, laid down by the ninth commandment: "We do not want to convert the Russians to National Socialism, but to make them our tools."

The "Commandments" were released on June 1, 1941, twenty days before Hitler unleashed Operation Barbarossa. But their cynical tone of unvarnished exploitation dominated Nazi economic policy throughout the occupation. In pursuit of Germany's profit, all other concerns became secondary, even to Ostminister Alfred Rosenberg. His directive on the employment of native labor in the economy of occupied territories tersely commands that "the handling of religious questions must be suspended."[79] Economic administrators would only be distracted from their tasks by getting themselves embroiled in cultural matters.

The shortsightedness of such a view was apparent to some lesser officials of the Ostministerium, as well as to the more perspicacious generals and diplomats. But against the regnant policies of Göring, Backe, and Koch their plaintive protests could not make a dent; they are epitomized in a secret memorandum by Otto Bräutigam, a section chief in the political department of Rosenberg's ministry, dated October 25, 1942.[80] He reviews the three German "war aims" in the Russian campaign and contends that if they had been limited to the first, "to destroy Bolshevism," the war would have ended long ago because it coincided with the wishes of the population, especially the peasantry. Even the second aim, "to smash the Great Russian empire," might have been accepted by most people as the price of their military defeat. But the final goal, "to win colonial territory for the purposes of settlement and economic exploitation," could not help but evoke widespread resistance, "since even a primitive man can realize that our slogan, 'Liberation from Bolshevism,' is only a pretext for applying techniques to enslave the Slavs."

Bräutigam defends this position against charges that it is "soft, sentimental, and humanitarian." On the contrary, he claims, it represents just sensible *Realpolitik* "to maintain the friendly welcome given us as liberators, in order to make military, political, and economic capital for Germany out of it." Yet the initial proposals of his office to dissolve the kolkhozy and introduce private farming had been rejected by the Four-Year Plan administration on the grounds that "organizational changes during the war were out of the question." The reform plan that was finally approved in February 1942 provided for a two-stage transition from collective to cooperative, then to individual farming. However, the Reich commissars held up its execution until the spring, when there were still reports of delays due to the lack of title books, surveyors, instruments, and so on.

It is clear from this account that agricultural reform did not have a chance, if only because Koch could sabotage the program in the rural heartland, the Ukraine. There, as Bräutigam notes, only ten percent of the kolkhozy had been converted into cooperatives after eight months of reform, and from all indications that was the point at which things would stall. He goes on to comment on the similar impasse in plans to promote religious freedom in the occupied territories. Although he casts no blame here, it is evident that the same constellation of administrative forces that had dashed liberal hopes when it came to economic questions was dooming genuine improvements in the cultural sphere. German "hard-liners" who insisted on the most rigid controls for the peasant had as little use for his churches as Soviet agricultural overseers had had in their time.

THE FOREIGN OFFICE

Among the German agencies that had some bearing on policy toward the Russian Orthodox Church, the Foreign Office is remarkable for the vast gap between the goodness of its intentions and its utter inability to put them into practice. Largely responsible for the former was Franz von Papen, the ex-chancellor who had been instrumental in negotiating Hitler's Concordat with the Vatican and had become one of a number of highly placed Catholics who rationalized the attack on Russia as a blow against atheism.[81] Advocates of the fostering of religion in occupied territories were the fairly sophisticated experts on Russia who had been assembled by Councillor Georg Grosskopf in a body known as the Russ-land-Gremium.[82] In short order they joined von Papen in the ranks of impotent bureaucrats whom Hitler suffered for no apparent reason except that they furnished the butt of his jokes. Their ineffectuality was abetted by their bumbling chief, Foreign Minister Joachim von Ribbentrop, whose rare attempts to relay the moderate views of his staff to Hitler invariably ended in servile retreat.

The notes of the July 1941 conference of Nazi leaders on the future administration of Russian lands contain the following entry: "By the way, the Führer emphasizes that church activity is entirely out of the question. Papen has already sent him via the Foreign Office a long memorandum in which it is claimed that now is the right moment to introduce churches again, but that is entirely out of the question."[83] The suggestion has been made that Ribbentrop fully expected Hitler's rebuff and, indeed, only passed along the proposal of his fierce enemy, von Papen, in order to have the roof fall in on him.[84] This seems a rather far-fetched hypothesis in view of the fact that von Papen had been out of favor with the leadership for some time by then.[85] It is also unlikely that Ribbentrop would have been unaware that by this move he was implicating himself in a project that would rouse Hitler's scorn. His own version of the incident admits no ulterior motive, though it must be read with the skepticism due such postwar accounts composed in the cells at Nuremberg. For what it is worth, he relates: "Papen was attacked by the Party, especially by Himmler, for his Catholicism and, if it hadn't been for my protection he would have been in deep trouble because of his work on behalf of the Catholic Action. I myself was favorably inclined when it came to church questions, if only because of foreign policy reasons."[86]

Although they were not spelled out by von Papen or Ribbentrop, these foreign policy reasons can be fairly well deduced in the case of the Russian Orthodox Church. Nazi diplomats could have recognized several profitable uses for a religious "liberation" in the occupied territories conducted under German auspices. News of it could have been transmitted to neutral countries and the United States (at least until its entry into the war) to offset the bad impressions created by stories of Nazi atrocities; it would have been particularly helpful in angling for the support of Greek Orthodox churches in these countries. A German modus vivendi with the Orthodox Church would also cement relations with pro-German Balkan governments of countries that had sizable contingents of believers. The dividends of such a venture were further indicated by the German alliance with the Grand Mufti, for which the groundwork had been laid by an extremely liberal policy in Berlin toward the Moslem nationalities, with religious toleration toward Islam constituting a vital part.[87] That alliance brought about the formation of German legions from Moslem areas of southern Russia and the closest collaboration the Germans received anywhere in their Eastern territories.

In any case, little more is heard on this subject from the diplomats beyond an occasional futile protest, such as the one tendered by the Russland-Gremium when the High Command barred further military assistance to Russian churches.[88] Russian questions as a whole were put outside the purview of the Foreign Office by 1942, on orders from Hitler.[89] Ribbentrop's staff remained only indirectly involved, through its dealings with the Vatican, which had for fifteen years "been quietly training priests to do missionary work in Russia" and wasn't about to recall them in the face of Rosenberg's orders not to admit them into occupied territories. Under the protection of some army officers, a number of the more persistent missionaries evidently managed to elude the ban. One source has gleaned from the Vatican that "the Germans were willing to allow the priests to carry out their duties because they believed that many Russians and Ukrainians secretly yearned for religion and, therefore, if the German army was followed by priests, it would help to reconcile the Russians to German occupation."[90] When the papal nuncio brought protests against official German harassment in the area, the Foreign Office would have the task of turning them aside, Lammers informed Rosenberg in October 1942.[91]

The desire of the Einsatzgruppen to keep Catholic missionaries from exploiting the disorganized church situation in Belorussia in order to win converts has already been noted. Security reports from the Ukraine also stress "the danger of Roman intervention . . . if no internal stabilization takes place in the traditional Eastern Church."[92] A further analysis in the summer of 1941 finds that "on former Polish territory, the Catholic Church is seeking to . . . gain political influence through the remaining Polish administrative machinery. Polish activity includes the baptism of Orthodox children, especially orphans, in the Polish Catholic area. With rare exceptions, there is no evidence of anti-German activity among the Polish clergy, but the latter probably identifies with Polish intellectuals who seek the re-establishment of an independent Poland."[93]

In the security police scale of values, Greek Orthodoxy, which might be kept from allying itself with nationalist groups, was relatively preferable to Catholicism, already fused with anti-German Polish patriotism or the extreme nationalism of the West Ukraine. Following an extensive survey of Ukrainian religious trends, an SD report concludes: "We need hardly add that Roman Catholicism and the whole Catholic way of thought evident among some Great Russian émigrés (naming the state as 'enemy' of the Church, declaring 'rights' of the Church) represents the real church-political danger in the East."[94] For the Einsatzgruppen, with their utilitarian approach to religion, the Orthodox churches, too, had their established predominance in the occupied territories to recommend them as candidates for collaboration; and they were no doubt influenced by the record of recent frictions between Germany and the Vatican, as well as by the anti-Catholic bias of the Nazi leadership that made them regard the incipient missionary effort as a direct ideological threat.

The papal see, outside the sphere of German hegemony, possessed enough power of independent action to issue widely circulated protests against Nazi inhumanities, at least on those rather rare occasions when it was deemed politic to do so. An Einsatzgruppen report which characterizes the Lvov clergy as chauvinistic and anti-German refers to such unfavorable publicity: "The Vatican reports alleged Nazi cruelties against the Polish clergy."[95] The second type of Vatican pressure conflicting with German interests, protests of the controls imposed by German church administrators, is also taken up in the report. Later dispatches reveal the paranoid strains in the Gestapo psyche, ranging from rumors that Belorussian missionary work was being done on the Pope's orders by Polish priests disguised as peasants, to the ultimate fantasy of an alliance forged by Catholic and Soviet leaders for their personal aggrandizement.[96]

If hamstringing the Catholic missionary effort was primarily the duty of the Einsatzgruppen with the unstinting support of the Ostministerium, the necessarily ruffled feelings of the Vatican meant that the Foreign Office had a new job to do, too. Thus the results of a meeting between Hitler and Rosenberg, on May 3, 1942, were transmitted to Ribbentrop to guide his Vatican diplomacy. At the meeting "it was mentioned . . . that the Vatican was already naming bishops for the Ostland Reichskommissariat who had become independently active, without liaison with the respective German administrations."[97] Hitler had assigned to Rosenberg's staff the handling of anticipated friction with these Catholic Church representatives, leaving it to Ribbentrop to ward off all such future requests and complaints expected from the papal nuncio—a task to which he sprang with alacrity.[98] In short, Foreign Office diplomats were deemed worthy of spinning red tape and deliberately "passing the buck" in response to Vatican remonstrances. By this time they had already been relegated to such minor service functions and excluded from genuine policy-making, for which their refusal to acknowledge the precedence of military-economic over political factors had made them unfit in the eyes of the Nazi leadership.

The sidelining of the Foreign Office represented a triumph for Rosenberg. He had won out, for once, over a rival. True, the vanquished was only Ribbentrop, an official with even fewer administrative talents and bureaucratic allies to marshal in his cause than Rosenberg could boast. To compound the hollowness of the victory, the Foreign Minister had been checkmated merely for trying to put into practice the theories of the Ostministerium. His debacle had come when he had tried to enlist anti-Russian nationalities in the German war effort by assembling émigré leaders, mainly from the Caucasus, at the Hotel Adlon in Berlin at the end of April 1942.[99] In persuading Hitler to call a halt to the proceedings, Rosenberg won the battle for his bureaucratic prerogatives but lost the war for his policies.

This example illustrates, if in an extreme form, how German occupation policy was permeated with struggles for personal power among the Nazi elite. If the failure to develop consistent policies is to be understood, one must begin here: with the feuds that pitted Rosenberg against Koch, Goebbels, and Ribbentrop; with the backstairs intrigues of Bormann and the temporary alliances between generals and Ostministerium officials, propagandists and security units; with the appetites of Göring, Himmler, and Koch for a lion's share of the prizes to be snatched from Russia. To the Eastern subjects of the Third Reich this meant being thrust into a role of pawns in a game they did not fathom. All they knew was that their aspirations counted for naught and that a bewildering succession of promises and threats from their German masters left them no option but to survive somehow beneath the clashing factions.

On the ideological plane, the battle lines of the bureaucrats were drawn in terms of the tension, recognized at the outset by Rosenberg, between long-range political and short-range military-economic advantages to be derived from the occupation. With fierce battles raging only a few miles away, it is small wonder that German officials in the field never managed to resolve this dilemma, especially since their chiefs persisted in coloring overall objectives in the light of their agency's peculiar

functions. The course of these divergent approaches as they were reflected in the microcosm of church policy has been traced here. In the
absence of any coordinating mechanism for ideological conflicts of this
type, it was perhaps inevitable that practices varied sharply and often
contradicted each other. The population, caught in the middle, saw
here but one more instance of grand promises matched by paltry fulfillment. Instead of becoming the tool the Germans had desired, the body
of the faithful, its hopes roused only to be frustrated, turned into another
of the potentially hostile forces that could be and was activated in the
Soviet favor by German repression and military defeats.

6

The Popular Reaction to German Religious Policy in the East

German agencies involved in the administration of occupied Russian territories shared a common assumption: the Russian Orthodox Church could in some fashion be molded to suit their purposes. At the very least, for the fanatic advocates of the master-race thesis, this meant seeing the Church as a means to make the populace tractable to the German yoke; in the more sanguine plans of the psychological warfare strategists, the Church was to play a positive role as a potential ally in the war against Bolshevism. The survey of German policies regarding the Church presented in this book suggests that they were too beset by contradictions, dilatoriness, and petty considerations to achieve any but chaotic results. The data must now be reviewed to reconstruct the picture of church life under Nazi rule from a different perspective—that of the believers—in order to focus on elements of order beneath the chaos.

At the outset, the extent to which patterns of popular reaction validated the German assumption should be determined. Four questions can be explored: To what degree did German church policy succeed in mobilizing popular resistance to the Soviet regime? If some Church groups did collaborate with the Germans, who were they and to what lengths did they go? If others were antagonized by German policies, were they moved beyond passive resistance to open friction with the authorities? If, apart from political factors, the people manifested a long-suppressed desire to express their faith, which strata were caught up in the religious revival? Definitive answers to these questions would do much to shed light on the inner workings of the Orthodox Church as an institution; however, the data are too fragmentary to lead to anything but tentative conclusions. As far as they do go, they indicate that the answer to each question cannot be an unequivocal yes or no, an unhesitating identification of clerical quislings and partisans or an unambiguous evaluation of motives for popular participation in Church activities.

The very qualification of such answers casts doubt on simpler deductions drawn, for example, by official Soviet historians who have taken the rarity of occurrence of overt collaboration as proof of pro-Soviet loyalties of the Church masses and leaders under the occupation.[1] On the other hand, it raises questions about the validity of contrary conclusions advanced by scholars whose sympathies for the pre-war plight of Russian believers may have predisposed them to over-rate pro-German sounds in the popular cheering that followed the removal of Soviet controls. Thus, David Dallin's judgment: "Many orthodox priests in occupied regions of Russia entered into collaboration with the German authorities. This was significant because the priests would not have ventured to act contrary to the sentiments of their parishioners."[2] Dallin's premise is subject to criticism because he limits his evidence for collaboration to the official thanks for their "liberation" that was tendered by a number of Church dignitaries to the Germans; his inference is the more dubious for not taking the unsettled social and political conditions of military occupation into account.

A critique would raise at least the following three objections: (1) much of the thanks poured out to Hitler by Church leaders bore the earmarks of extortion by German pressure; (2) some of the newly installed Church heads had been brought along by the Germans and were merely playing puppet roles according to a prepared script; (3) with the sudden need for priests to meet the upsurge of new congregations, many laymen (presumably more loyal to the Nazis, to whom they owed their offices, than to their parishioners) had to be invested. Except for the latter two groups, collaboration may have amounted to little more than rendering Caesar his due. Too much cannot be made of an occasional sermon written according to Nazi specifications. With the keen noses of the German political police sniffing out any signs of disaffection, the priests could hardly have been expected to preach insurrection.

Before examining in detail the three special factors that cast doubt on the genuineness of collaboration by the clergy, a qualification must be introduced. During the first few weeks of the four-year occupation period, priests and believers were caught up in the general euphoria of a transition period that had witnessed the overnight disappearance of Soviet controls but had not yet felt the brunt of German repression. The prevalent mood of the population, as recounted by several observers, was a mixture of hope and dread.[3] While the fears soon proved well founded, the aspirations were often rooted only in wishful thinking. "It can't be worse" was the byword of the moment.[4] Ukrainian believers greeted the Wehrmacht as a "punishing arm of God" and misread the black cross on tank turrets as a sign of Christian devotion.[5]

Where German military units helped to reopen churches, their unofficial and sporadic actions were interpreted by a confused populace as a harbinger of better days to come. The initial wave of welcoming speeches and "thank-you notes" was followed by swift disillusion. "We soon realized that the Germans hadn't come to liberate our people from Bolshevism but to subdue them for so-called *Lebensraum*," says one report.[6] The primary reason for the evaporation of popular gratitude after the first holiday flush lay in the worsening of material conditions, which far outweighed any of the spiritual concessions the Germans granted grudgingly. Religious freedom often remained a plus factor. "The church was overwhelmingly considered the sole area in which German rule brought decided improvement," concludes Alexander Dallin from his interviews of Russian escapees for the Harvard project.[7] Any thankfulness here was canceled out by four minuses: the brutal treatment of war prisoners, the harshness of German agricultural policy, starvation in the cities, and the ruthless labor draft.[8] Even in the church sphere, however, there was a growing resentment against heavy-handed administrators who extorted loyalist sermons, installed their puppets in leading church positions, and sanctioned arrests and executions of independent-minded clerics.

LIMITS OF PRESSURE: THE CASE OF SERGIUS

From the account of Gestapo and Propaganda Ministry practices in the last chapter, it is clear that the doctoring of sermons was no rarity; neither was the extraction of pro-Nazi appeals from reluctant church heads, at gunpoint if necessary. One of the most significant cases of such forced collaboration opens with a German Security Office report on July 11, 1941: "Metropolitan of the Russian Orthodox Church for the Baltic Lands, Sergei [Sergius] in Riga, is ready to release an appeal to the believers of Russia against Communism . . . Draft of the appeal is being prepared at this time."[9] The report does not bother to amplify the illustrious background of Sergius, merely noting that he has been "in Riga since 1941 . . . previously, 23 years in Moscow. He is a Great Russian. Civil name: Voskresensky."

Among the data not mentioned in the report was that the forty-two-year-old Sergius had risen meteorically in the Church, having been made a bishop twelve years before and soon becoming a chief adviser to his older namesake, who was to become patriarch.[10] On behalf of the latter, he had been sent to newly Soviet-occupied Volhynia in 1939 to sell the local clerics on the benefits of cooperating with Moscow. As principal liaison man to the Kremlin on behalf of the elder Sergius, he had shown the acumen which made him a logical choice for exarch, or supervisory bishop, for the Baltic states occupied by the Soviets in August 1940. When ordered to return to Russia because of the German advance, the younger Sergius made a crucial decision to disobey. Whatever his private reasons—perhaps the arrest of his father in the 1935 purges—he concealed himself for four days in the crypt of the Cathedral of Riga, emerging only to be arrested by the Gestapo.[11]

The pressures exerted by the German security officials on Sergius the Younger to make him issue the prepared text of his anti-Communist call to arms can only be conjectured. Evidently he was able to strike a bargain. During the next months he issued telegrams of greeting to Hitler, but he did not renounce his allegiance to the Church head in Moscow until his September 1942 denunciation by the Patriarchy made a rupture unavoidable.[12] In the meantime, his actions had made abundantly plain that his prime aim was the revival of religious life and the maintenance of a unified Church organization in his domain; pro-German prayers might be a necessary price, but they deliberately stopped short of a renunciation of his Russian national values. What they purchased was, first of all, the backing of the Ostland Reichskommissariat that overcame the resistance to Sergius' authority by Estonian bishops who had been supported by their Generalkommissar.[13] No sooner had his claim been validated for the Baltic than Sergius stretched it to cover the Russian areas to the east that the Wehrmacht had taken on its way to Leningrad. Particularly in the Pskov region, where not a single parish had survived, he built up a thriving mission with hastily commissioned lay priests and by 1943 was able to boast some two hundred congregations, workshops for religious objects, a parochial education system, record attendance at services, and a clerical journal.[14]

Perusal of Gestapo reports reveals that the exceptional success of the Orthodox mission in the Northern Military District, on the approaches to Leningrad, was no fluke. It is a tribute to the organizational skills of Sergius that he could make Pskov, as well as nearby centers at Ostrov and Luga, into economically thriving and well-staffed enterprises. No less does it bear witness to the Exarch's diplomatic skills in neutralizing his ecclesiastical competitors—particularly the nationalist clerics of Estonia and Latvia, who denounced Sergius for his Muscovite antecedents as a Bolshevik agent—while impressing his Nazi overseers as their potential tool or, at least, as a lesser evil than the local nationalists in the Baltic. The initial Einsatzgruppen dispatches from Pskov, Ostrov, and Luga depict the early spontaneous nature of the popular religious revival.[15] The German reaction is ambivalent, viewing the phenomenon as a clue to "pacification" of the countryside but discounting it as limited to the older peasantry. By February 1942, however, there was a reassessment: activities in the area between Lake Peipus and Lake Ilmen were attributed to the "Administration of the Orthodox Mission in the Liberated Areas of Russia," involving some forty priests under Sergius, whose position had presumably been underwritten by officials in Berlin.[16] The missionaries were promoting plans for religious instruction of children and they had recently staged (partly for German benefit) an admittedly imposing religious procession to the Pskov Cathedral with about two thousand celebrants (though mostly female), to dedicate an icon of the Madonna of Tikhvin that German troops had saved in recent battle.

Up to this time, the German security offices appear to have been skeptical about Latvian nationalist hostility to Sergius, even to charges that he was on the NKVD payroll and had ties to the Living Church.[17] As when Sergius repelled advances from the Karlovtsi émigrés operating through Bishop Seraphim in Berlin, or helped undercut the authority of Metropolitan Augustin in Latvia, the pragmatic Gestapo hesitated to back unreliable and weak competitors. After it had taken the measure of Sergius' organizational strength, however, it was happy to endorse the Reichskommissariat order of February 23, 1942, giving him ten days to move to Vilna, Lithuania, and putting Orthodox Church affairs in Latvia in the hands of his rival, the Estonian Archbishop Alexander, during an extended "vacation" of Metropolitan Augustin.[18] There can be little doubt that transferring Sergius from Riga was calculated to disrupt his communications with the Pskov area.

A month after his move to Vilna, Sergius was able to convince the security chief of Lithuania of a "pro-German direction in his speeches and actions," a tactical maneuver that appears to have enabled him to bring the economic and spiritual fortunes of the Pskov and Luga missions to new heights by autumn 1942. And the SS kept close watch over his balance sheet.[19] Thus an Einsatzgruppe reported on the operations of the Pskov organization that turned popular contributions into an income of 10,000 Reichsmark per month by tithing its parishes and transmitting half of this amount to Sergius. Kyrill Saitz, the priest in charge of the mission, requested German legitimation of administrators appointed by Sergius down to the parish level, as well as "all possible help" from German and local Russian government offices. His specific demands included permission for the Estonian diocese to resubmit to the Exarch's control, for "politically reliable" émigré priests to join the mission, and for theological courses to be set up in Riga, Vilna, and elsewhere to supply more priests. Along economic lines, he asked that taxes on parishes and "enterprises run for their benefit" be suspended and that procurement and transport of clerical supplies, such as wax for candles, be provided at fixed prices. The chief enterprise appears to have been a candle factory, whose sales account for eighty percent of mission income, though additional workshops produced icons and other items. In the town of Luga, churches were said to have taken in 9,000 rubles per month, with a savings account balance of 29,000 rubles by September 1942.

The German attitude implied in this report is wary, though not yet hostile enough to warrant the recommendation of drastic counter-measures. This fact can be gleaned from the report's deduction that a recent decline of sums spent on "charitable activities" by the Pskov mission from upwards of 10,000 rubles a month to one-tenth of that sum may have been due to the pocketing of funds by mission staff or to the siphoning off of a greater share by Sergius. Claims of an Orthodox priest strengthened Nazi suspicions that the mission had mishandled large sums and used a courier service to Sergius to escape German control of moneys and mail, indeed that Sergius may have been an NKVD agent after all. There is no gainsaying, however, the mission's hold over some ten thousand believers in the Pskov area; the thousands of baptisms and other religious rites performed; the ability of priests and deacons to support themselves entirely from ceremonial fees. Only occasionally did the Kommandatura betray skepticism about the operation, by presuming that some men and youth participating in services did so "out of curiosity rather than genuine faith." Only incidentally did it put up bureaucratic hurdles, by prohibiting churchly wedding services without prior civil registration. And though German officials turned down the mission's request to institute religious instruction in and out of school—since it would constitute official recognition they were not ready to grant—they accepted a revised proposal for religious courses given by teachers subordinate to local departments of education. They also took note of volunteer efforts by the people to restore churches but found labor and materials in too short supply to allow construction of new churches. As for the mission's desperate efforts to stave off impending income taxes on its employees and a turnover tax on its products, the Germans made no move to interfere. Neither did they seem particularly upset by the report that Bishop Pavel in a speech at Narva, Estonia, accused Pskov priests of meddling in his diocesan affairs, nor by Estonian clerics' resisting his offer to subordinate that state's church organization to Exarch Sergius, whom they considered "a tool of the Communists" unlike their national champion Metropolitan Alexander. Even with official reaction to Sergius shifting from benevolent neutrality to thinly veiled hostility, he managed to write a unique chapter in the church history of the occupation, thanks to his single-minded dedication no less than his charm, shrewdness, and administrative skill.

The successes of Sergius derived from the increasing strength of his bargaining position vis-à-vis the Germans, which in turn depended on his making the formal pronouncements of loyalty they demanded yet retaining enough independence of action to convince his flock that he was doing so under duress. The thin line he managed to tread is indicated by two examples. The first is the ingenious argument he used to justify not protesting the election of his old friend Patriarch Sergius as printed in the official German newspaper for the Ostland on March 4, 1943. It would be a mistake for bishops in the occupied territories to take such steps, he contended, since it would make them look like utter tools of German policy. By then the patriarchal elevation had been recognized by all high offices of the Church; rather than contest it, local bishops should hail it as a concession wrung from the Bolsheviks like their dissolution of the Comintern. "One has to play off the Patriarch of Moscow against Stalin," he advised. German propaganda should stress that "even today the Soviets have been forced to recognize a Church head as representative and symbol of the anti-Soviets . . . It is a sign of the bankruptcy of Bolshevism if its change in policy leads to the recognition of God and the Church."[20]

As relayed by the Ostland security police commander, the views of Sergius reflect an anti-Communism that falls far short of an espousal of Nazi aims; their only clear thrust is pro-Church. The same constellation of sentiments surrounds his response to an order by the Lithuanian puppet regime to have all parish councils prepare lists of men aged eighteen to forty-five for impressment into a special SS unit. Failure to comply with this order of April 7, 1943, by May 2 entailed "prompt shipment" of all derelict councillors to a concentration camp.[21] Sergius, evidently unable to forestall this action, telegraphed his bishops urging them to secure compliance and to explain to the population the severe sanctions for not answering an SS summons. However, he asked them to point out to the councillors that such measures were due to the absence of true popular representatives and that their participation was in the role of members of a social organization, not as church officials.[22]

As he dissociated himself more and more from their policy, Sergius must have made the Germans aware that they had grossly under-rated him. He had persuaded them that it would be better to deal with him than with the native Baltic archbishops who wore their nationalism on their sleeves. He had even cleverly turned the *Führerprinzip* to his own ends by using it to buttress his case for Church leadership.[23] Finally, he had gone behind their backs to contact leaders of the Belorussian Orthodox Church and keep them within his growing sphere of influence. The result of all these maneuvers was the heightened stature of Sergius and his organization. When it had transcended that of puppets, the Germans rang down the curtain. The climax is recounted by an acquaintance of Sergius in a Harvard Project interview: "Sergius was a determined Russian patriot. In his sermons he never mentioned the Germans, but implicitly his sermons did have a political character . . . He hated the Germans. Evidently there was a denunciation of him by somebody, perhaps through a special Einsatzkommando . . . Sergius, accompanied by a couple and the driver, was riding from Vilna, far from town, when a group of six or seven persons drove up in a car and barred his way. They shot all four of them with automatic pistols. The local peasants and partisans had no reason to dislike him so intensely. It seems more likely that the Germans did it themselves."[24]

There seems little doubt that the murder of Sergius on April 28, 1944, was indeed the product of a vendetta by the security troops. Not only did they have the motive and the opportunity, but they would have been advised of the travel plans which were to take Sergius to Riga; furthermore, the authorities remained conspicuously silent to naming any suspects or disclosing any efforts to track them down. The note of hypocrisy in the German epitaph for Sergius also strikes a familiar chord. The official publication of the Ostland Reichskommissariat cites the statement published by the "trustees" for Estonia, Latvia, and Lithuania in the June 15 issue of *Russki Vestnik* (Russian Herald) in

Riga. Arensburger, Alexeyev, and Stavrovsky, respectively, "bemoan the murder of Metropolitan Sergius, martyr against Judeo-Bolshevism. No threats will stop the Russian people in their struggle [against these forces]."[25]

For all its unusual features and somewhat mysterious ending, the story of Sergius may be taken as a model of the behavior many Russian priests strove to follow under the occupation. A plethora of verbal evidence supports a thesis for collaboration—greetings, sermons, and speeches on behalf of the Germans, most of them clearly delivered on demand—but very few actions lend them substantive meaning. It is on the basis of such data that Serge Bolshakoff comments on "the German advance, accompanied by the closing of the Godless museums and the reopening of the shut-up churches, where the Orthodox priests were invited to sing solemn thanksgiving services before the German officers." And he goes on to conclude that "the Uniate and the Orthodox clergy certainly abstained from supporting the German advance."[26]

LIMITS OF ARTIFICE: THE CASE
OF BELORUSSIAN AUTOCEPHALY

The Germans had originally gambled on Sergius because to them he seemed a known quantity, as opposed to the potentially more dangerous unknown factors, the nationalist bishops of the Baltic states. They took a different sort of risk in Belorussia, where neither of the prevailing forces—a Russian Orthodox Church loyal to the Moscow Patriarchate and a sizable group of Catholics and Uniates obedient to the Pope— was a likely prospect for collaboration, by fashioning a synthetic church organization to carry the twin banners of clerical independence and the swastika. The German Generalkommissar, old-time Nazi Gauleiter Wilhelm Kube, was charged with close guidance of this fledgling "Belorussian Autocephalous Orthodox National Church" in a unique example of official and total German support for a church group in the occupied territories.[27] At his disposal was the repressive machinery to stifle rival factions and to do away with those Belorussian nationalists who might try to bend the new movement to their purposes. The only thing he could not do was to blow life into his creature; that would be up to the ecclesiastical quislings and their enthusiastic followers who were supposed to have appeared at the appointed time but never did.

The German administration found it far easier to eliminate the competition than to market its product. The nationalists had never played a leading role in Belorussia; their sparse numbers were not equal to meeting the challenges of staffing local government posts, when allowed to do so by the Germans, or protesting the dismemberment of their territories, with chunks going to East Prussia, Lithuania, the Ukrainian Reichskommissariat, and the army-occupied territories to the east.[28] The only channel left open to them was the underground Party of Belorussian Independence (BNP), soon joined by a "People's Front" of Catholics reacting to German persecution, led by an old émigré from Vilna, Father Vincent Hadleŭski (Godlevski), who tried to rally anti-Communists who had accompanied Wehrmacht units into a force that could be led by him as bishop.[29] Their slogan, "Neither the Russians nor the Germans," lay tattered amid the German purges of the nationalists that began in summer 1942 and claimed Hadleŭski among its victims by the year's end. In the removal of Belorussian emblems and flags, the German-sponsored church, too, was ordered to drop the term "National" from its title.[30]

A similar fate was in store for the province's Uniates, some thirty thousand strong, organized in March 1942 by the Polish Metropolitan Szepticky as an Exarchate, under Father Anton Nemancevič (Nemantsevich), in a papal move suspiciously noted by the Gestapo.[31] This priest, with several years in Russian prisons and a round of Vatican studies to his credit, had at first been tolerated by the Germans in his missionary efforts, which included a decree on the use of the Belorussian language in sermons. Rosenberg's ministry, with its anti-Vatican bias, wasted no love on what it called "the Polish-influenced Roman Catholic Church" of Belorussia.[32] The crackdown came in November 1942 with the Gestapo arrest and presumed execution of Nemancevič and the dispersal of his forces.[33] When the Soviets recaptured Belorussia at the end of 1944, they found no Uniate organization left to liquidate.

The Germans' initial difficulty in trying to plant an autocephalous church in Belorussia lay in the absence of any native institution to graft it on. What there had been of an independent church movement was almost over before it started, and the legacy it had left was one of resistance to attempted modernization. It had begun on July 23, 1922, when Melchisedek (Payevski), the Bishop of Minsk, assumed the title of metropolitan of Belorussia to proclaim the independence of his administration. His grounds had not been nationalist, but ecclesiastical: to form a group of *starotserkovniki*, or "Old Church People," hearkening to the true faith. By the end of 1925, Metropolitan Sergius in Moscow had convinced him to renounce his title and call the whole thing off.

Melchisedek seems not to have been connected with the Minsk conference of churchmen and nationalists that tried to revive some form of autocephaly in 1927, only to meet a rebuff from the Patriarchate and to have most of its lay adherents disappear in the Soviet purges of Belorussian "National Democrats" in 1929.[34] The three other Belorussian bishops, Filaret of Bobruisk, Mikhail of Slutsk, and Ioann of Mozyr, were shut away in concentration camps in the 1937 Soviet "pogrom" that decimated the Belorussian clergy in small villages as well as urban centers. When the Soviets annexed the western part of the province in 1939, they met very little resistance in getting most of its church hierarchy to submit to the Patriarchate.

In short, not only did a new Belorussian church lack respectable antecedents, but it faced a serious staffing problem from the outset. For the German security police to proclaim in July 1941 that "the Greek-Orthodox Church is to be quickly activated and supported" was one thing.[35] To implement its premise that "priority be given to employment of Belorussian clergy" soon proved to be another, much more difficult matter. By September, it had become clear to the Germans that what religious revival had taken place was spontaneous, without any evidence of organization. In Minsk, only a few priests were concerned with regional developments; administrative considerations were far from their minds. One exception, noted in a report later that month, was Vladimir Finkovski, subsequently identified as an agent of Metropolitan Dionisius (Valedinski), head of the Polish Autocephalous Church. This priest had succeeded in ingratiating himself with the Germans by conducting services dedicated to the Führer, but he had also provoked the ire of local nationalists who saw in him a Great Russian with aspirations to the Belorussian archdiocese, promoted by the city's church council.

The Germans yielded to nationalist pressure and their own misgivings about admitting Polish influences into Belorussia. By the end of the year they had arrested Finkovski and shipped him back to Warsaw. To head the province church, they brought out of retirement seventy-four-year-old Archbishop Panteleimon (Rozhnovski) from the western region, who had been made exarch there under Soviet auspices in 1939. The choice merely led to a new dilemma, since Panteleimon (of half-Russian, half-Polish ancestry) proceeded to use all the power owing to his seniority and prestige to delay a proclamation of autocephaly, both on canonical and political grounds.[36] In January 1942, an Einsatzgruppen report announced the formation of a "Belorussian Autocephalous Orthodox National Church" but went on to accuse its leaders, Metropolitan

Panteleimon and his vicar, Bishop Benedict, of sympathies for the
Patriarchate of Moscow with whom they had been associated.[37] Though
nationalists in Warsaw made much of the "Communist past" of these
hierarchs, the Polish Church under Dionisius had recognized the legitimacy of the new church as within the bounds of the Constantinople
Patriarch's order of 1924 for a separate church administration in the
province. Along with this endorsement, Dionisius had evidently hoped
to influence the course of the new church by proposing to the Germans
three candidates for dioceses. One of them, Archimandrite Philotheus
(Narko), had already arrived in Minsk and paid a call, jointly with
Panteleimon, on Commissar Kube.[38] Among German specifications for
the new church were its canonical, politically neutral existence under
new statutes (to be drawn up), provision for services in Church Slavonic
rather than the vernacular, and the Germans' right to screen its bishops
and other officials, though "administrative matters" could be handled by
the Belorussians independently.[39]

Although his title as "Metropolitan of Minsk and all Belorussia" had
been validated by the Germans, Panteleimon may soon have begun to
doubt that they, no less than local nationalists or the circle around
Dionisius, were prepared to grant it much substance. His strategy seems
to have been to placate them when necessary in turn, but to rely on
procrastination when any of them tried to push him into what he felt
was an uncanonical posture. Thus he outflanked the Warsaw group by
making Philotheus a bishop but, to earn his loyalty rather than his
rivalry, appointed him his vicar in place of Benedict, who had been sent
to the Grodno diocese under East Prussian administration.[40] In March
1942, Panteleimon yielded to the combined pressures of nationalists and
Generalkommissariat officials by presiding at a bishops' council which
drew the structural outlines for the embryonic church in line with
German directives.[41] He also elevated another of Dionisius' nominees,
Athanasius (Martos) to the rank of bishop; but Athanasius' assignment
to the diocese of Vitebsk and Polotsk meant that, to the dismay of the
nationalists in Minsk, he would be far removed from the church center.[42]

It became clear to Germans and nationalists that, even though they
could wring concessions from Panteleimon, they were far from obtaining
his capitulation. Only a summons by the head of the Generalkommissariat's political section cut short Panteleimon's delays in appointing an
extreme nationalist, Bishop Stephen (Seŭba), to the Smolensk diocese.
On June 1, 1942, a German order exiled Panteleimon to the Liado
Monastery, his title intact, but his authority to be exercised temporarily

by Philotheus.[43] This vicar soon demonstrated that he would not gratify hopes pinned on him by the nationalists, when he resisted their attempts to call another sobor, in the Metropolitan's absence, in order to bring autocephaly of the church to fruition. A contemporary analysis of the security police blames a Great Russian conspiracy, with branches in Warsaw, Grodno, Vilna, Pinsk, and Riga, for Panteleimon's obstruction of Belorussian church developments. Its chief agent is Bishop Benedict, headquartered outside the province's jurisdiction. The real villain, according to the SD, is Exarch Sergius at Vilna, whose secretary contacted a priest close to Panteleimon. Among the communications passed on this occasion was word that autocephality of the Belorussian Orthodox Church was just a German fantasy running counter to Great Russian wishes, as well as advice to hold on till war's end made clear who would come out on top.[44] For the conspiratorial view of the Gestapo, in which all strands of Russian Orthodoxy ultimately led to Metropolitan Sergius in Moscow, one might substitute a pragmatic picture of Panteleimon: a prelate whose religious dedication and long-range vision of the Church steeled him against the importunate demands of Germans, Poles, and a small but vociferous band of Belorussian nationalists. As he told one of the latter—he had managed to survive Poles and Bolsheviks and would survive him, too.[45]

With Panteleimon in enforced retirement, nationalist hopes crested in summer 1942. Impatient Generalkommissariat officials pushed preparations for a church council that would take the final official step toward proclaiming Belorussian autocephaly. Philotheus, if somewhat reluctantly, agreed to take charge of a preparatory commission, which characteristically turned into a wrangle with the nationalists demanding a greater share of delegates to the sobor.[46] The commission submitted a draft of the new church statute to the Germans, who returned it with a detailed critique insisting that baptism of Jews be prohibited, that no extrareligious activities be provided for, and that plans for religious instruction in schools and the opening of new seminaries be reviewed by civil authorities to make sure the churches were not preparing youth for future resistance. With the qualified assent of the exiled Panteleimon, the nationalists, and the German administration, the sobor was finally held from August 30 to September 2, though several dioceses were not able to send delegates. It ratified the church statute and, in anticlimactic fashion, announced Belorussian autocephaly as fact but not canonical reality. Full church autonomy, it insisted, would be valid only if ratified by "all other Christian Orthodox Churches."[47] This meant addressing petitions to the several non-Russian Patriarchs, which was finally done on April 17, 1943 (the Generalkommissariat bringing Panteleimon back to Minsk just for the occasion), only to have the epistles mysteriously vanish once they had been handed to Kube's staff for forwarding.[48] The status of the new church was thus consigned to limbo.

Meanwhile, the German civil administration was encountering bizarre responses from the synthetic church body it had midwifed into existence. In the curious realignment of religious and nationalist groups in mid-1942, the ecclesiastics who had been coolest to the whole project now stood ready to pay lip service to the Nazis, while those who had seized upon it as a nationalist vehicle refused to do so. Evidently, the German clamp-down on the nationalists had disenchanted their sympathizers in the ranks of the clergy about the benefits of collaboration. A denationalized Church, however, appeared as a viable alternative to the politically neutral clerics. Collaboration was forthcoming from the "pro-Moscow" church heads, but not any longer from the would-be quislings who had greeted the Germans as liberators. Thus, just before his expulsion, Panteleimon apparently composed the following pastoral message in late May 1942: "The Almighty heard our prayers and, though we had lost every hope, worked a great and unexpected miracle: Our neighbors to the west, the German brothers, sent us with God's help their brave sons, the grand army that took the gruesome Bolshevik yoke from our shoulders, freed us from the Communist slave chains, and let White Ruthenia [Belorussia] breathe a new life . . . Our true patriots are only those who help the brave German army in the total liberation of our homeland."[49] In direct contrast was the record of his nationalist opponent, Bishop Stephen of Smolensk, who, according to an émigré account, "behaved very independently . . . The Germans requested Stephen to write a pro-German address; he refused and published a purely pastor-like message."[50] Panteleimon's plea may have been a desperate contortion to salvage his post, while Stephen could afford to play the ingrate from his newfound position of strength.

The Belorussian Autocephalous Church failed to live up to the hopes of Ostministerium officials under Kube for political as well as personnel reasons. The more they intervened in its affairs, the greater the resentment of clergy and parishioners; yet, whenever they loosened the reins, nationalists used it as a mouthpiece for their grandiose program. Moreover, a nonpolitical clergy without Russian sympathies seemed impossible to come by, as the Security Service—ever the critic of Rosenberg's "coddling" of anti-Russian nationalists—could gloat in a report to Berlin on June 5, 1942: "The General Commissar [Kube] brought the Auto-cephalous Orthodox Belorussian Church to life in order to split the Belo-russians from the Great Russians in the field of religion. It has become manifest that the Belorussian national church has become a catch basin for Great Russian priesthood; moreover, there is no national Belorussian clergy available to replace it."[51] Had there been some independent-minded priests to start with, the Gestapo purges of the nationalists would certainly have assured their elimination after the summer of 1942. A typical episode in this self-fulfilling prophecy is the SD arrest and execution of Alexander Koush, a Vilna priest and leading spokesman for Belorussian church autonomy, "under the absurd pretext of his being a Soviet agent."[52]

The anemic and refractory creature that Kube had on his hands by mid-1943 might well have been dropped by a less single-minded man; but instead, he recalled Panteleimon to Minsk in order to supervise a thorough renovation of the church. The doughty old Archbishop tried his best, but he was caught in a paralyzing cross fire of nationalist feuds and German rivalries. He could do little against the machinations of the nationalist circle around Bishop Stephen—especially when the German security forces and their agents in a "Belorussian Rada" were aiding his foes, and when most parishes evinced no enthusiasm for their compro-mised hierarchs or for the linguistic reform of services advocated by them. The position in which he was pinned down was particularly nebulous because the status of Belorussian autocephaly had never been ratified canonically or officially. An eleventh-hour sobor which the Ger-mans had Panteleimon assemble in May 1944 put off the issue for the duration of the war, blithely making plans for new eparchies made redundant by the Soviet advance. There continued to be no response from the Eastern patriarchs, who had been asked to acknowledge auto-cephaly, and even Kube kept hesitating to give it the official German seal of approval.

Only in June 1944, as the Germans prepared to withdraw from Minsk, would the Ostministerium admit that its erroneous estimates and half-hearted policies were partly to blame for the abortive church project: "It is a fact that the overwhelming part of the Belorussian clergy is Russian in spirit. The rearing of a Belorussian nationally conscious hierarchy meets with difficulties; it would be possible only if German initiative were deployed in the religious field. This, however, runs counter to the political directives now in force."[53] The political bars were lifted on June 27 to allow a Belorussian "central rada" to meet in Minsk, while Red Army guns were booming nearby. After Archbishop Philotheus offered greetings on behalf of the Orthodox Church, over a thousand delegates went through the meaningless motions certifying a Nazi puppet regime.[54] The ink was hardly dry on their anti-Semitic pronouncements before tainted nationalists and church leaders joined the retreating Germans. Even in emigration they found it impossible to raise aloft once more the tattered standard for Belorussian church independence.

LIMITS OF DISSENSION: THE CASE
OF UKRAINIAN AUTOCEPHALY

Where religious leaders in Belorussia cast their nationalist appeals on sterile ground, the churchmen of the Ukraine had much more fertile soil in which to plant an indigenous religious movement. If they suffered some of the same pressures—manipulation of their group by German administrators and internecine ecclesiastical rivalries carried to the point of gang warfare—the Ukrainians found a distinctive way out of their staffing problem. In Belorussia native hierarchs had been in short supply, and the shortage of clergy could only partly be satisfied by candidates from the fringes of legality, as "the new priests included many who had been arrested, exiled, or who had hidden out."[55] In the Ukraine men of this ilk were also drafted into service at the parish level, but the bulk of the leading positions was filled by a curious crew of adventurers, politicians, and Nazi fellow travelers imported from the western regions under Polish rule since 1920. They displayed none of the compunctions for canon law that had restrained the Baltic and Belorussian hierarchs, but simply consecrated each other in a bewildering succession of self-styled church councils. The resulting religious chaos was at times abetted by officials of Koch's Reichskommissariat, for it tallied with their general "divide and rule" prescription.

That the Ukraine had both a religious revival and a resurgence of nationalism far exceeding those of other provinces under German occupation is largely attributable to the strength of these forces in pre-Soviet days. Now they were rebounding from a generation of unremitting Communist repression, the distinctive features of which require a much closer scrutiny of the record than seems necessary for the Baltic and Belorussian cases. Russian Orthodoxy had been firmly entrenched by 1917, with about eight thousand parishes, nine dioceses, and two of the most renowned monastic shrines, the Pecherskaya Lavra in Kiev and the Lavra at Pochaev in western Volhynia.[56] As for national independence, it had been proclaimed by a central rada or council in June 1917, acknowledged by the Kerensky Provisional Government in July, and supplanted by a Soviet regime under Red Army auspices in February 1918. This was followed by the puppet regime of Hetman Paul Skoropadsky installed by the Germans and, after their military collapse, by a three-cornered struggle among remnants of the Rada who called themselves the Directorate, White Army forces under General A. I. Denikin, and the counterattacking Soviet troops who were eventually able to pacify the province by mid-1921.[57]

The historical record is of particular relevance in the Ukrainian case, first as it illustrates how the Church was drawn into the political arena, second as it bears on the genesis of an autocephalous faction. The Rada had announced the separation of church and state in a move parallel to that of the Provisional Government. To leftist nationalists, however, this seemed a de facto recognition of the russified hierarchy led by Metropolitan Vladimir, so they helped a small group of radical Kiev priests set up a rump council in the spring of 1917 with a platform calling for use of the vernacular in services, the selection of new bishops by eparchial meetings of priests and laymen, and total clerical independence from Moscow.[58] It was a more moderate group of churchmen, though, that obtained the approval of the Moscow Patriarchate to hold an All-Ukrainian Church Council in January 1918—providing a platform nonetheless to such nationalists as Ivan Ohienko (Ogienko), a former medical student and philology professor who had become involved in church affairs through his friendship with one of the rump council leaders, Vasili Lipkovsky. The council had been meeting for only a fortnight and had not yet voted on any resolutions before the advance of the Red Army caused it to disperse. On January 25, Vladimir was executed by a Communist squad either in a senseless fit of anticlericalism, since he had been a major foe of the anti-Moscow autocephalists, or in a trap set by nationalist provocateurs.

In April 1918, a German-sponsored coup enabled Skoropadsky to displace Soviet power and, true to his tsarist military antecedents, to reunite church and state in his first proclamation. With the nationalist bishop of Kiev, Nikodim, consecrating the hetmanate and with a minister of religion sympathetic to their cause, the autocephalists seemed about to triumph when the regime collapsed. They finally realized their hopes under the short-lived Directorate of Simon Petlyura. On January 1, 1919, the Petlyurovite leaders gave their blessings to an autocephalous church organization with a key feature of its program the severing of all political and cultural ties with Moscow.[59] The subsequent two years of civil war, however, put this claim in abeyance. When the smoke cleared in 1921, autocephaly was established only in the western territories that had been absorbed by Poland, and a Soviet-sponsored but uncanonical creation was installed in the central and eastern sections retaken by Russia.

Some four million Ukrainians and Belorussians of the Russian Orthodox rite had come under Polish rule in 1920, and they formed the major contingent of believers out of which arose, four years later, the Autocephalous Church of Poland, its independence duly certified by the Patriarch of Constantinople.[60] In the Russian-controlled area, Lipkovsky submitted a brief to the Moscow Patriarchate arguing that the Ukrainian dioceses had been wrongly put under its control in 1686 and should now be granted their autonomy. As might be expected, his plea was rejected; but, undeterred by this canonical rebuff and egged on by the Soviets who saw his movement as a potential ally in the fight against the Patriarchate's power, Lipkovsky assembled four hundred of his followers in a special Kiev sobor that made him a bishop of the new Ukrainian Autocephalous Orthodox Church in October 1921.[61] This meeting went on to consecrate another two bishops and to spell out a radical platform providing for married bishops, lay preachers, the conversion of monastic communities into working collectives, and the predominance of laymen in the church administration and liturgy in the vernacular.

Patriarch Tikhon excommunicated Lipkovsky in March 1922, but the Autocephalous Church merely entered a new period of hothouse growth. Two years later, it claimed some three thousand of the Ukraine's parishes, a clergy numbering twenty-five thousand, and twenty-six bishops.[62] This was the period of Lenin's New Economic Policy, during which nationalistically inclined Communist leaders such as N. A. Skrypnik in the Ukraine promoted indigenous education and culture; it was also a time of Soviet repression of Orthodox hierarchs in Russia and promotion of factionalism in such forms as the Living Church.[63] With the official odds thus stacked in their favor, the followers of Lipkovsky —Lipkovtsy, as they were known—had a clear field in which to exploit genuine popular desires for church reform. As the NEP drew to a close, Lipkovsky made a belated attempt to screen out the many poorly trained clerics in his ranks, but the Soviets forced him out of office in 1928 for a more tractable leader and, by the following year, withdrew their backing entirely from a church they had reclassified as a "bourgeois counterrevolutionary oganization."[64] The Lipkovtsy hierarchy was caught up with other Ukrainian nationalists in the purges and treason trials of 1929–1930; even a contrite confession of "anti-Soviet activity" at an extraordinary sobor in January 1930 could not stave off its doom.[65]

It was this defunct movement that the Polish Metropolitan Dionisius (Valedinski) now hoped to revive under German auspices in World War II. His agents were to be three bishops of his staff: Polykarp (Sikorski), Hilarion (Ohienko), and Palladius (Vydybida-Rudenko). It was a choice that meant, first, giving the revived Autocephalous Church a carpetbag character, since its leaders were to bring sizable missions of Galicians and West Volhynians with them into the Eastern Ukraine; second, guaranteeing that the new hierarchy would have a strongly political cast, for all three bishops had been officials in the days of the Directorate; third, setting the stage for an ecclesiastical struggle with the established bishops for control of key church centers. The evidence leaves little doubt that these consequences did indeed transpire, whether or not one agrees with analysts who blame the ultimate failure of the Autocephalous Church on its popular rejection as a tool of the Nazis or with others who say it met with popular acceptance until it was hamstrung by Koch's Reichskommissariat.[66]

The senior agent of the revival, Polykarp, could claim a church career covering two decades among the Orthodox of Poland. Presumably keeping in touch with the Lipkovtsy, Polykarp had served as archimandrite (monastery head) in Volhynia; in 1932 he had become Bishop of Lutsk, making that city a center of the Ukrainian Church brotherhood that inveighed against Slavonic rites and sermons.[67] That force had the backing of Polish authorities until 1938, when the regime launched a campaign to destroy Orthodox shrines and convert the faithful to Catholicism. When the Soviets occupied the West Ukraine in September 1939, the Patriarchate had sent first Bishop Sergius the Younger, then Bishop (later Metropolitan) Nikolai (Yarushevich) to call on the heads of all the newly acquired dioceses and secure their submission.[68] Polykarp rendered his pledge of obedience along with the rest to Nikolai, the official "Exarch of the Western Ukraine and Belorussia and Metropolitan of Volhynia." With Nikolai's flight at the advent of the Germans in 1941, a bishops' sobor had followed canon law in making Alexei (Gromadski) provisionally the Metropolitan, or acting church head, of the Ukraine.[69] Their organization, the Autonomous Ukrainian Church, was not ready to forswear totally its ties to the Patriarchate, so Polykarp and a second bishop who had boycotted the sobor, Archbishop Alexander (Inozemtsev) of Pinsk, the senior primate of Belorussia, whose Polessian diocese had been attached to the Ukraine, began laying plans for a rival, outspokenly nationalist organization. Dionisius instructed the two bishops in September to substitute the vernacular for Church Slavonic into services in a gradual fashion that would not antagonize the parishioners.[70]

Beside Polykarp and Alexander, the other two prime movers for autocephaly had more obvious political, rather than clerical, qualifications for their posts. Hilarion, who had been made Archbishop of Kholm (the Orthodox center of Poland) by Dionisius in October 1940, was the same philologist Ivan Ohienko who had been an active nationalist under the 1918 Rada. He had gone on, after a brief term as minister of religion under Petlyura, to become rector of Kamenets Podolsk University, as well as publisher of two Ukrainian journals in the area governed by Poland.[71] A month after the Germans invaded Russia, he obtained approval of their Ostministerium and counterintelligence officials to gather some two hundred Galician and West Volhynian priests to move into East Ukrainian parishes and promote the autocephalist movement. Even the Nazis were soon to characterize Hilarion as "more the politician than the prince of the church," and they found the reports of informers accusing him of NKVD ties unsubstantiated "but, in light of the bishop's character, not implausible."[72] Palladius had been vice-minister of finance in the Petlyura regime, then had mixed nationalist and monastic careers in the Polish territories until selected by Dionisius to be bishop of the small Orthodox population in the Lemko region in December 1940;[73] later he had been transferred to the see of Cracow. At his consecration in February 1941 he had pledged loyalty to Governor Frank and received a promise of German support in return.[74]

The rise of these bishops depended on the grace of Nazi administrators —the same arbitrary officialdom who restricted Dionisius, their superior, to Orthodox Church affairs in Frank's General-Gouvernement but permitted them to proselytize for their cause in Koch's Reichskommissariat. Their professions of loyalty carry a more voluntary and insistent note than the pro forma welcomes extended to the Germans by other churchmen. Hilarion, for example, offered the bronze bell of Kholm Cathedral as a donation to the German defense effort in 1941, transmitted Easter greetings to Governor Frank in 1942, and conducted thanksgiving services in April 1943 on the occasion of Hitler's birthday.[75] Since by then he had been able to put a sizable number of Ukrainian churches under his sway, such gratitude was evidently not misplaced.

The rebirth of autocephaly took place with little regard for canonical niceties. It began with the announcement of Dionisius in Warsaw on Christmas Eve 1941 that he was making Polykarp "Temporary Administrator of the Orthodox Autocephalous Church in the Liberated Areas of the Ukraine," with the rank of archbishop.[76] Not only did Dionisius thereby exceed the authority he had been granted in 1924 by the Constantinople Patriarch to minister to the Orthodox of Poland, but, as some indigenous bishops were quick to point out, he was also creating a title (Administrator) that had currency only in Catholic, not in Orthodox, church life.[77] There was also the technical objection raised by Alexei: Polykarp and any other regnant Volhynian bishops who joined him in the anti-Muscovite church were going back on their 1940 pledges of obedience to the Patriarchate.[78] The rebuttal of Dionisius, contending that those oaths had represented sinful acts "against Church and nation" which "wartime developments" now permitted them to recant, was not very convincing on legal grounds. The confidential notes of Dionisius further indicate that his appointment of Polykarp was neither an independent resolve nor one motivated primarily by canonical factors. He had merely responded to the demands of a Volhynian delegation that called on him in mid-December, and his initial scruples had been overcome by the assurances of a Berlin delegate that the Ostministerium was in favor of the move.[79] There Seraphim's hand seems to have helped push the switch starting the operation.

In any case, Polykarp had yet to be provided with a church to administer in the Ukraine. This was at last done by a sobor convened on February 8, 1942, at Pinsk by the Belorussian primate Archbishop Alexander. Here was the occasion for officially resurrecting the Ukrainian Autocephalous Orthodox Church (UAPTs) of 1921 vintage, peremptorily elevating two priests to flesh out its hierachy and filling the ranks with some fifteen hundred surviving Lipkovtsy.[80] The recruits were only too willing: Alexei's Autonomous synod had been requiring them to resubmit their shaky credentials for certification to their posts, while the UAPTs welcomed them back, no questions asked. After Erich Koch's Reichskommissariat had legitimized the new church on May 5, 1942, it held another sobor later that month in Kiev, where seven more bishops were installed and the political character of the organization became even more apparent.

Stephen Skrypnik was the most prominent of those who made the leap from layman to prelate. A nephew of Petlyura and a former member of the Polish Sejm, he had been selected by the Ostministerium in July

1941 to advise Army Group South on candidates for local administrative posts. The following month he had secured permission to set up a nationalist newspaper, *Volyn* (Volhynia), in Lvov, and later to transfer it to Rovno, the administrative center of the Reichskommissariat. This offered him a forum for virulent attacks on Orthodox priests who had not bowed to demands for the total Ukrainization of the church.[81] Now, as Bishop Mstyslav of Pereiaslav, he had the clerical as well as political means to enforce his program. His prowess in the latter regard eventually clashed with the prerogatives of Erich Koch, who insisted that his actions were more those of "a prominent Ukrainian politician" than a prince of the church.[82] As Koch complained to the Ostministerium in March 1943, Mstyslav's chief occupation seemed to be trying to turn Wehrmacht officers against the Reichskommissariat bureaucracy, in other words, trying to salvage his slipping power base by calling upon his old contacts in the army.

Outstanding among the priests who now held bishops' staffs, thanks to the liberal personnel policies of the UAPTs, was Fotius (Timoshchyk) in the Vinnitsa diocese. His case illustrates the scandal-ridden atmosphere which permeated the inflated new hierarchy. Fotius had popped up in Poland in 1932, passing himself off on Dionisius as a priestly refugee from the Bolsheviks. Two years later he was arrested as a Soviet spy, convicted of killing a Polish border guard on his way from Russia, and given a ten-year sentence, only to be freed by the Red Army in 1939 when it occupied Galicia.[83] His past seems to have escaped the notice of the Kiev sobor that sent him to Vinnitsa in May 1942, but in August it was brought to Polykarp's attention by Kendzeryavy-Pastuchiv, the priest in charge of the town's cathedral.[84] Polykarp ordered Fotius dismissed in September, but the Bishop's response the following month was to renounce UAPTs jurisdiction and proclaim himself head of a true church of his own. His coup had the backing of the Gebietskommissar in Zhitomir, who obliged him in November by decree to have Fotius become "Oberbishop" of the district reporting directly to him. At the end of the month, Fotius ordered Kendzeryavy-Pastuchiv to hand over control of the cathedral and its funds, which the hard-pressed vicar refused to do.

Polykarp found it considerably harder to remove a bishop than to install one as long as the German authorities turned their backs on this muddle. On December 14 Polykarp forbade "the former Bishop Fotius" to hold services, on pain of being read out of the church, and held out like punishment for all churchmen of the diocese who continued to "maintain religious contact" with him. Fotius ignored the order and even persuaded his patron, the Gebietskommissar, to give him additional powers in 1943 that included the convocation of church assemblies, the promulgation of canon law just for that district, and the nomination of another bishop in Zhitomir. When Fotius prepared leaflets accusing Polykarp of having sold out to pro-Moscow church factions, Polykarp addressed a desperate plea to the Reichskommissariat. The convincing part of his brief appears to have been the charge that the Orthodox population of the district was interpreting the Gebietskommissar's intervention as proof of Communist claims of German religious intolerance. In April 1943 Fotius, deprived of official support, finally surrendered his office to Gregory (Ohiychuk), the bishop of Zhitomir whom he had been trying to supplant.[85]

If the UAPTs allowed nationalists and an occasional adventurer to infiltrate its hierarchy, this was as much out of necessity as of choice. By far the greater part of previously ordained priests and bishops in the Ukraine wanted nothing to do with Polykarp's minions from formerly Polish areas.[86] The only exceptions among the leadership were Bishop Nikolai (Amasiiski) of Rostov-on-the-Don and Metropolitan Feofil (Buldovsky) of Kharkov.[87] Feofil's case seems to have been one that combined long-time alienation from the Patriarchate with new nationalist pressures. The eighty-year-old bishop had been involved with schismatics for fifteen years, earning himself the epithet "Sectarian of Lubny," when the German invasion gave him the chance to develop an independent church and, in November 1941, to make himself its "Metropolitan."[88] He extended its sway to the nationalist stronghold of Poltava, then in 1942 to the newly occupied areas of Kursk, Voronezh, and the Donbas. As long as these territories were under German military administration, he was spared the choice of affiliating with autonomous or autocephalous synods. Only in July 1942 did Mstyslav prevail on him to be his emissary to Polykarp and join his diocese to the UAPTs.

As for the middle and lower levels of the church, we have the expert testimony of Professor Hans Koch, active in Ukrainian religious affairs as a counterintelligence officer, that they were staffed by "many émigré priests" who "returned from the West" in the wake of the Germans.[89] Some, according to the Gestapo, accompanied Wehrmacht units in the role of interpreters.[90] Those who emerged from hiding under the Soviets were far too few to take care of the many reopened churches. "Priests were 'exhumed,' but the demand far exceeded the supply; yet more than I had expected did turn up—many had spent years as workers in the

Donbas, had sung as basses in factory choirs, etc. They themselves now offered their services, often so as to improve their social status." Even with the Reichskommissariat's restriction of church funds to the donations of believers, the priests maintained relative affluence in a starvation economy. "The priests were paid in kind by the population. Periodically, the *batiushka* would go around the villages of his parish, catch up with baptizing, marrying, burial for the past fifteen years. All these services were paid for—usually a loaf of bread being the unit of payment."[91] An Einsatzgruppen report from the Ukrainian frontal areas also points to the meteoric rise in popular prestige accorded the formerly déclassé clerics.[92]

Admissions standards for the priesthood were flexible in the extreme. In the Ukraine "the bishops consecrated many new priests: either plain, decent, literate people, or else former theology students, or else people whom the community desired."[93] Even these criteria, mentioned by an émigré who had himself entered the priesthood under the occupation, were probably flouted in practice. Data from all parts of the occupied territories point up the indiscriminateness of both the bishops investing new priests and the congregations accepting anyone willing to take on the accumulated backlog of rites. A Ukrainian nationalist recounts: "Our priest was a former dekulakized peasant who had hidden in the next village and had later worked as watchman in Kharkov and returned under the Germans."[94] The Gestapo was aware that the UAPTs used mass consecrations to pull ahead in the clerical competition with the Autonomous Church, as well as employing pressure on local government officials and terror on unaffiliated priests to make them turn over control of their parishes.[95]

It might be assumed that priests of such incongruous origin, like their superiors who had become bishops by grace of the Nazis, would be the church contingent most prone to overt collaboration. But there seem to have been two mitigating factors. First, the pressures to follow the German line impinged primarily on the clergy in district capitals where the understaffed Reichskommissariat bureaucracy maintained its offices.[96] In the "deaf corners" of the countryside, the sporadic sweeps of the Einsatzgruppen and the agricultural overseers proved inadequate to sustain native compliance. Second, once they had been ordained in impromptu fashion, the new priests found that their status and its perquisites depended exclusively upon their parishioners. Their tendency was to absolve themselves of any obligation to the occupation authorities by token verbal obeisance but, beneath this cover, to identify increasingly with the interests of their congregations. The latter in short order suffered from a succession of German repressive measures, leading to almost universal resentment expressed either in covert form or in the opening salvos of partisan warfare.

Thus, active collaborators among the priesthood constituted a distinct minority. In the Ukraine they appear to have been limited to a few of the "carpetbaggers" who had been funneled into the province by Bishops Seraphim, Polykarp, and Hilarion and who had been given their marching orders by Ostministerium officials intending them to be a fifth column for the takeover of the church and initially promoted by the Reichskommissariat in aid of its divisive policies. It was this group that Professor E. Markert, a German church administrator, had in mind when he attributed the low prestige of the UAPTs in the East Ukraine to the fact that some priests worked in the political secret service and the people found this out.[97] The most notorious quisling of the Church, Bishop Platon (Artemyuk), operated in the shadow of Erich Koch's headquarters at Rovno. He sought out and met several times with the youthful gangs of Bandera's partisans, dressed in Gestapo uniforms, who terrorized the area and may have been implicated in the assassination of the Autonomous Church head, Archbishop Alexei, in May 1943.[98]

Whatever the true facts of the Alexei case, it illustrates the way church rivalries became subsumed in the political struggle pitting extremist Ukrainian nationalists against all comers. In the process the UAPTs dissipated its energies in internecine warfare rather than devoting them to fortifying its religious base. The issues were even clearer cut in the murder of Bishop Manuil (Tarnavsky) by Bandera's men in August 1943. Hanged at their forest headquarters after they had abducted him from Vladimir Volynsk and found him guilty of "treason," Manuil seems to have committed no worse crime than to have transferred allegiance from the UAPTs, because he came to question its canonical validity, to the Autonomous Church in July 1942.[99] Though Autocephalous hierarchs could not be identified as accessories, the public drew contrary conclusions, as it did in the slaying of other priests who had resisted demands for total Ukrainization.[100]

Viewed in historical perspective, the vendettas of 1943 turn out to have been only a promontory of the iceberg symbolizing the two preceding years of "cold war" between Autonomous and Autocephalous church leaders. The platform of the former had called for gradual reforms, a fairly meaningless recognition of the Patriarchate's ultimate authority, and local option on Slavonic or Ukrainian services; that of the latter for immediate reforms, severance of all ties to Moscow, and insistence on employment of the vernacular. Operating against the Autocephalous reform program, as the Gestapo recognized, was the parishioners' adherence to traditional forms—as well as a shortage of priests able to speak Ukrainian and of prayer books written in that language.[101] These did not constitute the dramatic differences one might expect to find underlying a blood feud. Indeed, they were only the shibboleths of the power struggle between two clerical factions, abetted in the first instance by German administrators to whom a united Ukrainian church represented a political threat, in the second by nationalists who donned UAPTs cassocks as protective cover for their otherwise forbidden activities.[102] At stake was not merely a disputed point of canon law, but control of church organizations in the large towns and cities, with the material perquisites and the leverage on local administration that entailed.

One plum of the contest was the capital city of Kiev. At the outset of the occupation this was the temporary seat of Bishop Panteleimon (Rudyk), whom the Patriarchate had installed in Lvov after Soviet occupation of the West Ukraine. The Autonomous leader, Alexei, realized that such a cleric, while loyal to him, would never be accepted by the nationalists who prevailed in local religious councils. He worked out a compromise by which a bishops' council on November 25, 1941, selected Hilarion, who possessed all the proper nationalist credentials, to take over from Panteleimon, who was to be transferred to Poltava.[103] The carefully laid scheme never got off the ground because dissident Lipkovtsy refused to undergo the reconsecrations required by Panteleimon, he remained in the city to marshal the pro-Patriarchal forces, and the nationalists set up a rival UAPTs center that soon fell under the sway of the extremist Bishop Mstyslav. The city's nationalist mayor had turned the local Department for Religious Confessions into an Autocephalist center, taken up personal contact with Metropolitan Dionisius in Warsaw and Archbishop Hilarion in Kholm, and at the end of December 1941 communicated veiled threats to Panteleimon unless he took "a strong Ukrainian direction."[104] An odd aspect of the rivalry in the Kiev diocese was that a formidable revival of religious life developed in spite of it, and the two church factions shared its benefits almost equally. The 1,435 priests of pre-1917 vintage had dwindled to a mere 3 under the Bolsheviks; by the end of 1942, the Autonomous Church claimed 434 new ones and the Autocephalists 455, of whom 226 were newly invested laymen.[105]

The constellation of forces that allowed the UAPTs to hold its own in Kiev was composed of a favorably inclined German Stadtkommissar, an extreme nationalist mayor who was a former Lipkovtsy priest, and enough disgruntled priests and laymen aspiring to the cloth to staff hundreds of parishes. In the city of Dnepropetrovsk, the latter two elements were absent, so that intervention of German officials, who recognized that a majority of the populace favored the Autonomous Church, was much more pronounced.[106] Indeed, the bishop sent by the UAPTs, Gennady (Shirpikevich), was handed his staff at a marketplace assembly by the Gebietskommissar, who followed up this welcoming gesture by seizing most of the Autonomous churches and turning them over to the Autocephalists.[107] The indigenous members of the press and the city administration did not take kindly to the imported bishop; neither did the population, as shown by acts of vandalism against some of the transferred churches.[108] Gennady was apparently able to carry on only with the help of the liaison he set up with local partisans under the commands of both Melnyk and Bandera. It was the Melnyk group's influence, for example, that convinced the city university to begin training clergymen for Gennady's staff.

Such instances of German benevolence to the UAPTs, as Heyer points out, represent a fairly consistent policy of the Reichskommissariat of supporting bishops whose unpopularity was a measure of their openness to manipulation by German officials.[109] At least until 1943 this meant only a modicum of toleration for the Autonomous congregations that, according to most German and Russian sources, accorded with the desires of the bulk of the population.[110] A writer for a Kiev newspaper under the occupation paints the following picture: "The last citadel of the Ukrainian extremists was the Autocephalous Church. This was purely a political affair, which included many Petlyurovites. The Germans tried to conduct themselves 'diplomatically' in this matter; they permitted both the Centralist [Autonomous] and the Autocephalous Church to exist, but the Autocephalous had the inside track with the Germans."[111] From his inside position in the German bureaucracy, Markert, too, concluded that, in the formerly Soviet areas of the Ukraine at any rate, the population proved to be "pro-Autonomy and preferred its own Eastern Ukrainian clergy."[112] To a specialist on the UAPTs, Raevski, the new Autocephalous hierarchs permanently compromised themselves in the eyes of the people when they turned to the German district commissars to supply them with facilities.[113]

The paradox of German policy consisted in its foisting the UAPTs clergy on the unwilling faithful, then condemning the clerics for taking the only avenue open to them out of their social isolation by making common cause with the ultranationalists. The Reichskommissariat's safeguards proved of no avail in blocking this alliance, which was after all merely the natural outcome of the process set in motion when the Ostministerium sped the West Ukrainians on their way east. By April 1942, the district commissar at Nikolaev was already warning Koch that the UAPTs was threatening to become a "national church" in the northern area of his jurisdiction, so that he was putting all its priests under close surveillance.[114] As noted in Chapter 4, Koch's "toleration edict" in June had limited the ecclesiastical organization of both Autonomous and Autocephalous churches to district levels; his October edict in effect dissolved the respective sobors. A further reprimand was in store for the UAPTs. On March 29, 1943, the Reichskommissariat sternly reminded Polykarp "to have no connection with his eparchial bishops, since these bishops received their orders from the district commissars."[115] Koch's fragmentation policy was, of course, related to his earlier discussed veto of the proposed merger between Autonomous and Autocephalous churches in October 1942. An Einsatzgruppen analysis of this abortive union indicates the vested interests that made churchmen of both factions relinquish their support of the projected union.[116] The stage for negotations had been set by the desperation of Alexei, who headed the Autonomous Church, at nationalist pressures, including UAPTs penetration of the monkhood at Pochaev, and his failure to secure mediation from Metropolitan Seraphim in Berlin. A synod of the UAPTs, held in contravention of Reichskommissariat orders at Lutsk from October 4 to 8, sent Bishops Mstyslav and Nikanor to utilize Alexei's vulnerability by having him sign a document recognizing autocephaly and placing Metropolitan Dionisius of Warsaw at the head of a united church synod in which they controlled four of six seats. Panteleimon was thunderstruck when he learned of the signature by which Alexei appeared to have wiped out a year's objection to autocephaly, and he planned an Autonomous bishops' council to decide how to dissolve the pact. The retired but still prestigious senior bishop in the province, Antony, denounced the accord from the Kievo-Pecherskaya Lavra. Even the Autocephalous "Administrator" Polykarp was unhappy at the implied loss of his title and instructed his clergy that the agreement was only a preliminary step toward eventual union. Erich Koch settled the issue by calling in Mstyslav, the would-be "secretary" of the new synod, and informing him that the decision of an illegal council could not stand. While Koch, hypocritically no doubt, expressed satisfaction with the church rapprochement, he claimed that the Reichskommissariat could not allow the Ukraine to establish its church hierarchy until the province had been "finally pacified." Even then, the participants in the present illicit accord would be barred from participation. And for good measure, he ordered Mstyslav into exile at Pryluki in the West Ukraine on October 22, to begin a "probation period" during which he was to refrain from political and religious activites.

Following this interlude, the three-cornered drama between the two church factions and the German administration started up again. The denouement was perhaps inevitable. The nationalist leaders Bandera and Melnyk had been groomed for puppet roles by the Nazis, but by autumn 1943 had recouped sufficient forces to bid once more for an independent part. The German response was to clap them, together with a host of more respectable nationalist intelligentsia, into concentration camps for a cooling-off period. Their allies in the UAPTs hierarchy were, willy-nilly, caught in the same squeeze play. The Lutsk commissariat broke off relations with Polykarp, while Professor Ivan Vlasovsky, his associate and the leading Autocephalous theologian, was jailed along with a number of other churchmen.[117] The official black cloud was to follow the UAPTs to the end of the German occupation in the Ukraine.

Only after they had fled the Red Army to Warsaw in the spring of 1944 did UAPTs leaders obtain a brief reprieve, thanks to their old friends in the General-Gouvernement and the Ostministerium. In this epilogue of comic-opera proportions, the hierarchs with the least church experience were deemed worthiest of concluding a union with the émigré Autonomous clerics on terms that would guarantee Nazi control. As Rosenberg's agent reported to him, "the nonclerical background of Hilarion and Mstyslav explains their lack of religious fanaticism and willingness to consider political factors."[118] These two—a former philologist and a former politician—were supposed to have concluded the agreement that more reputable bishops had been forced to retract by Koch in October 1942. The Germans set the stage by circumventing Polykarp in favor of more pliable UAPTs bishops and by trying to ship the independent-minded Autonomous leader Panteleimon, who had succeeded the murdered Alexei, off to Riga, where the assassination of Sergius had created a diocesan vacancy. Even these desperate shuffles, however, could not bring off the shotgun marriage, since Autonomous churchmen refused to settle for the minor role assigned them by the Ostministerium.[119] The UAPTs bishops urged Ukrainians to keep fighting as Nazi allies and went on to give Dionisius the empty title of Patriarch of the province retaken by the Soviets. In a final bit of irony, the UAPTs synod in West German exile temporarily defrocked Polykarp—who had been instrumental in elevating them to bishops' rank—and took over the direction of the émigré church from him in April 1945.[120]

RELIGIOUS REVIVAL AMID POLITICAL CONSTRAINTS

The preceding three cases illustrate the predilection of German administrators for church movements in the occupied territories that could be kept sufficiently weak and fragmented to be manipulated by them with minimal effort. Religious organizations such as that of Sergius in the Baltic or of the UAPTs in the Ukraine, which committed the cardinal sins of becoming either too popular or too embroiled in political causes, were subject to arrests and executions; only the isolated, nonideological church, such as that conjured up in Belorussia, was given sustained blessing. Implicit in these generalizations is the hypothesis that the great majority of Orthodox believers did not follow the lead of clerical puppets. They were kept from so doing primarily by the disastrous living conditions under German rule and secondarily by their absence from two of the groups that did improve their status during the occupation. One such group was composed of younger, Soviet-trained men, especially those of urban background, put in charge of local government, workshops, and police units. The other includes representatives of those nationalities later punished by the Soviets for wartime collaboration by having their sovereignty abolished. All of these—the Kalmyk Autonomous Soviet Socialist Republic, the Crimean ASSR, the Chechen-Ingush ASSR, the Karachai and Balkarian areas—represent non-Slavic, non-Orthodox populations. This leaves no Orthodox congregations predisposed to the pro-Nazi side, with one exception: that wing of the UAPTs which became linked to nationalist extremists in the Ukraine.

Virtually all sources agree that a substantial religious revival did take place in the occupied territories; they diverge when it comes to identifying the causes. Emigré accounts uniformly attest to its spontaneous nature, based on local initiative. Some German reports insist that a major role was played by German troops and civilian administrators, who lent assistance to the faithful who had welcomed them as liberators. On balance, the latter view appears heavily larded with wishful thinking. In the words of a typical example: "The German advance forces were greeted at every village and town entrance by representatives of the population with bread and salt, while priests prayed for the new masters of the country in the reopened churches and cathedrals."[121] If such prayers were indeed offered out of fear or misplaced hope, the true nature of the occupation regime soon turned them into pleas of relief from compulsory labor edicts that made no allowance for religious holidays. In response to these measures, "the deeply religious peoples of the Eastern Ukraine were incensed. A good many joined the partisans; others were forcibly evacuated by the Germans, like a funeral expedition."[122]

Any subsequent popular expressions of gratitude to the Germans for their religious policy lacked positive, concrete steps on which to rest. At best, a church group might have been thankful for the fact that German administrators, preoccupied with more pressing matters, left it alone to reconstitute local religious life. Possibly, if the officials had not immediately hedged their backing of some congregations for fear that unfettered candidates for popular allegiance were bound to turn against them, there might have been a great deal more clerical collaboration. As it was, even the friendliest German agency displayed nothing warmer than an attitude of skeptical neutrality to the churches, while others showed only callousness when believers could not get services under way with available facilities, as in the following example: "Wherever possible, the Army tolerated the restoration of old churches, but many had been used as museums, hospitals, to store tractors and other equipment. Then cemetery chapels were used (in general, these were the only untouched church nuclei left intact under the Soviets) . . . We wanted to reopen the Kievo-Pecherskaya Lavra but found no volunteer monks. Then the Lavra was blown up."[123]

On the whole, believers did better when left to their own devices than when subjected to German intervention, which tended to be either negative or heavy-handed. A Belorussian account typifies the ingenuity shown by a congregation that found itself without a usable church: "The village club again became a church. The dome was repaired and the inside painted. Many people were baptized and married in the church."[124] One Ukrainian report comes in two versions: first, the authorized German form, in which Protopriest Vladimir Benevsky, head of the Poltava Church Administration, expresses "ineffable thanks" to the forces of the Nazis "who have opened the door of the Church of God with their blood"; then, the historical treatise of Friedrich Heyer, devoid of such credits. Benevsky may have stuck to the truth when he related that "the German occupation became the signal for a great flocking of the masses to services, occasioning the reopening of several churches" and that some believers walked more than seven kilometers to participate, while there were cases of "grown children whom we were asked to christen."[125] But this gratitude seems misplaced when one learns from Heyer's account that it was Benevsky himself who reopened the main church of the city, the Makarievskaya, on September 8, 1941, the day after the city fell.[126] Then this priest, who had been forced to take up mason's work under the Soviets, rounded up eighteen other clerics who had gone underground, put five more churches back into operation, and performed some twenty-five hundred overdue christenings in the first fifteen months of the occupation. Here the German role appears limited to giving the green light for the revival, then extorting public thanks while lending no concrete help.

The population groups behind the religious resurgence, according to eyewitness accounts, turn out to be the same rural, female, and older age groups identified in Chapter 2 as the main force of the Church in prewar Russia. The exigencies of German rule brought them even more to the fore of the faithful. The peasantry, spatially and administratively, occupied a position at the furthest remove from the urban bases of the Nazi control system. Three other factors were at work to assure the religious predominance of women and the elderly: (1) many young males had been drafted into the Red Army; (2) most Soviet officials and party members had fled or been evacuated; (3) agents of the German labor draft rounded up fit young men as they were leaving church. How widespread the latter practice was cannot be ascertained, but it is mentioned in several accounts, notably that of a former Ukrainian priest, possibly as a rationalization, to explain the absence from services of physically fit males.[127]

When it comes to speculating on the motives of believers who did crowd into the reopened churches, some analysts focus on the nationwide thirst for a long-denied faith. Thus Nikita Struve concludes: "After twenty-four years of persecution, the people grasped the first opportunity to give free rein to religious feelings which were all the stronger for having been so long repressed."[128] Others, like Walter Kolarz, feel that there was more at stake: the population of the occupied territories "spontaneously reopened the secularized churches . . . with the connivance of the military authorities . . . not only for religious reasons but also in the search for a political third solution, neither Soviet nor German."[129] Alexander Dallin would go so far as to relegate religious motives to secondary significance: "If the Church under the occupation acquired considerable 'popularity,' one dares suspect that it was not so much because of an inherent faith as because it became a symbol of change and improvement over the Soviet era, and at the same time the only licit focus of national sentiments tolerated by the Germans."[130]

The trouble with shifting the stress to ulterior motives is that, in two respects at least, it would leave unresolved doubts about why the tail was able to wag the dog. First, in order to evaluate the Church as "a symbol of change and improvement," one must recognize the potential following it brought along from prewar times. It was this legitimacy, enhanced rather than tarnished by Soviet repression, that could now make the Church—not some other institution, like local government—into a popular symbol. Similarly, the strong undercurrent of religious feeling must be considered in order to explain how the Church could become a "focus of national sentiments," especially since a more logical nexus would seem to have been provided by nationalist groups themselves. Thus, one is forced to fall back on the deduction borne out by Gestapo reports, that the people's desires for a reconstructed church must have been sufficiently basic to permit them to subsume other aspirations.[131]

Some qualifications also need to be introduced when dealing with the subject of "national sentiments." In the Ukrainian case, the degree to which nationalist leaders used the cassock as protective cover from the Germans has been noted, as has the considerable extent to which the Autocephalous clergy was a German import from former Polish territories into the East Ukraine, rather than an expression of indigenous sentiments. Under such circumstances, alliances between the UAPTs hierarchy and extreme nationalist leaders may be viewed as a tactic by the leaders of two relatively weak forces to combine their command, a move that bore little relation to the wishes of the people. I have found only one case in the record showing that religious and nationalist motives were able to fuse at the grass-roots level: this took place in the Polotsk area, where a priest known as Father John became the focus of Russian nationalism among his parishioners, who rejected both Nazism and Bolshevism.[132] Such a phenomenon is not likely to have been widely duplicated in other parts of the occupied territories, if only because the pervasive German control system stripped the Church of any affiliation save one that might be of direct exploitative value. Even the sole documented instance of a messianic movement—processions of women and children from the Kiev area, inspired by a vision to reach the front lines with icons and bring peace by June 1943—led to "quiet suppression" by Einsatzgruppen even though they could find no church or other organization behind it.[133]

Undoubtedly, the pressures impinging on believers did propel them in the direction of becoming a "third force," in the same sense that Dallin observes that a revulsion against Soviet and Nazi controls gripped all other sectors of the population. The Orthodox faithful had no reason to long for a return to the restrictive conditions of worship under Communism. Once their incipient hope for improvements under the "New Order" had quickly dissipated under the rigors of the occupation, they could find little in Nazi arbitrariness to prefer as a lesser evil which at times promoted, but far more often threatened, their status. As one priest reports: "With the Germans, a lot depended on the individual; I was beaten up by one German in the railway station; in other places I found a lot of respect toward me." The laity, ever uncertain about the next reversal of German policy, had to rely on rumor: "The Germans authorized the opening of churches from the beginning . . . there was a rumor that the Germans would shoot all those who were not baptized."[134] But when these supposed protectors of the faith put top priority on the exploitation of native labor, "the Germans did not allow the holding of church holidays, not even the 'twelve high' holidays . . . The German Catholics and the SS-SD were intolerant of the Orthodox Church."

The power of attraction displayed by the Church under the occupation was too strong to be explained by negative factors alone—the refuge it provided from material hardships or the resistance it offered to arbitrary German regulations. At least four positive factors enhancing its formidability can be hypothesized: (1) the genuine faith, particularly of the older generation in the countryside, (2) the drawing power of the one institution in which, despite German restrictions, the population could observe a distinct improvement over Soviet conditions, (3) the only indigenous group in which membership was fully legitimized by the authorities, (4) the sole means available to most of the people for unburdening themselves of their grievances. And, as Samarin has pointed out, virtually everyone could find plentiful grounds for prayer:

> Those who sought relief filled the churches to overflowing . . . They prayed as they had not for a long time. There wasn't a family without its woes, without its sacrifices: those who had been arrested

by the NKVD and sent to die in Siberia, those forcibly evacuated east, those conscripted into the army and missing without a trace, those who had perished in prisoner-of-war camps, those killed by Soviet bombs that fell nightly on peaceful Russian towns, those doing forced labor in Germany, those who had vanished into Gestapo camps, those who had remained on the front lines.[135]

Partly because the momentum of its explosive growth carried it into new fields, the Church found itself playing a political role as well as a spiritual one. At times, this was done of its own accord as the Church enlisted allies among other groups like the peasantry or local intelligentsia—which were also striving for autonomy—in order to build a broader base for its position. At other times, the nonreligious role was thrust upon it, either by nationalist infiltrators or by German authorities with their insistent demands for professions of loyalty. In either case, the Church invariably did not yield to the pressures of political forces with the intent of becoming subservient to them. By keeping its own interests paramount, the Church became fully entitled to be judged a "third force" in its own right. The crowded services and the sacrifices made by the people to maintain their congregations represent independent variables, not the mere products of German manipulation or spectacles staged as camouflage by assorted nationalists. This conclusion is reinforced by the fact that the Soviets, after recapturing the German-held territories, did not attempt to undo the effects of the religious revival and that this area survived that war's end as the center of religious life in Russia. Even in the midst of the war, the Kremlin had implicitly acknowledged the potency and independence of this institution in the occupied zone by the dramatic launching of a "New Religious Policy" that would reverse twenty-five years of Communist hostility to the Russian Orthodox Church.

7

Soviet Response: The "New Religious Policy" in Full Flower

Stalin's decision in September 1943 to allow the Russian Orthodox Church to call a bishops' council for the election of a Patriarch was as dramatic a reversal as any in the annals of Soviet policy. As observed in Chapter 1, in the two decades following the Revolution the regime merely shifted tactics along what seemed an inexorable march to the destruction of the Church from which it could not be diverted either by the resistance or submission of religious leaders. By 1939, the institution of Russian Orthodoxy appeared on the verge of extinction, its 163 bishops reduced to seven, its 50,000 priests down to a few hundred, the 1,000 monasteries and 60 seminaries of prerevolutionary times totally shut down.[1] Now, midway through World War II, the Church was not just being granted a reprieve—a ceremonial occasion to utter its dying words; instead, it was given the seal of legitimacy that let it rise from the ashes during the next decade with the help of 74 bishops, some 30,000 priests, 67 monasteries, and 10 schools of theology. Even if some of these gains were canceled by as much as fifty percent during the last four years of the Khrushchev era, the plight of the Church could scarcely approach its previous hopelessness when, bereft of legal status, its tenuous existence had been at the mercy of the next assault on "counter-revolutionaries."

The genesis of the so-called "New Religious Policy" owes a great deal to events in the western areas which lent the Patriarchate three grounds to justify having its lease on life officially renewed. First, it was needed to keep the population in the path of the advancing German army from welcoming the Nazis as liberators; second, it had to steer the resurgent mass of believers in the occupied territories away from temptation to collaborate with the Germans; third, it had to reassert its authority over the churches in areas retaken by the Red Army. In all these respects, the Church had to convince Soviet decision-makers that it had a unique political contribution to make, one of sufficient weight in determining the outcome of the war and the reestablishment of peacetime controls to earn it a place at the negotiations which would consider the legitimacy of its survival. In passing the first two of its tests, the Russian hierarchy received the unwitting aid of the German warmakers who, by fusing anti-Slavic racism with their fight against Communism, left the population little choice but to rally behind the Kremlin's "Great Patriotic War."[2] Passage of the final test was facilitated by the Soviet imposition of political controls in Eastern Europe.[3] This helped to persuade local Orthodox leaders, schooled in a loyalist tradition, to rejoin the Muscovite fold.

My hypothesis is that the reorientation of Soviet religious policy was essentially influenced by church developments in what were for a time German-occupied territories. The nature of the causal relation varied according to the conditions of each of the four phases the New Religious Policy described. The preparatory period, 1938–1941, witnessed a modulation of antireligious propaganda that may be viewed as part of the trimming process that mobilized Soviet society for war threats from the west. The initial phrase, 1941–1943, found the Church as comrade in arms of a regime concerned with appeals to its citizens under enemy rule. In the peak phase, 1943–1945, the Church was rewarded for its wartime contributions, not the least of which was having kept collaboration by its forces with the Germans to a minimum. More substantial rewards came with the secondary phase, 1945–1947, as the Church was allowed to consolidate most of the organizational gains made by dioceses formerly under Nazi rule. Its status had changed during the course of the war from probationary servant to junior partner of the state. Churchmen who had begun the period by thankfully grasping the chance to address patriotic broadcasts to the people ended it by assuming such privileges as government-sponsored flights to visit fellow prelates abroad.[4]

PREPARING FOR WAR

During the two or three years preceding World War II, the Church became the indirect beneficiary of government measures to mobilize the society around themes of national unity. The Great Purge had petered out with the removal of Yezhov as head of the NKVD in July 1938; and the eclipse of the purgers also cast a shadow on other divisive forces, such as the League of Militant Atheists, whose paper successes had just been underscored by the large number of believers turned up by the 1937 census. It is hardly likely that strictures on the League were intended by the regime to yield any profit to the Church. It is only by hindsight that they can be pointed out as portents of fundamental change. At the time it must have appeared to Church leaders that they were enjoying a brief respite only until the government selected a more efficient instrument for their destruction. Weapons had been alternated before, the atheistic timetable on occasion extended as well as contracted, but there had never been doubt about the ultimate destination: the extinction of religion in Russia.

If a more subtly conducted atheist campaign posed a graver threat in the long run than had the vulgar demonstrations just past, the Church nonetheless derived some short-run advantages from the shifting of gears. First, it gained a new measure of respectability regarding its origins. Thus, the revised credo of the Atheist League announced that it was a mistake to automatically identify Christianity with capitalism; the cultural contributions of the former, especially its beneficial influence on morality and the development of family relations should not be denied.[5] The Church also could bask in the light reflected from the rediscovered glories of the Russian past. Commenting on the filmed portrayal of Alexander Nevsky in which the clergy had been conspicuous by its absence, the League advised that "there is . . . no reason to be afraid of objectively showing the role of the Church in Russian history. Antireligious propaganda is permissible in films of this kind; however, it must be directed not against the Orthodox clergy but against Catholic monks and the Roman Pope."[6]

The Communist leadership, in taking up the theme, betrayed the fact that the League's change of heart had not been entirely spontaneous. By the spring of 1940 the official word went out that the League and some overzealous Party members had strayed from the true Marxist path by denying the rightful place of the Church and falsely tracing the roots of religion to ignorance of the masses and their betrayal by priests.[7] The League, in its turn, joined in the rewriting of history by claiming that, indeed, it had "never fought" religion, but merely its prerogatives as a private affair of citizens. Quite to the contrary, it had been

the true champion of religion "against those who exaggerated its importance and demanded its extermination by administrative measures."[8]

Finally, in being once more relegated to the status of a secondary target, the Church gained a little breathing space to recover from the latest
round of repression. The League was told to sheathe its weapons for the
time being and subordinate its activities to the major political tasks that
were currently engrossing the regime's attention. Party members who advocated the closing of churches were punished; others who had been
disrupting services and exposing religious objects to public ridicule
were said to have "caused immense harm to the Soviet government . . .
The result was not a decrease in religious sentiment but an increase
in anti-Soviet feeling."[9] Atheist propaganda was couched in more civil
tones, and the trials of churchmen came to a halt. The last one took
place in eastern Siberia in April 1939, perhaps because the Party line
could not be so efficiently transmitted to such a distant spot, when clergy
and kulaks were charged with conspiring to overthrow the Soviet government at the instance of Japan.[10]

The muzzling of rabid atheists before World War II did not at the
time seem to presage a rapprochement between state and Church. The
churchmen could merely expect that, in accordance with the previous
twenty-year pattern, the regime was shifting from a frontal attack to
more subtle enveloping tactics against the die-hard remnants of the
faithful. In order to extend the truce, they would need an occasion to
justify their existence in terms of positive service to the state. This was
furnished by Stalin's decision of September 17, 1939, to annex the
eastern half of Poland in the wake of the Nazi-Soviet pact. By this move
and, to a lesser degree, the incorporation of Bessarabia and the three
Baltic states into the Soviet Union during the summer of 1940, "several
millions of Orthodox Christians, active members of Churches that were
very much alive," were inadvertently allowed to infuse fresh life into
the ailing body of the Church within Russia.[11]

The Orthodox establishment reaped a twofold benefit from the an-
nexations. It gained new cadres—some thousand priests whose vigor had
not been diminished by decades of Soviet control, now available to
staff untended parishes within Russia.[12] Of even greater import was
Stalin's call on the Patriarchate to bring the churches of the newly
acquired areas under its control.[13] This pro-Soviet coordinating mission
took Bishop Nikolai (Yarushevich) to the lands carved out of Poland,
Bishop Sergius the Younger to the Baltic, Bishop Alexis of Tula to

Bessarabia. Local prelates were pressured into rendering submission to Acting Patriarch Sergius—some at the forced invitation of Moscow, from whence they returned rather shaken, telling their subordinates back home to "be glad you're not a bishop."[14]

At first glance, the Russian hierarchy would seem to have done little to be proud of in performing such menial tasks on behalf of the Kremlin's imperialism. But the pawn's role they accepted marked a vital transition from that of the arch-villian to that of bargaining partner. Muting of the atheist campaign had meant, according to the Party line, lightening the image of blackness that had been projected onto the Church; to a limited extent it could now emerge from its twilight world, projecting the colors of Russian nationalism in the western borderlands. If the Church was not yet considered, in official eyes, a positive force, at least it was clearly a lesser evil than non-Orthodox denominations, particularly Catholicism. The latter felt the full force of Soviet suppression, while Orthodox churches in the new dioceses, though stripped of their real property and monastic centers, enjoyed a vital relative advantage—their right to survive for the time being.[15]

As long as they had their new chore to do, the Russian hierarchs could feel secure from further state harassment. There was yet no question of any major rewards or of a long-term lease to Russian religion, but by 1940 some legal crumbs fell to the lot of the faithful. Official restoration of the regular workweek, while justified on grounds of workingman efficiency, did again leave Sundays open for attendance at services.[16] Other government dispensations included supplying oil for icon lamps, permitting the restoration of icons, and allowing the celebration of Easter once more.[17] Still only faint indications, rather than clear proofs of a policy change, such measures may nevertheless be taken as indications of Stalin's dawning awareness that, to meet the Nazi threat now at his gates, he might have to enlist the legions of believers in his cause.

It is surprising that the Soviet regime did not go beyond a grudging degree of tolerance in the immediate prewar period, since it must have known of the early successes of the Berlin diocese and the promotion of the Church in the General-Gouvernement under Nazi auspices. Perhaps Stalin deluded himself with the permanency of the Nazi-Soviet pact to an extent that kept him from appreciating the potential of the Church as a wartime ally. Anyway, his excision of virulent atheism removed a chronic irritant from Soviet international relations and facilitated the search for Western allies. The pan-Orthodox slogans, which the Church was now allowed to issue, further meant garnering an appreciative audience in the crucial neighboring countries of the Balkans and the Middle East. It can be concluded now, in retrospect, that much more could have been asked of the Church and far greater use made of it as a national rallying point.

What the Church did accomplish in the prewar period was to pass muster as a candidate for political probation; on the opening day of the war it was allowed to add its voice to the call for defense of the fatherland. That the real test was put off until the first two years under fire does not diminish the essential nature of the preliminary relaxation—part of the general letup following the bloodbath of the mid-thirties. Analyses of the New Religious Policy that see it merely as a reward for political services well rendered would seem to put the cart before the horse.[18] If the official opprobrium over the Church had not lifted before June 1941, it would hardly have been given a chance to redeem itself by its wartime conduct any more than were kulaks or "counter-revolutionaries" in labor camps, whose chance at rehabilitation came only later and in more circumscribed fashion when some were enrolled in "death battalions" of the embattled Red Army. Further, a Church which had experienced only unrelieved repression at the time of the Nazi invasion would have had little inclination to throw its forces to the Soviet side, to reject out of hand the German promises for relief from Stalinism. The small but distinct change in Soviet religious policy from 1939 to 1941 represented a straw at which the embattled hierarchs had to clutch for a chance at survival. Also, a Church whose prestige was beginning to be refurbished, along with the glories of the Russian past, could link its interests with that of the nation and be dissuaded from looking to foreign intervention for restatement of its viability.

CONTRIBUTING TO DEFENSE

In the light of the patriotic traditions of the Russian Orthodox Church, it might not appear especially remarkable that its leaders rallied round the flag during a struggle in which national existence was evidently at stake. There are, however, two noteworthy features of the part played by the Church in the period from mid-1941 to mid-1943: (1) the celerity and unstinting effort that marked the contributions, with virtually no concessions by the state to spur the drive; (2) the acceptance by the regime of this unlikely volunteer, whom official antireligious publications were still castigating until October 1941, after twenty-four years of ideologically grounded repression. Of course, these first two years of World War II were critical ones for state as well as Church, and the leaders of both operated under extraordinary pressures that facilitated a break in their set pattern of relations. The hierarchs were not so much pursuing a period of trial as accommodating themselves to the test thrust upon them; if they could not keep their followers in line, their doom would be imminent. Political leaders, by the same token, did not go out of their way to enlist the support of the Church, but this aid, once offered, could be rejected by them only at the peril of driving a substantial segment of the population into the arms of the enemy. Collaboration, then, took place not by choice, but by necessity; not because of advantages anticipated by either side at the outset, but in reaction to the suicidal aspects of other alternatives.

Acting Patriarch Sergius apparently wasted no time checking with the authorities on June 22, 1941, to issue a proclamation "To the Whole Church," damning the "Fascist bandits" who had invaded Russia and blessing "with heavenly grace the people for their heroic battle."[19] He condemned any laggard clerics shrinking from wartime involvement for personal advantage, for they would thereby "betray their duties to the fatherland as well as their pastoral responsibilities." Even Stalin waited another ten days, in the belief that the Nazi move was merely an act of provocation, before making his first appeal to the people.[20] By then, Sergius had already spoken out a second time, at a Te Deum for Russia's victory on June 26 that attracted an estimated twelve thousand worshipers to the Cathedral of the Epiphany. Once more his theme was broadly patriotic, with no reference to the Soviet government, but this time he took cognizance of the danger that his hard-pressed flock might welcome the Germans as liberators.[21] Such a turn of events, by implication, would unloosen the ultimate in Soviet religious purges. Therefore, he admonished the Orthodox not to commit the "sin" of lagging in the defense of their country and assured them, out of his own knowledge of German conditions, that they would soon prove terribly mistaken if they thought "the enemy will not attack our sanctuaries or our beliefs." Metropolitan Nikolai elaborated on the theme in a speech of August 8, reminding believers of the "well-known fact that Hitler brings with him his atheist world view and his cult of the pagan god Wotan."[22]

On October 14, another proclamation by Sergius shows him aghast at "rumors that there may be, even among our Orthodox clergy, some who are ready to enroll in the service of the enemies of our fatherland

and Church—to be under the shadow of the pagan swastika instead of the holy cross."[23] Those unnamed persons—whose ranks Sergius must by then have known included his younger namesake in the Baltic, as well as the Autocephalists of the Ukraine—were admonished to "repent" under threat of being defrocked, excommunicated, and subjected to divine punishment for breaking their oaths of clerical obedience. The analysts who see in such loyalist appeals a desperate attempt by Sergius to save himself and his Church do not mean to derogate the genuineness of his patriotic fervor.[24] They simply note that Sergius was safely evacuated from embattled Moscow to Ulyanovsk after this last proclamation, while persons whose loyalty had been in doubt were executed by the Red Army before it gave up towns to the Germans—and some four hundred priests may have been among their number.[25]

From his wartime refuge, the Acting Patriarch kept up a stream of patriotic exhortations, with a special appeal to the Orthodox under German rule to stay loyal to the Kremlin so that they would not expose the Church to charges of treasonable conduct. In January 1942, he warned them against the lure of "faint-hearted service to the enemy" for material gain, a course of action condemned as constituting "treason to Church and fatherland."[26] In June, on the anniversary of the invasion, he went on to urge all the faithful in the occupied territories to support the partisans fighting the Nazis. In his Christmas message that year, they were told not to become discouraged, but to "be patient a little while longer and the light will once more shine upon you." The same note was sounded by the other hierarchy, particularly Metropolitan Nikolai, whose Kiev diocese had been taken by the Germans and who had been allowed to return to Moscow to administer Church affairs in the capital. His greetings to Stalin on November 7, 1942, the twenty-fifth anniversary of the Revolution, brought wishes for a long life "to cleanse the Ukraine of the German filth."[27]

During 1942, the statements of Orthodox Church leaders in Russia assumed an increasing tone of confidence as they must have become aware that the great majority of the clergy was refraining from coming out for the Germans. Sergius had at first hesitated to admit the existence of clerical collaborators, then to deny they carried any churchly weight. He opened his letter to Bishop Polykarp on February 5, 1942, by saying there really was no Autocephalous "movement" embracing any priests or believers. "Sikorski's action," he wrote, "seems to me of an exclusively political and not a Church nature. He has done what he has done . . . under orders from a political party," and his use of Ukrainian instead of Old Slavonic in the liturgy has stirred the resentment of congregations among whom "he enjoys neither love nor authority." If Polykarp continues to extort confessions "in the wake of the German armed forces," he will be liable to "deprival of all priesthood."[28]

On March 28, the Acting Patriarch in a second letter admitted the seriousness of the schism and Polykarp's heightened defiance but still suspended final judgment. Sergius abandoned the element of personal vindictiveness of his preceding note, which had characterized Polykarp as "a fresh wolf in sheep's clothing," "zealous like a lackey to Hitler," and "guilty of simony" and other crimes which "it is difficult to find words harsh enough to express"; now his focus shifted to the Ukrainian Autocephalists' breaches of Church discipline. Polykarp was ordered to desist from celebrating services until he either repented or underwent an ecclesiastical trial—although the preceding note had charged him with "exclusively political" misdeeds. Sergius conceded that the Autocephalists touched a sore spot when, in their countercharges, they questioned the legitimacy of his status. He has heard "reports . . . that in answer to my letter Bishop Polykarp calls me an impostor, as if I had obtained the office of Acting Patriarch by illegal means," yet he promises to be "magnanimous, and the affair shall be investigated by a Church Council and my judgment either will be confirmed or corrected."[29] Slurs on his office were not an unmixed curse for Sergius: he could convert them into a bargaining point with Soviet leaders to have a sobor convoked that would officially enthrone him in the Patriarchy—an event that did at last transpire in September 1943.

Until the limited contours of clerical collaboration with the Germans had become apparent, Sergius had to play his hand with caution. At the start, he could not be certain that a bolder attitude of recriminations would not push pro-Nazi sympathizers in the Church beyond the point of no return. Thus he put off until September 23, 1942, his condemnation of the Baltic Exarch Sergius the Younger.[30] Not only did ecclesiastic punishment of collaborators by the Patriarchy come remarkably late, but it was reserved for only a small fraction of their number, apparently no more than four in all.[31] Even though the two main antireligious journals, *Bezbozhnik* and *Antireligioznik,* had ceased publication in September and October 1941, respectively, because of "paper shortages," the fate of the Church hung in the balance, and a pro-Nazi swing in the occupied territories would have brought swift Soviet retribution.[32] This remained true in 1942, when a de luxe edition of patriarchal proclamations was printed, evidently by the same press that had been used for antireligious works in prewar days.[33] In his preface to *The Truth About Religion in Russia*, Sergius took pains to debunk "the 'crusade' of the Fascists, undertaken by them supposedly for the 'liberation' of our people and of our Orthodox Church from the Bolsheviks."[34]

For the first eighteen months of the war, the regime did little beyond looking the other way while the hierarchs set about frantically establishing an incontrovertible case for their loyalty under fire. The regime offered no ideological justification for the quiet demise of the League of Militant Atheists and other antireligious forums in late 1941, nor for the religious hour that Radio Moscow began to broadcast.[35] Unofficially, however, it demonstrated a willingness to exploit the propaganda potential of its clerical volunteers. Soviet aircraft were used, according to émigré reports, to disillusion the population of the occupied territories about any impending Nazi "liberation" by dropping leaflets announcing the support of Church leaders for the war effort.[36] Other media were made available to Sergius and Nikolai to broadcast appeals to Rumanian soldiers in November 1942 and to Orthodox audiences in Yugoslavia, Czechoslovakia, and Greece the following Easter.[37] Metropolitan Nikolai had been named to an extraordinary state commission charged with the investigation of German war crimes in November 1941, in another obvious move to put the lie to talk of any German "crusade."[38]

In circulating reports of German atrocities against religion, Soviet leaders may have sought to expunge memories of their own campaigns against the Church, besides trying for special effects in the West and at home.[39] Reports published in English frequently refer to desecrations of artistic cathedrals, as in the following example: "The Nazi invaders do not spare the religious feelings of believers among the Soviet population. They have burned down, plundered, blown up, and befouled hundreds of churches on Soviet territory, including certain unique examples of ancient church architecture."[40] The authors of such accounts do not pretend to give a balanced picture. They do not cite witnesses, nor do they admit any relief in the black image of German soldiers depicted in every paragraph as "beasts," "two-legged jackals," and "depraved tools of the master gangster Goebbels." They are filled with gruesome incidents, as in this typical excerpt from an official report: "When an aged priest, Pomaznev, cross in hand, tried to prevent the rape of young girls, the Fascists beat him up. They tore off his cassock, burned his beard, and bayoneted him to death."[41] Nazi intelligence coldly took notice of such alleged atrocities and attributed them to Soviet desires to placate critics among the Allies and in neutral countries, as well as to exploit popular religious feelings at home.[42]

Lurid colors also mark Soviet dispatches released for home consumption, although they carry a unique extra charge: that the Germans were making *Kirchen* out of the Orthodox churches under their rule. Metropolitan Nikolai furnishes an example of such forced Protestantization at Trubino (Ugodsk-Zavod). There the Germans are said to have thrown out icons, burned the priests' vestments, and installed a German pastor with a revolver and grenades stuck in his belt.[43] Russian publications also carry accounts of other kinds of desecration, such as reports that Germans used church buildings as barns, in what seems to have been an attempt to trump memories of sacrilegious acts committed by Militant Atheists under Soviet auspices a decade before. It was all part of a gigantic effort at rewriting history to which the hierarchs lent their imprimatur by shrugging off all clerical victims of past purges as having merited their fate as undercover counter-revolutionaries.[44]

A curious feature of the new Party line on religion was that, in portraying the legions of Hitler as the embodiment of antichrist, Soviet leaders found themselves cast by contrast in the unwonted role of true protectors of the faith. In such a setting, their old antireligious reflexes had to be extinguished. Victor Kravchenko describes an official rationalizing the softer line on the Church at a Party meeting in 1942 in this way: "The enemy is making use of our antireligious attitudes for propaganda purposes, and the improved relations with the Russian Church cut the ground from under them."[45] Though Kravchenko's veracity is a matter of conjecture, it is not unlikely that some explanation of this sort was given when Party members asked embarrassing questions about the need for a modus vivendi with Church forces. The new course took a long time to emerge clearly. Even in late 1943 the veteran Bolshevik leader M. I. Kalinin was still telling Party propagandists that it was all right for younger men to laugh at middle-aged recruits in the Red Army who turned up wearing crosses.[46]

Only by the end of 1942 did Church leaders feel secure enough to address their pledges of loyalty to Stalin personally, in what was soon to become a veritable chorus of beatification, and to go beyond their legally prescribed rights by beginning to collect funds for the Red Army in a drive that netted 150,000,000 rubles during the next two years.[47] A detailed analysis of either activity would be out of place here; what is noteworthy is that, in its response to what appears to have been the clerics' initiative, the regime moved from tacit approval to explicit recognition. When on January 5, 1943, Sergei offered the first 100,000 rubles to equip a tank column named for the sainted medieval hero Dimitri Donskoi and requested permission to open an account in the State Bank for this project, Stalin personally granted it in a note of thanks that constitutes the first official communication between the Soviet government and the Church since the Revolution.[48] By certifying its status as a depositor, Stalin was also in a backhanded way conceding that the Church, denied the rights of a juridical person since the 1918 decree on the separation of Church and state, was entitled to a new legal lease on life. With the exchange of telegrams between the Patriarchate and Stalin in March, on the twenty-fifth anniversary of the Red Army, yet another sign pointed to rapprochement of state and Church, as the Gestapo was quick to note.[49]

During the first two years of the war, the Church gave much to the regime and asked little in return. It was a model probationer. Its moral and material contributions to the war effort were epitomized by the clergy of Leningrad, led by Metropolitan Alexis, which not only steeled the populace to withstand the bitter German siege, but collected over 3,000,000 rubles for a defense fund by January 1943.[50] By April, the Germans had become aware that Red partisans were adopting a new proreligious line; by May, they recognized the efficacy of Soviet appeals for a "Holy War" and of the Acting Patriarch's blessing of resistance efforts, even to the death.[51] The Church had made no claims on the state for losses sustained in three waves of repression and, in the manner of Soviet political prisoners of the Stalin era, confessed that the whole thing had been its fault. It willingly served the ends of propaganda at home, in the Balkans, and among Russia's allies in the West. Its signal achievement, however, lay in retaining the loyalties of the Orthodox who formed the bulk of the population in the German-occupied territories. In light of this record, the hierarchs could hardly be accused of making immodest demands by asking the regime to certify that they had lived down their status as political suspects.

COLLECTING THE REWARDS

Shortly after his return from Ulyanovsk to Moscow in August 1943, Acting Patriarch Sergius, together with Metropolitans Nikolai and Alexis, was able to secure an unprecedented privilege for a Russian Church head: a meeting with Joseph Stalin, at which something like a concordat could be worked out to supply the Church with a minimum of essential means—a flow of fresh believers, priests, and bishops—to keep it from atrophy. Since no details have ever been released regarding this historic meeting, analysts must surmise the nature of the bargain the hierarchs were able to drive from progress the Church made in the next few months. Probably the session of September 4 only formalized an agreement worked out in principle beforehand, since Stalin's curt announcement "that there will be no objections from the Government" to the election of a new Patriarch was followed posthaste by the assembly of nineteen bishops four days later, and arrangements for their travel from distant parts of the country would have required more time.[52]

It can further be inferred that in their session with Stalin the hierarchs obtained agreement only on the broad outlines of the Church's regeneration, for it took the better part of a year to fill in the all-important details: setting up the first of a series of new theological academies and seminaries,[53] reopening a limited number of new churches,[54] consecrating some three dozen new bishops,[55] and restoring the right of priests to proselytize and to give religious instruction to children.[56] All of this was evidently worked out by the Council for the Affairs of the Russian Orthodox Church, which had been set up on September 14 to become the first public body of the Soviet state dealing with religious matters. It seems fairly well established that the nucleus of the new council was made up of the NKVD section that had theretofore supervised churches.[57] Its first chairman, Georgi Karpov, an avowed Communist and nonbeliever, was promptly nicknamed Narkombog (People's Commissar for God) and Narkomopium (People's Commissar for Opium).[58] The council's tainted antecedents, however, do not detract from the importance of its establishment as signaling rebirth of the Church as a full-fledged Soviet institution. Karpov may have formerly commanded a secret police squad to conduct surveillance of church organizations and restrict their activities;[59] now he directed a field force in all Soviet republics and provinces charged with a totally different mission, to effect a liaison between religious groups and local government organizations, to see that ten new seminaries were opened, and to facilitate the licensing of religious societies.[60]

In the context of this study, what is of particular interest is the extent to which the new course in Soviet religious policy was determined by developments in the German-occupied territories. Why bother hastily assembling the bishops to elect Sergius to the Patriarchy by acclamation, when he himself admitted it changed nothing—"In fact, I have borne the patriarchal responsibilities for the past seventeen years"?[61] One pressing reason for the conclave's action was the need to lay at rest the doubts that had been raised by Polykarp and other restive churchmen about the validity of Sergius' slipping into the office of Acting Patriarch. Why, indeed reward the Church at all for wartime services at a juncture when Russian victory seemed certain and clerical volunteers were no longer needed on the home front? Again, the resurgent church life of areas being recaptured from the Germans seems to supply a logical link. One analyst argues that Soviet spies must have reported on the Orthodox renaissance in the occupied zone, so that one may "view all Soviet measures as an attempt to offer something like that of the enemy, even to trump him."[62] Furthermore, rooting out the multitude of churches that had been flowering under Nazi rule would have represented a virtually insuperable task for Soviet forces in pursuit of the Wehrmacht. It was a much simpler strategy to reimpose Communist controls on existing institutions such as the Church—which had remained essentially apolitical at its base, since most of its pro-German leaders had fled and the rest were ready to recant.

The bishops who assembled for the command performance of formalizing the status of Sergius indicated their awareness of their future duties in the retaking of the western lands. They took time in their brief proceedings to condemn any bishop, priest, or layman who had "renounced the faith and fatherland by going over to the enemy," and to apply the appropriate punishments: defrocking and excommunication.[63] An ecclesiastical purge was thus coordinated with the political one and its guidance entrusted to a permanent Holy Synod that was to replace the temporary body set up in 1927. To carry the relevant announcements, the Patriarchate was permitted to begin printing a monthly bulletin, *Zhurnal Moskovskoi Patriarkhi,* in September 1943, its first periodical in eight years.[64]

During the critical first half of the war, the Church proved itself a trustworthy ally of the regime. During the downhill second half, it could collect the rewards facilitating its further employment "particularly essential in the fight against centrifugal forces in the borderlands from the Baltic states to Bessarabia."[65] If the Church was to fulfill its new political assignment, it would have to speak with authority. To this end, it was given the ceremonial prestige of Patriarch and Synod and of churchmen in Leningrad, Moscow, Tula, and other front-line cities, who began receiving medals in October 1943 for their heroic defense efforts.[66] To overcome religious separatism in the borderlands the Church would also have to stand on a unified base; it is for this purpose that we can infer political pressure to have been exerted on pro-Communist clerics of the Living Church to render submission to the Patriarch. The terms of their penance included stripping some bishops of their ranks, reordaining most of the clergy, and turning over prestigious icons and churches that had been under their control in Moscow, Leningrad, Tula, and other centers of the schism.[67]

The reintegration of Living Churchmen foreshadowed the forced "homecoming" to the central hierarchy of priests in areas retaken from the Germans. There were shotgun unions—particularly in the Ukraine, where patriarchal emissaries took no heed of local desires for some sort of clerical self-government that were held even by the moderate majority constituting that Autonomous Church. Postwar return of the Uniates to the fold could only be achieved after a military tribunal had dealt with Archbishop Joseph Slipy and other members of the hierarchy in April 1945 and the Soviet secret police had arrested hundreds of priests.[68] Among the liberated Orthodox the official spotlight fell only on clerics and laymen who had helped the partisans or otherwise proved a loyalty that could now be rewarded with medals and citations. Scant mention was made of wartime disaffection by priests who stayed behind, presumably to vanish into prisons;[69] nor was any cognizance taken of the "third force" churchmen who had sought to forswear subservience to Soviet as well as German masters.

In the reconquest of the western lands, the Soviets picked up, at times with hardly a break, where German occupation authorities had left off. Russian regulations followed almost literally the texts of German orders which had banned the semisecret "Whitsuntide Congregations" and the use of "glossolalia," a kind of tongue speech in some parishes that had been condemned as "too mystical" by an SS office.[70] Churches that had sprung up under the occupation were being turned over to the Patriarchy purged of all schismatics and mystics who might resist marching in lock step to the Soviet drum. The Moscow hierarchs were in no position to cavil at strings attached to this gift: the regained western lands were to supply them with more than half of all parishes in the Soviet Union, nearly all of the sixty-nine monastic institutions they could claim as late as 1958, and a vital middle level of organization that had no parallel in the shattered ecclesiastical structure of central and eastern Russia.[71]

In a real sense, all the contributions by Russian churchmen to the regime during the war, all of what seemed to unsympathetic foreign eyes like their groveling at the feet of Stalin, was justified in order to gain this new heartland for Orthodoxy. In the areas that had never left Soviet control, there may also have occurred something like a religious revival, though in a much more constricted form than of that in the German-occupied territories, as far as one can tell from the admittedly skimpy data. During the war, official publications ignored the resurgence of belief. Only by the late 1950's did they admit it, rationalizing it as a phenomenon limited to "a few weak-willed and ideologically unstable people" whose wartime suffering had driven them "to seek 'solace' in the churches."[72] Contemporary observations come primarily from two sources, each with its own bias: Church announcements of record attendance at holidays in the Moscow congregations and reports of foreign visitors focusing on the limits to religious liberty.

The Patriarchate proudly reported the lifting of the Moscow curfew just in time to let celebrants attend Easter Eve services in 1942.[73] A repetition of this measure the next year brought some fifty thousand to midnight worship, only a third of whom could squeeze inside the thirty churches still open in the city.[74] Alexander Werth noted a marked difference in the two observances, the first held in rundown buildings by priests in shabby robes for mostly elderly worshippers, the second in renovated quarters with "many more soldiers" in the churches in 1943 than there had been in previous years.[75] Even the Gestapo took note of the "significant attendance" at these services and commented on Red Army personnel at reopened Moscow churches.[76] Eve Curie, on a French journalistic mission through many Russian cities in 1942, concluded that, after twenty-five years of antireligious propaganda, the regime could afford to relax controls, since "on the whole, the young Russian generation had parted with Christianity . . . had been converted to a new faith that left room for no other faith."[77] In a *New York Times* account of Christmas services in Moscow as late as 1944, the overflow congregation was characterized as consisting of "a normal sample of Moscow's housewives and middle-aged men," devoid of youth except for a few soldiers.[78] In the previous fall, Maurice Hindus had commented on the absence of males and youth at a special service conducted by the Patriarch.[79]

What emerges from these impressionistic data is a pale shadow of that recrudescence of faith under German occupation: this came two years later, took in a smaller fraction of the population, and was marked by a much greater shortage of church facilities and cadres.[80] It can be hypothesized that three critical factors account for this divergence. First, compared to the social conditions of areas that remained under Soviet rule, those of the occupied zone were extremely fluid. Upheavals in the system became the norm as the strict Communist order was replaced more often by disorder than by the "New Order." New social forces, such as the nascent religious organizations, were relatively free to organize themselves, at least on a regional level, as long as they stripped themselves of lingering Soviet ties. Second, there was a difference in the nature of controls imposed on these emergent groups. In the occupied areas, there was substituted for pervasive Soviet rule a German martial law which focused its sporadic surveillance on aspects of behavior that bore watching for possible rebellion. The Kremlin's church policy had consistently set limits to the growth of organized religion. Even by the time the "New Religious Policy" was a year old, a Central Committee directive was launching a new wave of antireligious activities under the more subtle label of "scientific educational propaganda."[81]

On the one hand, then, Soviet policy-makers limited the benefits of religious toleration to the lowest and least mobile social stratum, the older peasantry.[82] Urban youth was to remain hostile to what the Party termed "survivals of ignorance, superstition, and prejudice." Its textbooks in 1944–1945 still talked of religion as superstition, the stupefying of people, and a means to enslave the masses.[83] On the other hand, the regime forced the rehabilitated Church to concern itself exclusively with what it called "practice of the cult." This means, according to William Fletcher, making the Church turn "her back on the great social issues of the day" in a narrowing of the mission to a "purely spiritual, supernatural calling."[84] As Alfred G. Meyer views it, the 1943 modus vivendi allowed the churches to engage in activities "so long as they had a purely sacramental character" but at the same time prevented them "from extending their work into areas such as education, social work, charity, or even social life."[85]

Here is found the third respect in which believers of the occupied area gained a critical advantage. German religious measures were—at times intentionally, generally as a result of bureaucratic confusion—a welter of contradictions. Yet there was no sustained attempt to suppress Orthodoxy in any part of the population; only the church cadres were under pressure to keep out of politics or to issue pro-Nazi sermons. In the fluid occupation society the Church won an opportunity for cohesion and communication without the strictures on its appeal that were never relaxed by the Soviets. German controls in their very contradictions permitted this vital force free movement, except at its apex. As Alexander Werth has noted, the churches almost at once transcended the anti-Communist mission for which the Germans had primed them, to aid prisoners of war, offer relief to the poor, organize "mutual aid circles," and, to their administrators' consternation, become "active centers of Russian national consciousness."[86]

CONSOLIDATING THE JUNIOR PARTNERSHIP

In the two or three years following the war, the movement of the Church in the new direction opened by the 1943 concordat gathered momentum. The hierarchs assumed added measures of prestige. Their conclaves held in an aura of luxury, their offices richly appointed, their messages carried in official publications, and their encounters with the political elite a matter of course, they could be considered to have taken their place among the privileged classes of Soviet society. They also rose to new prominence as junior partners of the state. As the cold war dawned, they tightened their connections with Orthodox congregations in the East European states which were being drawn into the Soviet bloc, and their foreign missions carried them to "Peace Congresses" and to meetings with prelates of the Middle East and Western Europe again in aid of Soviet foreign policy. Coordination of this new political task devolved upon Metropolitan Nikolai, until 1960 head of the Church's Department of External Relations, who apparently was personally assigned to it by Stalin in April 1945.[87] Nikolai's biographer, William Fletcher, has ably analyzed the ethical dilemmas of this churchman, who went to great lengths even in the service of Soviet intelligence objectives until a crisis of conscience in 1956 appears to have set him on the road to resistance and eventual martyrdom.

With the death of Patriarch Sergius on May 15, 1944, temporary leadership of the Church passed to Metropolitan Alexis, who hastened at once to notify Stalin of the "very deep love . . ." and devotion borne the "Godgiven leader" by himself and all his "churchly colleagues."[88] This was a guarantee of political trustworthiness, evidently a necessary preliminary to having the regime permit convocation of a sobor to formally elect a new patriarch in February 1945. The outcome was once more a foregone conclusion, once Karpov had paid tribute to "the esteemed churchman and fervent patriot Alexis."[89] Rather more unexpected was the attendant pomp and circumstance: the full complement of clergy and laity that accompanied the forty-four prelates, the large contingent of foreign clerics, the splendor of the installation ceremony, and the concert of church music performed at the Moscow Conservatory afterward.[90]

By its pronouncements, this sobor also offered a clue to the nature of the modus vivendi that the Church was being allowed to extend into the postwar period. Prior to the election, it had passed a statute (on January 31) giving in outline form the first rules since the Revolution for internal government of the Church.[91] A regularized administration was a prerequisite for an institution that had hopes of growth, of adding to its hierarchy, and, as a result of Stalin's sympathetic hearing of the Patriarch's requests in April, of setting up new facilities to replenish its chronically short supply of priests.[92] The new statute further put the financial affairs of the parishes in more permanent order by organizing the production of candles, whose sale was to provide an essential supplement to donations by the faithful. These very real gains must, of course, be balanced against the setting of the centralized Church administration presupposed by the statute, which in effect enabled "the Soviet Government to remove and get rid of any bishop whom it finds undesirable."[93]

Finally, the sobor indicated clearly the political price the Church would have to pay unstintingly to earn its future viability. It did so, in the first instance, by intoning praise to "our beloved leader of the Soviet state and Supreme Commander of our glorious troops, Joseph Vissarionovich Stalin."[94] Such paeans had already become a customary preamble to ecclesiastical messages; their effusiveness grew with Stalin's advancing years, reaching something of an apogee in the seventieth birthday wishes tendered by all the bishops in 1949.[95] Even at Stalin's death in 1953, the Patriarch still took time to bless his "eternal memory" and, together with two archbishops, to be among the guard of honor at the bier.[96] In such gestures the hierarchs showed that they were relying on Stalin to honor his word to them; by countenancing them, Stalin implied that he saw some value in enhancing his legitimacy in the eyes of the faithful.

The second side of the coin tendered by the Church in 1945 represented its contribution to Soviet objectives abroad. The sobor appealed to "the people of the whole world" to "raise their voices against the efforts of those, particularly the Vatican, who, seeking by their utterances to shield Hitlerite Germany from responsibility for all the crimes committed by it" were said to be perpetuating anti-Christian, fascist doctrines into the postwar period.[97] The Vatican's role as the bête noire of Orthodoxy was to last until the collective leadership that followed Stalin adopted a "peaceful coexistence" line. By the end of the 1950's the Church had made the requisite accommodation, displaying a new taste for the ecumenical movement which, to the surprise of foreign churchmen, eventually brought its observers to the Vatican Council and made it join the World Council of Churches in 1961.[98]

Just as the attacks on the Vatican were noteworthy for their political rather than ecclesiastical grounds, so the churchly exhortations to punish the Germans were notably devoid of Christian precepts. Archbishop Lucas of Tambov declared in the patriarchal journal that the Golden Rule was not a valid standard for the case: "The despicable Germans are not merely our enemies but also God's, and who dares to speak of love for God's enemies?"[99] In a later issue, a priest named M. Sernov found it equally expedient to justify the Nuremberg trials of Nazi war criminals: "There are deeds on earth for which there is no forgiveness. The Redeemer prayed for his persecutors because they knew not what they did. But our enemies knew very well what *they* did. Therefore, they deserve no forgiveness."[100]

If such vengefulness appears unseemly, it is at the same time consonant with the official Church view of the German occupation, in which exaggerated accounts of war crimes crowded out the least mention of the substantial gains made by religious organizations. In the ecclesiastical history of the period, as subsequently rewritten, the Orthodox under German rule have a monopoly on the gallery of heroes. The stigma of collaborators was reserved for other sects, particularly the Ukrainian Uniates whose misconduct could be attributed to their Vatican links, severed at Moscow's insistence in 1945. The following spring, a loyalist delegation of Uniates rationalized the imprisonment of scores of their fellows in the Communist postwar purge as due punishment for treasonable collaboration with the Germans.[101] The leader of this rump group, Archpriest Gabriel Kostelnyk, may not have been in a position to do otherwise, for two of his sons are supposed to have fled to the West after having served with the Ukrainian SS Division, while a third was held hostage by the Soviets.[102] Kostelnyk was assassinated in Lvov on September 20, 1948, a crime the Patriarchate was quick to blame on German-Ukrainian nationalists acting at the instigation of the Vatican.[103]

In general, it was a much easier matter for Orthodox groups, guilty of a moderate degree of involvement with the Axis powers during the war, to have their political sins quietly forgiven upon rendering their submissions to the Patriarchate. The inducement to do so was particularly strong in the lands that had fallen under the shadow of the Red Army. Thus, in the Russian zones of Germany and Austria, the congregations of Berlin, Potsdam, Dresden, Leipzig, and Vienna quickly embraced

Moscow's hegemony.[104] Soon after the Soviet occupation of Manchuria in the summer of 1945, the clergy in the former White Guard stronghold of Harbin also returned to the fold.[105] Even the head of the Polish Auto-cephalous Church, Metropolitan Dionisius, who had once hoped to dominate Ukrainian Orthodoxy under German auspices, was released from the Warsaw jail where he had been awaiting trial after issuing a penitential letter, though he lost most of his dioceses as a result of Russia's seizure of the eastern third of Poland. A nationalist Polish bishop, Timofei, had become acting Church head, but the final step to a russified hierarchy was delayed until June 1951, when a Soviet bishop, Macarius of Lvov, a much more pliable figure in the hands of the Patri-arch, was installed at Warsaw.[106]

Encouraged by such successfully conducted "homecomings" by the Orthodox beyond the borders, and reacting as well, perhaps, to the limits on religious growth set by the regime at home, the Moscow hierarchs began to revive a forgotten piece of tsarist ideology: that the Patriarchy could claim to be the "Third Rome." The subject had been broached by the North American Exarch, Metropolitan Benjamin, at the 1945 sobor.[107] He had proposed that an advisory central council be set up in Moscow to service Orthodox churches around the world. Ambitions along this line had swelled by the spring of 1947 to the point where the Patriarch invited the heads of all Orthodox Churches to a Moscow meeting at which ecumenicism was to be high on the agenda.[108] Dreams of such global unity were punctured rudely by the realities of the cold war. The session scheduled for November had to be canceled after a number of anti-Soviet hierarchs, including the Patriarchs of Constantinople and Alexandria and the Church heads of Greece and Cyprus, begged off.

The Patriarch had to content himself with revised invitations to the foreign prelates to a conference in July 1948, in connection with the celebration of the five-hundredth anniversary of Russian Church auto-cephaly. The hierarchs from non-Communist countries were conspicu-ously absent. Speeches were monotonously cast in the clichés of the cold war vocabulary: denunciations of capitalism, American imperialism, and, for good measure, the Vatican and the World Council of Churches.[109] Karpov accused "the heads of some ancient Greek Churches" of having boycotted the meeting for nonecclesiastical reasons, but this was no less than sour grapes. The aspirations of the Moscow Church to become the "Third Rome" lay shattered. Its subservience to the Soviet state bound it to a far more modest role in the foreseeable future.

THE POSTWAR OUTLOOK FOR THE CHURCH

If the Church embarked in the postwar era as a newly certified Soviet institution, there still remained grounds for speculation on the amount and direction of the diffusion taking place between it and other social structures in Russia. One extreme view, taken by Serge Bolshakoff, held that the Church, which had "Christianized the most unlikely societies and institutions," might in time "Christianize the Soviet State as well."[110] The antipodal opinion is represented by Miklos Nyarady, who concluded on the basis of his 1947 diplomatic mission to the Soviet Union that the Church had simply become the mouthpiece of the government.[111] The true nature of the postwar trend seemed to lie somewhere between these polar analyses.

Christianization of the state seemed the less likely of the two prospects, since in 1946 its proponents were ignoring the "considerable evidence showing that the Soviet authorities still regard religion as an error which should be combatted."[112] The regime was no less determined to prevent "contamination" of its cadres by religion, as it barred believers from the Party and Komsomol—both of which continued to espouse antireligious propaganda, now put on a par with the inculcation of "scientific notions."[113] Sunday schools were still prohibited, and parents had no easy choice in arranging for private religious instruction of their offspring; they knew that the step could incur sanctions for themselves and impede their children's careers. Though the Militant Atheist League had faded away, it had apparently been succeeded by the Society for the Dissemination of Scientific and Political Knowledge. For the grotesque museums and demonstrations of the League, the Society had at least temporarily substituted lectures and pamphlets to drive out religious error without direct mention of the Church.

Among the restrictive controls on the Church, there was a continued hiatus in the cultural activities that had flourished in prerevolutionary Russia, a ban on public meetings of a religious nature, and a further dearth of Church literature beyond the limited circulation of the *Journal of the Moscow Patriarchate* to ecclesiastical subscribers.[114] Christianization of the Soviet state remained little more than the fond hope of those arguing from the premise that "good always triumphs over evil" and others who saw the Kremlin adopting and shedding policies to suit its whims. An example of the latter is Stephen Graham, who depicted Stalin as secretly a Church sympathizer from his Tiflis seminary days, forced into an irreligious stance by Lenin's uncompromising hostility to the

Church and then, upon receiving a plea for religious liberty from a priest named Vissarion like his father, returning to the faith—a stray lamb.[115] Lenin was, of course, out of touch with the Yezhovshchina, and Stalin, whose memories of his father were probably replete with the beatings he had administered, was not seen attending any of the Moscow cathedrals.

The second postwar prospect, Sovietization of the Church, cannot be dismissed as easily as a figment of wishful thinking. But its extreme interpreters cannot be taken too seriously when they contend that in 1947 Patriarch Alexis was "in constant touch with Stalin and the Politburo members" and had become "an ardent supporter of Soviet imperialistic policies because he believes that a Russian victory in the East-West conflict finally would bring about a long-awaited triumph of 'the only true church against the heretic Catholic or Protestant churches of the world' after a thousand-year enmity."[116] Equally far-fetched was the Vatican broadcast claiming that the Orthodox Church, under Kremlin orders, had transformed forty thousand secret police agents into priests in order to listen in on confessions.

A much more balanced picture is painted by a German Jesuit priest, Wilhelm DeVries. He makes a case for political secularization by citing the absence of religious terminology in the Church leaders' call to arms for the defense of Russia; the Patriarch's attack on the late Metropolitan Benjamin, head of the Petrograd diocese who had been executed in 1922 for "having cloaked counterrevolutionary activities by church schism" and having invoked "state power to assist against clerical enemies"; and by a like couching of charges against the Ukrainian Autocephalists led by Bishop Polykarp.[117] DeVries seems to have gone astray, however, by accepting at face value declarations of the hierarchs attesting to the contentedness of their subservient status. He is on surer ground when returning to his main theme, one corroborated by other data: high clerics have played a vital diplomatic role in Soviet foreign relations, especially within the East European bloc; Church publications, such as the Patriarchate's journal, were carrying affirmations of loyalty to the regime and the "God-chosen Leader," Stalin; Church calendars were made to include Soviet holidays; special services were held on state occasions, such as Stalin's birthday, according to émigré interviews. Patriarch Alexis was supposed to have preached in 1947: "Every true Christian in the Soviet Union should be ready for a 'holy war' to repel an eventual attack by the 'American capitalists and Western imperialists.'"[118] Although the text is perhaps apocryphal, the likelihood for

Church messages in this vein increased as, amid the exacerbated cold war, a layman wrote in the patriarchal journal: "The camp of world reaction, headed by the United States of America, fiercely opposes the establishment of a stable peace on a democratic basis. The Wall Street billionaires, who dream of a dollar-dominated world, the colonizers who make gold and diamonds from human blood, military spies, and provocateurs—these are primarily responsible before humanity, history, and culture for the propaganda and preparation of a new war."[119]

After the war, Church leaders found themselves in a privileged position, surrounded by the material comforts and perquisites furnished by the government. Even the base level of clerical salaries exceeded the earnings of skilled workers or civil servants with senior priests in Moscow making 300 rubles a month and the lowly village priest relatively well off.[120] That, in this context, they should acquire a vested interest in the regime and, in their historical role as "junior partners" of the state, perform the domestic and diplomatic tasks assigned them is not surprising. But, according to an interview with N. S. Timasheff, the infiltration of Soviet standards tends to be limited to the top levels of the Church. Local priests and believers discounted the loyal protestations of their superiors, and in their reading of Church publications like the *Journal of the Moscow Patriarchate* skipped the first few pages devoted to the praise of Communism in order to reach the purely theological discussions that formed the bulk of their contents. Adoption of pro-Soviet positions by the Church leaders could be viewed as a corollary of their status. With religious forces concentrated in strata of the population alien to the cadres of other institutions, the Church was robbed of the means for independent action. It had to placate the leadership upon whose favor its future rested by constantly demonstrating that it "knew its place" and would perform whatever duties might be reserved for a Soviet institution, still slated to wither away sooner or later according to official ideology.

The hierarchs could not be expected to face their moribundity with joy. By performing the regime's assignments with alacrity, they tried to secure their status as indispensable allies of the state. By displaying "Communist consciousness," they averted association with "backwardness" and attempted to reach a stage of "enlightened religion," in the hope that the Marxist formulation would eventually be revised. Only when the Church could declare the "bourgeois superstitious forms of religion" to have withered away inside Russia might the stage be set for a permanent rapprochement, the ideology be once again remolded to current Soviet needs. Not till then could the Church hope to earn its place beyond question as a fully legitimate component of Communist society.

IN CLOSING

An attempt has been made in the separate sections of this book to evaluate the largely scattered and fragmentary data, to explore some hypotheses regarding causal relations in German and Soviet policies toward the Orthodox Church, and to reach conclusions on the political sociology of religion in Russia. A summary of the findings might seem in order; but, on second thought, it appears advisable to allow the conclusions reached en route to stand by themselves. Their tentative and partial nature is in keeping with materials that, for obvious reasons, could not lay claim to comprehensiveness, due to the impossibility of interviewing Nazi and Stalinist decision-makers or of conducting field surveys among the survivors of the occupation period. It may be of interest, nonetheless, to return to the purposes of the inquiry outlined in the Preface and to assess the extent to which they have been fulfilled: How much light on the institutional characteristics of the Church has been shed by regarding its wartime experiences as a "controlled experiment"?

At the primary level of popular participation, the "experimental group" of believers in the German-occupied territories ran true to expectation by staging a religious revival of proportions unprecedented and unparalleled in the areas remaining under Soviet control. This phenomenon took place in spite of, rather than because of, intervention by the Nazi authorities. Indeed, at the level of policy, one witnesses the failures of these officials to come to grips realistically with the resurgent Church and sees in them the major source for the frustration of German hopes to exploit Russian religious forces. Arbitrary as it was, the Nazi system of cultural controls did not match the pervasiveness of the Soviet network. Within the looser confines of the former, Orthodox congregations were able to thrive on the peripheries of society under the occupation. The price they had to pay for survival amidst economic and political repression was relatively modest: delivering occasional tributes to their German masters and not venturing into areas of potential opposition.

At the secondary level of the role and status of the Church and its hierarchy, one somewhat unexpectedly finds that the really dramatic changes affected the "control group," the Church in the Soviet Union during the same period. Except for the fairly unsuccessful revolt engineered by outsiders in the Ukrainian Autocephalous movement, there was no marked transformation of the institution's position under German rule. In the Soviet area, on the other hand, a policy reversal led to the proclamation of religious peace for the first time at a moment of overt national danger. The Church received a reprieve, perhaps permanently, from execution as an endemic enemy of the regime. It was elevated to the status of an ally, and the ecclesiastical leaders were "sovietized" by assuming roles in the state. Ironically, the Germans, by their policy of negativism, at best neutrality, toward the Church, had furnished the Moscow Patriarchate the proof it required of the political reliability of its forces to convince Stalin that a fresh start in Soviet religious policy was in order.

The objective, unified view of the Church sought at the outset of the book has not come into focus during an analysis of either Nazi or Soviet policies. The makers of each brought to their subject only fitful attention and a set of preconceptions that tell us less about the institution than about the agencies that tried to manipulate it. In the case of the Germans, the blinders are provided by the *Untermenschen* stereotype into which they forced all Russians and by the preoccupation with its primary mission shown by each of the bureaucratic machines engaged in the occupation. All agreed that some form of exploitation should be applied to native religious organizations, but differences in their respective orders of priorities led them to adopt tactics at odds with each other. Soviet decision-makers displayed a similar obsession with manipulative strategy, although in their case this desire was checked by the ideological assumption on the incompatibility of religion and communism. Furthermore, their actions were fitted into a more or less unified "line" enunciated by the Politburo, with none of the semiautonomous agencies the Germans relied on to execute their policies.

If there is something like a true institutional nature of the Church, it must be reconstructed from blind spots in the official images—from the areas of resistance to Nazi as well as Soviet pressures. According to the specialists I consulted, especially Timasheff, the Russian Orthodox Church is inherently ill-suited to become a tool of any kind. Services emphasize ritual, and sermons are as a rule devoted to purely spiritual, otherwordly topics. This hypothesis on the political neutrality of most Orthodox congregations is corroborated by the spontaneous and autonomous nature of their revival under the occupation. Yet these were the very characteristics that could not be countenanced by the German authorities, who were functionally incapable of exploiting popular feeling that, to the extent it was left unfettered, the religious sphere was *the* area in which significant improvement had been brought about by Nazi rule. Instead, these officials hinged their measures on the few priests who could be forced to lend verbal support to the New Order (and shooting those who were politically suspect), just as postwar Soviet judgments of church life under the occupation singled out the handful who had aided the partisans—or served as quislings. In neither case was the Church permitted to assert its right to an independent existence, as a "third force."

Though the sections on Nazi and Stalinist policies toward the Church have been devoted to contrasting theories and methods, it should be noted that they also illustrate a common denominator of the totalitarian approach to cultural controls. In the black and white categories of such a system, even the most "inherently neutral" institution, as a locus of popular loyalty, is forced to choose sides. It must become a pillar of support for the regime (if policy is to change from repression to tolerance, as in the Soviet case, and if organization is to be allowed to transcend local limits, in the German) or it is marked as an obstacle to be overturned. That the bulk of the believers might not desire to be transformed into pillars or obstacles was a thought alien to the minds of Soviet and German decision-makers on the Church.

If this study has an antitotalitarian bias, I am nevertheless hopeful that it has detached itself from the coloring that overlay much of the data. Apart from the obviously subjective accounts found in Nazi and Soviet sources, less direct distortions called for correction. It further became apparent that, when predicting the future of the Orthodox Church in the Soviet Union, the writers who foresaw Christianization of the state turned out to be of Protestant background, the prophets of a "sovietized" Church of Catholic origin. In another vein, politically oriented analysts often laid undue stress on the expression of loyalty or disloyalty by an individual cleric to the German or Soviet regime; others, of a "pro-Orthodox" bent, overemphasized Soviet religious concessions, representing them as Church triumphs. Finally, the believers among the respondents to the Harvard Refugee Interview Project appear also to have overestimated the strength of religious forces. To the extent this essay has discounted such preconceptions it may add to a more valid estimate of the Orthodox Church, of popular religious patterns in Russia, and of the determinants that governed Nazi and Stalinist policies in this field.

Bibliography

Notes

Index

Bibliography

Books

Alexeev, Vasili. *Russian Orthodox Bishops in the Soviet Union, 1941–1953.* New York, Research Program on the USSR, mimeographed series No. 61, 1954 (in Russian).

Anderson, Paul B. *People, Church and State in Modern Russia.* New York: The Macmillan Co., 1944.

Anderson, Paul B., ed. *Major Portions of the Proceedings of the Conference of Heads and Representatives of Autocephalous Orthodox Churches in Connection with the Celebration of 500 Years of Autocephalicity of the Russian Orthodox Church, 8–18 July, 1948.* Paris, YMCA Press, 1952.

Anisimov, Oleg. *The German Occupation in Northern Russia During World War II: Political and Administrative Aspects.* New York, Research Program on the USSR, mimeographed series No. 56, 1954 (in Russian).

Arendt, Hannah. *Eichmann in Jerusalem.* New York, Viking Press, 1963.

Armstrong, John A. *Ukrainian Nationalism,* 2nd ed. New York, Columbia University Press, 1963.

Bade, Wilfred, and Wilmont Haacke, eds. *Das heldische Jahr.* 2nd ed. Berlin, Zeitgeschichte Verlag, 1943.

Baran, Stepan, *Mitropolit Andrei Sheptitski.* Munich, Vernigora, 1947.

Bauer, Joseph M. *Die Kraniche der Nogaia.* Munich, R. Piper & Co., 1942.

Bauer, Raymond A., Alex Inkeles, and Clyde Kluckhohn. *How the Soviet System Works.* Cambridge, Harvard University Press, 1956.

Beckmann, Joachim. *Kirchliches Jahrbuch für die Evangelische Kirche in Deutschland 1933–1944.* Gütersloh, Evangelische Kirche im Dritten Reich, 1948.

Bell, Daniel. *The End of Ideology,* rev., ed. New York, The Free Press, 1962.

Bernstein, Victor H. *Final Judgment.* New York, Liveright Publishing Corp., 1947.

Birnbaum, Walter. *Christenheit in Sowjetrussland.* Tübingen, Katzmann Verlag, 1961.

Black, Cyril E., ed. *The Transformation of Russian Society.* Cambridge, Harvard University Press, 1960.

Bolshakoff, Serge. *The Christian Church and the Soviet State.* New York, The Macmillan Co., 1942.

―――― *Russian Nonconformity.* Philadelphia, Westminster Press, 1950.

Bonch-Bruevich, V. D. *Izbrannye sochineniya,* vol. I: O religi, religioznom *sektantstve i tserkvi.* Moscow, Academy of Sciences, 1959–1963.

Bottomore, T. B., ed. *Karl Marx: Early Writings.* London, C. A. Watts & Co., Ltd., 1963.

Bourdeaux, Michael. *Opium of the People: The Christian Religion in the U.S.S.R.* Indianapolis, The Bobbs-Merrill Co., Inc., 1966.

Bracher, Karl D. *Die Auflösung der Weimarer Republik.* 3rd ed. Villingen, Ring Verlag, 1960.

Braun, Leopold L. *Religion in Russia, from Lenin to Khrushchev: An Uncensored Account.* Patterson, N.J., St. Anthony's Guild Press, 1959.

Briem, Efraim. *Kommunismus und Religion in der Sowjetunion, ein Ideenkampf.* Basel, F. Reinhardt, 1948.

Bullock, Alan. *Hitler: A Study in Tyranny,* rev. ed. New York, Harper & Row, 1962.

Carroll, Wallace. *We're in This with Russia.* Boston, Houghton Mifflin Co., 1942.

Casey, Robert P. *Religion in Russia.* New York, Harper & Row, 1946.

Chamberlin, W. H. *Russia's Iron Age.* Boston, Little, Brown & Co., 1934.

Chandler, Albert R. *Rosenberg's Nazi Myth.* Ithaca, N.Y., Cornell University Press, 1945.

Cochrane, Arthur C. *The Church's Confession under Hitler.* Philadelphia, Westminster Press, 1962.

Conway, J. S. *The Nazi Persecution of the Churches 1933–45.* London, Weidenfeld & Nicolson, 1968.

Corsten, Wilhelm. *Kölner Aktenstücke zur Lage der Katholischen Kirche in Deutschland 1933–1945.* Cologne, W. Corsten, 1949.

Curie, Eve. *Journey Among Warriors.* Garden City, N.Y., Doubleday & Co., Inc., 1943.

Curtiss, John S. *Church and State in Russia.* New York, Columbia University Press, 1940.

―――― *The Russian Church and the Soviet State: 1917–1950.* Boston, Little, Brown & Co., 1953.

Dallin, Alexander. *German Rule in Russia, 1941–1945.* London, Macmillan & Co., Ltd., 1957.

Dallin, Alexander, and Alan F. Westin, eds. *Politics in the Soviet Union: 7 Cases.* New York, Harcourt, Brace & World, Inc., 1966.

Dallin, David J. *The Real Soviet Russia.* New Haven, Yale University Press, 1944.

Davidson, Eugene, *The Trial of the Germans.* New York, The Macmillan Co., 1966.

DeVries, Wilhelm. *Christentum in der Sowjetunion.* Heidelberg, Kemper Verlag, 1950.

―――― *Kirche und Staat in der Sowjetunion.* Munich, Verlag Anton Pustet, 1959.

Dwinger, Edwin E. *Wiedersehen mit Sowjetrussland.* Jena, E. Diederichs, 1943.

Emhardt, William C. *Religion in Soviet Russia.* Milwaukee, Morehouse Publishing Co., 1929.

Engelhard, Walter. *Klinzy, Bildnis einer russischen Stadt nach ihrer Befreiung vom Bolschewismus.* Berlin, Nibelungen Verlag, 1943.

Engelhardt, Eugen. *Weissruthenien: Volk und Land.* Berlin, Volk und Reich Verlag, 1943.

Engels, Frederick, "*Anti-Duehring.*" Chicago, Charles H. Kerr & Co., 1907.

Europas Soldaten berichten über die Sowjetunion. Berlin, Erasmusdruck, 1942.

Fainsod, Merle. *How Russia Is Ruled.* Cambridge, Harvard University Press, 1953; rev. ed., 1963.

Fedotov, Georgi P. *The Russian Church Since the Revolution.* London, Society for Promoting Christian Knowledge, 1928.

———— *The Russian Religious Mind.* 2 vols. Cambridge, Harvard University Press, 1946.

Feuer, Lewis S., ed. *Marx and Engels: Basic Writings on Politics and Philosophy.* Garden City, N.Y., Doubleday & Co., Inc., 1959.

Fevr, Nikolai M. *Solntse voskhodit na zapade.* Buenos Aires, Novoe Slovo, 1950.

Fjodorow, O. *Die Religion in der UdSSR.* Berlin, SWA Verlag, 1947.

Fletcher, William C. *Nikolai: Portrait of a Dilemma.* New York, The Macmillan Co., 1968.

———— *A Study in Survival: The Church in Russia 1927–1943.* New York, The Macmillan Co., 1965.

Fredborg, Arvid. *Behind the Steel Wall: A Swedish Journalist in Berlin, 1941–43.* New York, Viking Press, 1944.

Gauger, Joachim. *Chronik der Kirchenwirren.* Elberfeld, Gotthard-Briefe, 1934.

Goebbels, Joseph. *Diaries, 1942–1943.* Garden City, N.Y., Doubleday & Co., Inc., 1948.

Graham, Stephen. *Summing-Up on Russia.* London, E. Benn, Ltd., 1951.

Guderian, Heinz. *Erinnerungen eines Soldaten.* Heidelberg, Vowinckel, 1951.

———— *Panzer Leader.* London, M. Joseph, 1952.

Gurian, Waldemar, ed. *The Soviet Union: Background, Ideology, Reality.* Notre Dame, Ind., Notre Dame University Press, 1951.

Gustavson, Arfved. *Die Katakombenkirche.* Stuttgart, Evangelisches Verlagswerk, 1954.

Hagen, Walter [Wilhelm Hoettl]. *Die geheime Front.* Linz, Nibelungen Verlag, 1950.

Haussleiter, August. *An der mittleren Ostfront.* Nuremberg, J. L. Schrag, 1942.

Hecker, Julius F. *Religion under the Soviets.* New York, Vanguard Press, Inc., 1927.

Hermelink, Heinrich. *Kirche im Kampf.* Tübingen, Wunderlich Verlag, 1950.

Heyer, Friedrich. *Die orthodoxe Kirche in der Ukraine von 1917 bis 1945.* Cologne, Rudolf Müller, 1953.

Hitler, Adolf. *Mein Kampf.* Munich, F. Eher, 220/224 ed., 1936. Translation by James Murphy, London, Hurst & Blackett, 1939.

Hitler's Table Talk, 1941–1944. London, Weidenfeld and Nicolson, 1953. Translation by Norman Cameron and R. H. Stevens. See also Henry Picker.

Hochhuth, Rolf. *The Deputy.* New York, Grove Press, Inc., 1964.

Hofer, Walther. *Der Nationalsozialismus: Dokumente 1933–1945.* Frankfurt, Fischer Bücherei, 1957.

Hunt, R. N. Carew. *The Theory and Practice of Communism.* London, Geoffrey Bles, 1957.

Inkeles, Alex, and Raymond A. Bauer. *The Soviet Citizen: Daily Life in a Totalitarian Society.* Cambridge, Harvard University Press, 1959.

Jackson, Robert H. *The Nürnberg Case.* New York, Alfred A. Knopf, Inc., 1947.

Jarman, T. L. *The Rise and Fall of Nazi Germany.* New York, New York University Press, 1956.

Jessop, T. E., R. L. Calhoun, *et al. The Christian Understanding of Man.* Chicago, Willett, Clark & Co., 1938.

Kandidov, Boris P. *Tserkov i shpionazh.* Moscow, State Antireligious Publishing House, 1937.

Kasyak, I. *Z gistory Pravaslaunai Tsarkvi Belaruskaga Narodu.* New York, Belorussian Central Rada, 1956.

Khudyakov, Semyon N. *Vsegda li budet sushchestvovat religiya?* Moscow, Znanie Publishing House, 1958.

Kleist, Peter. *Zwischen Hitler und Stalin, 1939–1945.* Bonn, Athenäum, 1950.

Kolarz, Walter. *Religion in the Soviet Union.* New York, St. Martin's Press, 1961.

Kravchenko, Victor. *I Chose Freedom.* New York, Charles Scribner's Sons, 1946.

Kryvelev, I. A. *Lenin o religi.* Moscow, Academy of Sciences, 1960.

Kuznetsov, Anatoly. *Babi Yar.* New York, Dial Press, 1967.

Leibbrandt, Gottlieb. *Bolschewismus und Abendland.* Berlin, Junker und Dünnhaupt, 1943.

Lemkin, Rafael. *Axis Rule in Occupied Europe.* Washington, Carnegie Endowment for International Peace, Division of International Law, 1944.

Lenin, V. I. *Sochineniya.* 4th ed. 43 vols. Moscow, State Publishing House of Political Literature, 1942–1966.

Lewy, Guenter. *The Catholic Church and Nazi Germany.* New York, McGraw-Hill Book Co., 1964.

Lichtheim, George. *Marxism: An Historical and Critical Study.* New York, Frederick A. Praeger, Inc., 1961.

Lieb, Fritz. *Russland unterwegs.* Berne, Francke, 1945.

Littel, Franklin H. *The German Phoenix.* Garden City, N.Y., Doubleday & Co., Inc., 1960.

Lochner, Louis P., ed. *The Goebbels Diaries.* Garden City, N.Y., Doubleday & Co., Inc., 1948.

Luther, Martin. *The Works of Martin Luther.* Philadelphia, A. J. Holman Co., 1915–1932.

Magidoff, Robert. *The Kremlin vs. the People.* Garden City, N.Y., Doubleday & Co., Inc., 1953.

Marx, Karl. *Capital: A Critique of Political Economy.* New York, Random House, Inc., 1936.

———— *Selected Works.* 2 vols. New York, International Publishers, 1933.

Marx, Karl, and Friedrich Engels. *On Religion.* New York, Schocken Books, 1964.

Maynard, John. *Russia in Flux.* New York, The Macmillan Co., 1948.

Meier, Kurt. *Die Deutschen Christen,* Göttingen, Vandenhoeck & Ruprecht, 1964.

Meyer, Alfred, ed. *Das Recht der besetzten Ostgebiete.* Munich, F. Eher, 1943.

Meyer, Alfred G. *The Soviet Political System: An Interpretation.* New York, Random House, Inc., 1965.

Micklem, Nathaniel. *National Socialism and the Roman Catholic Church.* London, Oxford University Press, 1939.

Moore, Barrington, Jr. *Soviet Politics: The Dilemma of Power.* Cambridge, Harvard University Press, 1951.

———— *Terror and Progress USSR.* Cambridge, Harvard University Press, 1954.

Moscow Patriarchate. *The Truth about Religion in Russia.* London, Hutchinson, 1942.

Msgr. A. M. [Bishop Athanasius]. *Materialy da history Pravaslaunae Belaruskae Tsarkvy.* 1948. N.p.

Müller, Artur. *Ich begleite einen General.* Dresden, W. Heyne, 1942.

Müller, Hans. *Katholische Kirche und Nationalsozialismus.* Munich, Nymphenburger Verlagshandlung, 1963.

Neuhäusler, Johann. *Kreuz und Hakenkreuz.* 2nd ed. Munich, Katholische Kirche Bayerns, 1946.

Neumann, Franz. *Behemoth: The Structure and Practice of National Socialism.* New York, Oxford University Press, 1942.

Nikitin, M. U., and P. I. Vagin. *The Crimes of the German Fascists in the Leningrad Region.* London, Hutchinson, n.d.

Nikolai, Metropolitan. *The Russian Orthodox Church and the War against Fascism.* Moscow, Patriarchate of Moscow, 1943.

———— *Slova, rechi, poslaniya: 1941–1946 gg.* Moscow, Patriarchate of Moscow, 1947.

Nyarady, Miklos. *My Ringside Seat in Moscow.* New York, Crowell-Collier, Inc., 1952.

Oberkommando der Wehrmacht. *Kampf gegen die Sowjets: Berichte und Bilder bis zum Frühjahr 1942.* Berlin, 1943.

Orlowski, Slawomir. *Erich Koch pered polskim sudom.* Moscow, Institute of International Relations, 1961.

Packard, Reynolds and Eleanor. *Balcony Empire.* New York, Oxford University Press, 1942.

Paléologue, Maurice. *An Ambassador's Memoirs.* 3 vols. London, Hutchinson & Co., 1925.

Palmer, Gretta. *God's Underground by "Father George."* New York, Appleton-Century-Crofts, 1949.

Papen, Franz von. *Memoirs.* London, A. Deutsch, 1952.

Pares, Bernard. *A History of Russia.* New York, Alfred A. Knopf, Inc., 1949.

Picker, Henry, ed. *Hitlers Tischgespräche im Führerhauptquartier, 1941–1942.* First ed. Bonn, Athenäum, 1951; 2nd ed. Stuttgart, Seewald Verlag, 1965.

Polski, Mikhail. *Novye mucheniki rossiiskie.* Jordanville, N.Y., Holy Trinity Monastery, 1949.

Probleme des Ostraumes. Berlin, Reich Ministry for the Occupied Eastern Territories, 1942.

Propotschuk, Gregor. *Der Metropolit.* Munich, Verlag Ukraine, 1955.

Raevski, S. *Ukrainskaya Avtokefalnaya Tserkov.* Jordanville, N.Y., Holy Trinity Monastery, 1948.

Rauschning, Hermann. *Hitler Speaks.* London, Eyre & Spottiswoode Publishers, Ltd., 1939.

———— *The Revolution of Nihilism.* New York, Longmans, Green, 1939.

———— *The Voice of Destruction,* New York, G. P. Putnam's Sons, 1940.

Ribbentrop, Joachim von. *Zwischen London und Moskau.* Leoni, Druffel, 1954.

Richthofen, Bolko von, ed. *Bolschewistiche Wissenschaft und "Kulturpolitik."* 2nd ed. Königsberg, Ost-Europa Verlag, 1942.

Riess, Curt. *Joseph Goebbels.* Garden City, N.Y., Doubleday & Co., Inc., 1948.

Rosenberg, Alfred. *Memoirs.* Chicago, Ziff-Davis, 1949.

———— *Der Mythus des 20. Jahrhunderts.* Munich, Hoheneichen, 1935.

———— *Das Wesensfüge des Nationalsozialismus.* Munich, F. Eher, 1933.

Russian Orthodox Church. *Patriarkh Sergi i ego dukhovnoe nasledstvo.* Moscow, Patriarchate of Moscow, 1947.

———— *Pravda o religi v Rossii.* Moscow, Patriarchate of Moscow, 1942.

———— *The Russian Orthodox Church, Organization, Situation, Activity.* Moscow, Patriarchate of Moscow, 1959.

———— *Russkaya pravoslavnaya tserkov i velikaya otechestvennaya voina.* Moscow, Central State Publishing House, 1943[?].

Samarin, Vladimir D. *Civilian Life under the German Occupation, 1942–1944.* New York, Research Program on the USSR, mimeographed series, No. 58, 1954 (in Russian).

Schlesinger, Rudolf. *The Spirit of Post-war Russia: Soviet Ideology, 1917–1946.* London, D. Dobson, 1947.

Seraphim, Hans-Günther, ed. *Das politische Tagebuch Alfred Rosenbergs.* Göttingen, Musterschmidt Verlag, 1956.

Soviet Government Statements on Nazi Atrocities. London, Hutchinson, n.d.

Soviet War Documents. Washington, Embassy of the USSR, 1943.

Spinka, Matthew. *The Church and the Russian Revolution.* New York, The Macmillan Co., 1927.

———— *The Church in Soviet Russia.* New York, Oxford University Press, 1956.

Stratonov, I. *Russkaya tserkovnaya smuta, 1921–1931.* Berlin, Parabola, 1932.

Strauss, Leo, and Joseph Cropsey. *History of Political Philosophy.* Chicago, Rand McNally & Co., 1963.

Strik-Strikfeldt, Hauptmann. *Unser Verhalten zum Russen.* Berlin, Deutscher Verlag, n.d.

Struve, Nikita. *Les Chrétiens en U.R.S.S.* Paris, Editions du Seuil, 1963.

———— *Christians in Contemporary Russia.* New York, Charles Scribner's Sons, 1967.

Timasheff, Nicholas S. *Religion in Soviet Russia: 1917–1942.* London, Sheed & Ward, 1944.

Ulam, Adam B. *The Bolsheviks.* New York, The Macmillan Co., 1965.

Vakar, Nicholas P. *Belorussia.* Cambridge, Harvard University Press, 1956.

Valentinov, A. A., comp. *Chernaya kniga.* Paris, Russian National Students' Union, 1925.

Valori, Aldo. *Campagna di Russia.* 2 vols. Rome, Grafica Nazionale, 1951.

Werner, Paul. *Ein schweizer Journalist sieht Russland.* Olten, Walter, 1942.

Werth, Alexander, *Russia at War, 1941–1945.* New York, E. P. Dutton & Co., Inc., 1964.

Wiedmann, Hanns. *Landser, Tod und Teufel: Aufzeichnungen aus dem Feldzug im Osten.* Munich, R. Piper & Co., 1943.

Wolin, Simon, and Robert M. Slusser. *The Soviet Secret Police.* New York, Frederick A. Praeger, Inc., 1957.

Articles, Documents, Periodicals

Akten zur deutschen auswärtigen Politik, Series D (1937–1945). 7 vols. Baden-Baden (1950).

American Historical Association. Committee for the Study of War Documents, *Guides to German Records Microfilmed at Alexandria, Virginia,* Nos. 28, 31–33, 38–39, U.S. National Archives and Records Service, Washington, D.C.

Amtsblatt des Generalkommissars für Weissruthenien. Minsk.

Antireligioznik (Moscow), Nos. 1, 4, 5 (1939).

Antireligioznik sbornik (collection of antireligious articles "to aid propagandists and agitators"). Moscow: Workers' Press (1940).

Benevsky, Vladimir. "The Church Policy of Bolshevism. Report of October 12, 1941" (German ms.), Riga (1942). Several such ms. sources given here were consulted in private files; for further information see Dallin, "The German Occupation."

Bezbozhnik (Moscow), Nos. 4 (1924), 12 (1938).

Central Committee, Communist Party of the Soviet Union. "On the Organization of Scientific-Educational Propaganda," *Propagandist,* No. 18 (1944), 1–5.

"Circular of 'Trustees' for the Russian Population in the General District of Lithuania, April 7, 1943" (Russian ms.), in Archive of Russian and East European History and Culture, Columbia University.

Commander of the Security Police and the Security Service, Ostland. "Letter on Comments of Exarch Sergius in the *Deutsche Zeitung im Ostland,* March 4, 1943" (German ms.), in Yivo Institute for Jewish Research.

Curtiss, John S. "Non-Orthodox Religions in the U.S.S.R.," *American Review on the Soviet Union,* 8, No. 1 (1946), 3–14.

————— "The Russian Orthodox Church During the War," *American Review on the Soviet Union,* 7, No. 4 (1946), 33–44.

Dallin, Alexander. "Popular Attitudes and Behavior under the German Occupation, 1941–1944," Cambridge: Harvard Russian Research Center, Project on the Soviet Social System (Mar. 31, 1952).

————— "Summary Statement of B-Schedule on Wartime Occupation," Cambridge: Harvard University Refugee Interview Project, mimeograph (n.d.).

Dallin, Alexander, comp. "The German Occupation of the U.S.S.R. in World War II: A Bibliography," Washington: Department of State, External Research Paper No. 122 (1955).

Deutsche Bug-Zeitung. Amtsblatt des Generalkommissars für den Generalbezirk Nikolajew (March 1942-November 1943, semiweekly).

Deutsche Post aus dem Osten, Berlin: Verband der Russlandsdeutschen (1941–1942, monthly).

Der Deutsche in Transnistrien, Odessa (July 1942-January 1944, weekly).

Dienststelle Rosenberg. Memorandum on the "Ostland" (German ms.) (November 1942[?]), in Yivo Institute for Jewish Research.

Dionisius, Metropolitan. "Memorandum, July 15, 1942" (Russian ms.), in Archive of Russian and East European History and Culture, Columbia University.

Etzdorf, Hasso von. "Notes on Koch Speech at Rovno Conference, August 26, 1942" (German ms.).

Friedberg, B. "Alfred Rosenberg Named Reichsminister for the Eastern Territories" (German ms., n.d.), in Yivo Institute for Jewish Research.

Gesetzblatt der deutschen evangelischen Kirche (Aug. 10, 1934).

Hadamowsky, Eugen, and Eberhard Taubert. "Report on the Propaganda Situation in the East, September 17, 1942," (German ms.) in Yivo Institute for Jewish Research.

Harvard Refugee Interview Project. "A-Schedules" (n.d.) Items from this source on file at Harvard University Russian Research Center, Cambridge, Mass.

————— "B-Schedules on Wartime Occupation" (n.d.).

————— "Hans Koch," Protocol of June 1, 1951.

————— "Interview with Professor Markert," Protocol G-10 (n.d.).

Himmler, Heinrich. "Aktennotiz 5329. Führerhauptquartier, November 15, 1941" (German ms.). International Military Tribunal, Document NO-5329.

Inkeles, Alex. "Family and Church in the Postwar USSR," *Annals of the American Academy of Political and Social Sciences,* 263 (May 1949), 32–44.

International Military Tribunal. *The Trial of German Major War Criminals. Proceedings of the International Military Tribunal Sitting at Nuremberg.* 22 parts. London: H.M.S.O. (1946–1950).

———— *Trial of the Major War Criminals.* 42 vols. Nuremberg, International Military Tribunal (1947–1949). Abbreviated in notes as *TMWC.*

———— *Trials of War Criminals Before the Nürnberg Military Tribunals.* 15 vols. Washington: Government Printing Office (1949–1954).

Kempner, Robert. "The Nuremberg Trials as Sources," *American Political Science Review,* 44, No. 2 (June 1950), 447–459.

"Die Kirchenpolitik des Bolschewismus," Riga (1942), in Yivo Institute for Jewish Research.

Lammers, Hans-Heinrich. Memorandum of Aug. 21, 1943, on Führer's order Aug. 15 regarding Goebbels-Rosenberg jurisdictions (German ms.), in Yivo Institute for Jewish Research.

Lohse, Hinrich. Speech of Feb. 23, 1943, at conference of Reichskommissariat Ostland, Dept. III (German ms.), in Yivo Institute for Jewish Research.

Milwe-Schröden, "The Soviet Church and Religious Policy since June 22, 1941." See Reich Ministry for the Occupied Eastern Territories.

Minsker Zeitung (1942–1944).

"Minutes of the Conference of the Reich Minister for the Occupied Eastern Territories and Commanders of Army-Occupied Areas—Top Secret" (German ms.), Berlin (Jan. 4, 1943).

Müller, Major O. W. "Report No. 21—Secret" (German ms.) (October 8, 1942), in Yivo Institute for Jewish Research.

Muravev, E. F., and Iu. V. Dmitriev. "On Concreteness in the Study and Overcoming of Religious Survivals," *Voprosy Filosofi,* No. 3 (1961), trans. in *Soviet Review,* No. 2 (July 1961), 41–56.

Neumann, Inge S., comp. "European War Crimes Trials: A Bibliography," New York: Carnegie Endowment for International Peace (1951).

New York Herald-Tribune (Sept. 25, 1943).

The New York Times (Oct. 1, 7, 1941; Nov. 10, 1942; Jan. 8, Aug. 12, 18, Sept. 5, 1944; June 7, 1945).

Novoe Slovo, Berlin (1941–1944).

Oleshchuk, F. "For Concreteness of Scientific-Atheistic Propaganda," *Kommunist,* 5 (April 1958), 111–118.

Orthodox Church Bulletin, London (May 1943).

Die Ostkartei. Grundriss des Heraufbaus im Osten, Berlin, Nos. 1–6 (1943).

Ostland: Halbmonatsschrift für Ostpolitik, Berlin (1943–1944).

Ostland: Monatsschrift des Reichskommissars für das Ostland, Riga (1942–1944).

Pravoslavny Khristianin, Pskov (1942–1944).

"Preliminary Inventory of the Records of the U.S. Counsel for the Prosecution of Axis Criminality," Washington, D.C.: U.S. National Archives (1949).

Reich Chief Security Office. *Ereignismeldungen. UdSSR* (1941–1942). See U.S. National Archives and Records Service.

Reich Minister and Chief of the Reich Chancellery. "To the Reich Minister for Foreign Affairs, Mr. von Ribbentrop" (German ms.) (May 3, 1942).

"Reich Minister Rosenberg Visits the Ostland" (German ms.), press release (May 15, 1942), in Yivo Institute for Jewish Research.

Reich Ministry for the Occupied Eastern Territories. "Instructions on Attitudes Toward Eastern European Peoples Employed in Economic Enterprises of the Occupied Eastern Territories" (German ms.).

—— Letter of June 28, 1943, to Reichskommissariat Ostland, transmitting essay of Milwe-Schröden, "The Soviet Church and Religious Policy since June 22, 1941" (German ms.), in Yivo Institute for Jewish Research.

—— "Memorandum of June 1, 1944" (German ms.).

—— Press Chief. Memorandum of March 1942, "Improvement of Enlightment and Propaganda in the Eastern Space" (German ms.), in Yivo Institute for Jewish Research.

—— *Verkündungsblatt für das Ostland* (1941–1942).

—— *Verordnungsblatt* (1941–1944).

—— Department East. "Politics of the Ukraine. Report by Professor Pavel Saitsev to Taubert" (German ms.), Berlin (Mar. 29, 1943).

Reich Ministry for Popular Enlightenment and Propaganda. "Directives and Guidelines for Propaganda Work in the Occupied Eastern Areas—Strictly Confidential" (German ms.), 1st ed. (April 1944).

—— "Entry No. 500/43g. in Diary of Press Section Chief—Secret: Report on the Trip of Dr. Kausch to the Ukraine and Crimea from June 3 to 22, 1943" (German ms.), Berlin (June 26, 1943), in Yivo Institute for Jewish Research.

—— Letters of May 22 and June 5, 1943, regarding jurisdictional disputes with the Ostministerium (German ms.), in Yivo Institute for Jewish Research.

Reichsgesetzblatt, Part I, No. 20 (1937).

Reichskommissar for the Ostland. *Lagebericht* (pamphlet), Riga (n.d.).

Reichskommissariat Ostland. Letter of May 26, 1942, transmitting memorandum on Berlin conference with Ostministerium representatives of May 12–16 (German ms.), in Yivo Institute for Jewish Research.

—— *Stimmen aus der Ostland Presse*, Riga (1944).

—— *Verordnungsblatt* (1941–1944).

Reichskommissariat Ukraine. *Verordnungsblatt*, Pt. 1, "Verordnungen"; Pt. 2, "Bekanntmachungen." Rovno (1942–1943).

—— *Zentralblatt des Reichskommissars für die Ukraine*, Rovno (1941–1942).

Rosenberg, Alfred. Letter of Aug. 31, 1943, to Lammers, protesting Goebbels' exceeding his jurisdiction (German ms.), in Yivo Institute for Jewish Research.

—— "Speech at the Reception for Representatives of the German Administration in the Eastern Territories and Representatives of Latvian Economy, Science, and Art" (German ms.) (May 5, 1942), in Yivo Institute for Jewish Research.

Sauckel, Fritz. Speech on labor draft at conference with Lohse (German ms.) (Apr. 21, 1943), in Yivo Institute for Jewish Research.

Security Service, Ostland. Letter of Aug. 10, 1942, to Reichskommissariat Ostland (German ms.), in Yivo Institute for Jewish Research.

Seraphim, Metropolitan. "Appeal to All Russian Believers" (Russian ms.) (June 22, 1941) in Archive of Russian and East European History and Culture, Columbia University.

Sergius, Metropolitan. "Christmas Greetings to Parishes" (German ms.) (December 1942), in Yivo Institute for Jewish Research.

Seventh Army Interrogation Center (APO 758). "Facts and Opinions as Reported by Field Marshall von Weichs" (Oct. 12, 1945), No. SAIC/FIR/55.

Signal, "Special Issue on Troops at the Eastern Front" (December 1943).

Skinner, G. William. "China." Paper presented at September 1965 meeting of the American Political Science Association, Washington, D.C. (University Microfilms, Ann Arbor, Mich.)

Slinsky, Pavel. "Life in the Polotsk Area, 1941–44" (Russian ms.) (1952).

Spuler, Berthold. "Die orthodoxen Kirchen," *Internationale Kirchliche Zeitschrift* (Berne), 30 (1940), 94–106, 154–170; 31 (1941), 46–69, 158–168; 32 (1942), 38–60, 165–185; 33 (1943), 28–49, 159–172; 34 (1944), 50–74, 163–183.

Sputnik Agitatora, No. 10 (1943).

Svitich, Alexander. "The Orthodox Church in Poland and Its Autocephaly" (Russian ms.), 1959, in Archive of Russian and East European History and Culture, Columbia University.

"Telegram from Lithuanian Metropolitan Sergius to Lithuanian Bishops, April 7, 1943" (Russian ms.), in Archive of Russian and East European History and Culture, Columbia University.

"To All Peoples of the East" (German ms.) (n.d.), in Yivo Institute for Jewish Research.

[U.S. Department of the Army] Adjutant General's Office, Departmental Records Branch. "General List of Seized Records Available for Unofficial Research," Reference Aid No. 15, Washington, D.C. (1954).

U.S. Military Tribunals, Nuremberg. *Documents and Staff Evidence Analysis* (mimeographed), Nuremberg (1947–1948). On file in Library of Congress.

U.S. National Archives and Records Service. "Records of the Reich Ministry for the Occupied Eastern Territories, 1941–45," microfilm, Washington, D.C.: The American Historical Association, Committee for the Study of War Documents (1960).

———— Reich Chief Security Office. *Ereignismeldungen. UdSSR.,* Nos. 1–195 (June 1941-April 1942). *Meldungen aus den besetzten Ostgebieten,* Nos. 1–55 (May 1942-May 1943). Microfilms, Washington, D.C.: The American Historical Association, Committee for the Study of War Documents (1960).

War Documentation Project [Columbia University, Bureau of Applied Social Research]. "Guide to Captured German Documents," comp. Gerhard L. Weinberg *et al.,* Maxwell Air Force Base, Ala.: Human Resources Research Institute (1952).

Who's Who in Occupied Europe. London: British War Office (1944).

Zeitschriftendienst (1941–1945).

Zhurnal Moskovskoi Patriarkhi (1943–1953).

Notes

Chapter 1. The Background of Soviet Religious Policy

1. See John Maynard, *Russia in Flux* (New York, 1948), p. 35.

2. Maurice Paléologue, *An Ambassador's Memoirs* (London, 1925), III, 208–209.

3. G. P. Fedotov, *The Russian Religious Mind* (Cambridge, Mass., 1946), I, xii.

4. Nicholas S. Timasheff, "The Inner Life of the Russian Orthodox Church," in Cyril E. Black, ed., *The Transformation of Russian Society* (Cambridge, Mass., 1960), p. 426.

5. *Ibid.*, p. 431.

6. Alfred G. Meyer, *The Soviet Political System* (New York, 1965), chap. iv.

7. Walter Kolarz, *Religion in the Soviet Union* (New York, 1961), p. 48.

8. Karl Marx, "Contribution to the Critique of Hegel's Philosophy of Right." in T. B. Bottomore, ed., *Karl Marx: Early Writings* (London, 1963), pp. 43–44. (His italics).

9. Marx and Engels, *On Religion* (New York, 1964); I. A. Kryvelev, *Lenin o religi* (Moscow, 1960).

10. Karl Marx and Friedrich Engels, "Manifesto of the Communist Party," in Karl Marx, *Selected Works* (New York, 1933), I, 231.

11. *Ibid.*, p. 226.

12. Karl Marx, "The Communism of the Paper Rheinischer Beobachter," in Marx and Engels, *On Religion* (New York, 1964), pp. 83–84. This edition contains a number of important passages translated for the first time.

13. Karl Marx, *Capital: A Critique of Political Economy* (New York, 1936), p. 91.

14. Frederick Engels, *"Anti-Duehring"* (Chicago, 1907), p. 258.

15. *Ibid.*, pp. 140, 143–144.

16. Frederick Engels, "On the History of Early Christianity," in Marx and Engels, *On Religion*, p. 316.

17. Kryvelev, pp. 3–4.

18. *Ibid.*, pp. 6–7.

19. Adam B. Ulam, *The Bolsheviks* (New York, 1965), p. 9.

20. Kryvelev, p. 19.

21. V. I. Lenin, "Classes and Parties in their Relation to Religion and Churches" (*Sotsial-Demokrat,* No. 6, June 4, 1909), in his *Sochineniya,* 4th ed. (Moscow, 1942–1966), XV, 377–378.

22. Kryvelev, pp. 16–17.

23. John S. Curtiss, "Church and State," in Black, p. 409.

24. Lenin, "Proposed Speech on the Agrarian Question at the Second State Duma" (Mar. 21–25, 1908, entry in "Notebooks"), in *Sochineniya,* XII, 261.

25. Lenin, "Father Gapon" (*Vpered,* No. 31, January 1905), in *ibid.,* VIII, 86.

26. Lenin, "Socialism and Religion" (*Novaya Zhizn,* No. 28, Dec. 3, 1905), in *ibid.,* X, 68–69.

27. Lenin, "The Third Congress" (*Proletari,* No. 1, May 27, 1905), in *ibid.,* VIII, 414.

28. "Decree of the RSFSR Council of People's Commissars on the Separation of Church and State, and Schools and Church," in Kryvelev, p. 142.

29. *Ibid.,* p. 183.

30. See V. D. Bonch-Bruevich, *Izbrannye sochineniya* (Moscow, 1959–1963), vol. I: *O religi, religioznom sektantstve i tserkvi,* p. 65 n. 2 and pp. 200–213.

31. Lenin, "Results of Reaction" (*Proletari,* No. 33, July 23, 1908), in *Sochineniya,* XV, 166, 379.

32. Lenin, "On the Village Poor" (1903), in *ibid.,* VI, 384.

33. Lenin, "Classes and Parties," in *ibid.,* XV, 387.

34. Lenin, "On the Relations of the Workers Party to Religion" (*Proletari,* no. 45, May 13, 1909), in *ibid.,* XV, 379.

35. *Ibid.,* p. 380.

36. Lenin, "Classes and Parties," in *ibid.,* p. 387.

37. Lenin, "Socialism and Religion," in *ibid.,* X, 65–66.

38. Lenin, "Letters from Afar" (*Kommunisticheski international,* No. 3–4, 1924), in *ibid.,* XXIII, 327.

39. Lenin, "The Zubatov Men of Moscow in Petersburg," in *ibid.,* VI, 272.

40. Lenin, "The State and the Revolution" (September 1917), in *ibid.,* XXV, 392.

41. Lenin, "Socialism and Religion," in *ibid.,* X, 67.

42. Lenin, "On the Relations," in *ibid.,* XV, 372.

43. *Bezbozhnik,* no. 4, 1924, cited in Kryvelev, p. 18.

44. This has been noted by Nicholas S. Timasheff, in *Religion in Soviet Russia: 1917–1942* (London, 1944), and by David J. Dallin, in *The Real Soviet Russia* (New Haven, 1944).

45. For a similar geometrical representation of Red China's cultural revolution, see G. William Skinner's paper "China," presented at the September 1965 meeting of the American Political Science Association, Washington, D.C.

46. Kolarz, pp. 26–30.

47. Matthew Spinka, *The Church in Soviet Russia* (New York, 1956), pp. 10–11.

48. John S. Curtiss, *Church and State in Russia* (New York, 1940), p. 409.

49. John S. Curtiss, *The Russian Church and the Soviet State: 1917–1950* (Boston, 1953), p. 46.

50. Matthew Spinka, *The Church and the Russian Revolution* (New York, 1927), p. 120.

51. Timasheff, *Religion in Soviet Russia*, p. 23.

52. Curtiss, *Russian Church*, pp. 57, 63.

53. I. Stratonov, *Russkaya tserkovnaya smuta, 1921–1931* (Berlin, 1932), p. 13.

54. William C. Fletcher, *A Study in Survival: The Church in Russia 1927–1943* (New York, 1965), p. 16.

55. Wilhelm DeVries, *Kirche und Staat in der Sowjetunion* (Munich, 1959), p. 12.

56. See Georgi P. Fedotoff, *The Russian Church Since the Revolution* (London, 1928), p. 62.

57. Spinka, *Church in Soviet Russia*, pp. 36–37; see also William C. Emhardt, *Religion in Soviet Russia* (Milwaukee, 1929), p. 66.

58. See Emhardt, p. 134.

59. See Spinka, *Church in Soviet Russia*, p. 61, for reference to the secret Department for Church affairs in the Council of People's Commissars.

60. See Stratonov, pp. 150–151.

61. For list of 66 jailed bishops including Sergius, see A. A. Valentinov, comp., *Chernaya kniga* (Paris, 1925), p. 257.

62. See Spinka, *Church in Soviet Russia*, p. 63 and Appendix I (for text of announcement by Sergius).

63. See *ibid.*, pp. 66–67 and Appendix II (for text of "Declaration"). On the organization and aims of the Karlovtsi Synod, see also Stratonov, pp. 32–34.

64. Spinka, *Church in Soviet Russia*, pp. 70, 73.

65. Robert V. Daniels, "Stalin's Rise to Dictatorship, 1922–29," in Alexander Dallin and Alan F. Westin, eds., *Politics in the Soviet Union: 7 Cases* (New York, 1966), p. 29.

66. Spinka, *Church in Soviet Russia*, p. 73.

67. Fletcher, *Study in Survival*, p. 46.

68. DeVries, p. 14. For official protests of Sergius, see Paul B. Anderson, *People, Church and State in Modern Russia* (New York, 1944), pp. 106–110.

69. See Alex Inkeles, "Family and Church in the Postwar USSR," in *Annals of the American Academy of Political and Social Sciences*, May 1949, p. 42; also Julius F. Hecker, *Religion Under the Soviets* (New York, 1927).

70. Bernard Pares, *A History of Russia* (New York, 1949), p. 512.

71. Inkeles, "Family and Church," p. 43.

72. Pares, p. 515.

73. Dallin, *The Real Soviet Russia*, p. 61.

74. See, for example, Boris P. Kandidov, *Tserkov i shpionazh* (Moscow, 1937).

Chapter 2. Soviet Believers on the Eve of the War

1. William C. Fletcher, *A Study in Survival: The Church in Russia 1927–1943* (New York, 1965), pp. 46–48.

2. *Ibid.*, pp. 84–96. See also Mikhail Polski, *Novye mucheniki rossiiskie* (Jordanville, N.Y., 1949). For more fanciful versions of catacomb churchdom, see Arfved Gustavson, *Die Katakombenkirche* (Stuttgart, 1954), and in even less believable fashion, Gretta Palmer, *God's Underground by "Father George"* (New York, 1949).

3. Done under contract for the Air Force, this work, known as the Harvard Project on the Soviet Social System, is summarized by Raymond A. Bauer, Alex Inkeles, and Clyde Kluckhohn in *How the Soviet System Works* (Cambridge, 1956), as well as by Inkeles and Bauer in *The Soviet Citizen: Daily Life in a Totalitarian Society* (Cambridge, 1959). A critique by Daniel Bell entitled "How the Harvard System Works" appeared in his *The End of Ideology*, rev. ed. (New York, 1962), pp. 337–341.

4. For special effects on families of nonmanual workers, see Inkeles and Bauer, pp. 216–217, 222–223.

5. Harvard Refugee Interview Project, "A-Schedules," No. 131, pp. 40, 55. For an example of generational conflict between grandmother and child, see Anatoly Kuznetsov, *Babi Yar* (New York, 1967), pp. 24–25.

6. Harvard Refugee Interview Project, "A-Schedules," No. 447, p. 25.

7. Alfred G. Meyer, *The Soviet Political System* (New York, 1965), pp. 439–440.

8. Walter Kolarz, *Religion in the Soviet Union* (New York, 1961), p. 4.

9. Harvard Refugee Interview Project, "A-Schedules," No. 1664, p. 21.

10. Walter Birnbaum, *Christenheit in Sowjetrussland* (Tübingen, 1961), pp. 187–188.

11. Kolarz, pp. 27–28.

12. Harvard Refugee Interview Project, "A-Schedules," No. 139, p. 16.

13. *Ibid.*, No. 241, p. 24.

14. Kolarz, pp. 3–33. See also John S. Curtiss, *The Russian Church and the Soviet State: 1917–1950* (Boston, 1953), pp. 279–288.

15. Kolarz, pp. 11–14. See also Curtiss, *Russian Church*, p. 279, for League's growth from 1.9 million in 1938 to 2.9 million in 1940. For reports of stepped-up atheist campaigns in 1940 and appointment of Molotov's wife to head the League's women's division following Krupskaya's death in 1939, see Berthold Spuler, "Die orthodoxen Kirchen," *Internationale Kirchliche Zeitschrift* (Berne, 1940), 30: 155–157.

16. Curtiss, *Russian Church*, p. 289.

17. See Spuler, p. 155.

18. Harvard Refugee Interview Project, "A-Schedules," No. 136, p. 51.

19. W. H. Chamberlin, *Russia's Iron Age* (Boston, 1934), pp. 323–324.

20. Harvard Refugee Interview Project, "A-Schedules," No. 241, p. 11.

21. Cited by Curtiss, *Russian Church*, p. 288.

22. Wilhelm DeVries, *Kirche und Staat in der Sowjetunion* (Munich, 1959), p. 16.

23. Fletcher, *Study in Survival,* pp. 60–62.

24. Harvard Refugee Interview Project, "A-Schedules," No. 318, p. 13.

25. O. Fjodorow, *Die Religion in der UdSSR* (Berlin, 1947), pp. 20–21.

26. Cited by Fletcher, *Study in Survival,* p. 86.

27. *Ibid.,* p. 66.

28. Harvard Refugee Interview Project, "A-Schedules," Nos. 113, 191, cited by Barrington Moore, Jr., *Terror and Progress USSR* (Cambridge, Mass., 1954), p. 94.

29. Matthew Spinka, *The Church in Soviet Russia* (New York, 1956), p. 96.

Chapter 3. Nazi Ideology and Administrative Practice on Religion

1. T. L. Jarman, *The Rise and Fall of Nazi Germany* (New York, 1956), p. 55.

2. Franz Neumann, *Behemoth: The Structure and Practice of National Socialism* (New York, 1942), pp. 127–129.

3. Hermann Rauschning, *The Revolution of Nihilism* (New York, 1939).

4. Walter Birnbaum, *Christenheit in Sowjetrussland* (Tübingen, 1961), p. 180.

5. *Hitler's Table Talk, 1941–1944* (London, 1953), p. 322.

6. Walter Kolarz, *Religion in the Soviet Union* (New York, 1961), p. 20.

7. *Reichsgesetzblatt,* Part I, No. 20 (1937), p. 203.

8. For some outstanding examples, see "Sermon of Bishop Clemens August von Galen at St. Lamberti Church, Münster, on Aug. 3, 1941," in Johann Neuhäusler, *Kreuz und Hakenkreuz* (Munich, 1946), Part II, pp. 365–366; "Final Basic Appeal of Bishop D. Wurm to Hitler and Members of the Cabinet in the Case Against 'Privileged Non-Aryans,' July 16, 1943," in Heinrich Hermelink, *Kirche im Kampf* (Tübingen, 1950), pp. 654–656; "Speech of the Archbishop of Cologne at the Papal Coronation Mass in St. Martin's Cathedral, Cologne, March 12, 1944," in Wilhelm Corsten, *Kölner Aktenstücke zur Lage der Katholischen Kirche in Deutschland 1933–1945* (Cologne, 1949), p. 310.

9. *Hitler's Table Talk,* p. 304; see also J. S. Conway, *The Nazi Persecution of the Churches 1933–45* (London, 1968), pp. 284–285.

10. See, for example, Barrington Moore, Jr., *Soviet Politics: The Dilemma of Power* (Cambridge, Mass., 1951); R. N. Carew Hunt, *The Theory and Practice of Communism* (London, 1957), chap. xviii; George Lichtheim, *Marxism: An Historical and Critical Study* (New York, 1961).

11. Merle Fainsod, *How Russia Is Ruled* (Cambridge, Mass., 1953), p. 445.

12. Karl D. Bracher, *Die Auflösung der Weimarer Republik* (Villingen, 1960), pp. 407–414, 438–442.

13. See Hannah Arendt, *Eichmann in Jerusalem* (New York, 1963), p. 180.

14. For an evaluation of *Mein Kampf,* see Alan Bullock, *Hitler: A Study in Tyranny* (New York, 1962), pp. 121–122; for Hitler's own low estimate of Rosenberg's *Mythus,* see *Hitler's Table Talk,* p. 422.

15. Bullock, pp. 139–140.

16. *Ibid.,* pp. 284–307.

17. See Walther Hofer, *Der Nationalsozialismus: Dokumente 1933–1945* (Frankfurt, 1957), pp. 124–125, for a summary of such measures. For individual actions, see the following documents in International Military Tribunal, *Trial of the Major War Criminals,* 42 vols. (Nuremberg, 1947–1949) (cited hereafter as *TMWC*): 116-PS, Bormann's letter to Rosenberg enclosing copy of letter, Jan. 24, 1949, to Minister of Education, requesting restriction or elimination of theological academies; 122-PS, Bormann's letter to Rosenberg, Apr. 17, 1939, enclosing copy of Minister of Education letter, Apr. 6, 1939, on elimination of theological faculties in various universities; R-145, State Police Order, May 28, 1934, at Düsseldorf, signed Schmid, concerning sanction of denominational youth and professional associations and distribution of publications in churches. See also Neuhäusler, for order of Munich police headquarters banning Catholic Youth Organization, Apr. 23, 1934 (in Part I, p. 170), Order of Interior Minister of Oldenburg prohibiting religious newspaper supplements, June 1934 (Part II, p. 199), and Order of Munich Police Presidium banning religious publications, Feb. 29, 1936 (Part I, p. 215). For detailed documentation of the 1930–1935 period see also Hans Müller, *Katholische Kirche und Nationalsozialismus* (Munich, 1963).

18. Joseph Goebbels, *Diaries, 1942–1943* (Garden City, 1948), pp. 141–142.

19. Adolf Hitler, *Mein Kampf,* trans. James Murphy (London, 1939), p. 110.

20. *Ibid.,* p. 95.

21. Bullock, pp. 128–129.

22. Alfred Rosenberg, *Das Wesensfüge des Nationalsozialismus* (Munich, 1933), p. 76.

All translations of German and Russian sources are mine unless otherwise indicated.

23. Cited in Hofer, p. 121.

24. See Corsten, p. 63.

25. Cited in Neuhäusler, Part I, pp. 111–112.

26. Cited in Corsten, p. 63.

27. On negotiation of the Concordat, see Guenter Lewy, *The Catholic Church and Nazi Germany* (New York, 1964), chap. iii; for a somewhat self-serving account, see Franz von Papen, *Memoirs* (London, 1952), pp. 279–282; for a more balanced picture, see Conway, pp. 23–30.

28. For restrictions on Caritas, see Hofer, p. 124. See also the following documents in *TMWC*: 1482-PS, Secret letter, July 20, 1933, to provincial governments and the Prussian Gestapo from Frick concerning Confessional Youth Organizations; 1481-PS, Gestapo order, Jan. 20, 1938, dissolving and confiscating property of Catholic Youth Women's Organization in Bavaria. For censorship and ban on Catholic youth movements, see also n. 17, above.

29. Henry Picker, ed., *Hitlers Tischgespräche im Führerhauptquartier, 1941–1942* (Stuttgart, 1965), p. 150.

30. See Minutes of Foreign Office Meeting, June 22, 1942, in U.S. National Archives and Records Service, "Records of the Reich Ministry for the Occupied Eastern Territories, 1941–45," microfilm (Washington, 1960), Roll 22, Frames 813–819.

31. Letter of Lammers to Rosenberg, May 15, 1942, transmitting Ribbentrop memorandum of May 10, in *ibid.*, Frames 807–810.

32. For letter of Minister for Church Affairs to bishops of German dioceses, Mar. 23, 1937, see *Akten zur deutschen auswärtigen Politik 1918–1945*, Series D (1937–1945), vol. I (September 1937 to September 1938) (Baden-Baden, 1950), p. 761. For Gestapo order prohibiting circulation of papal message, Mar. 27, 1937, see Neühausler, Part I, pp. 230–231.

33. Credo of the "German Christian Denomination," Nov. 13, 1933, in Joachim Gauger, *Chronik der Kirchenwirren* (Elberfeld, 1934), Part I, p. 111. For a detailed history of the movement, see Kurt Meier, *Die Deutschen Christen* (Göttingen, 1964); see also the summary in Conway, chap. ii.

34. *Gesetzblatt der Deutschen Evangelischen Kirche,* August 10, 1934.

35. Gauger, p. 103.

36. "Theological Declaration on the Present Condition of the German Evangelical Church, issued by the Reichs-Confessional Church at Barmen-Gemarke, May 29–31, 1934," in Joachim Beckmann, *Kirchliches Jahrbuch für die Evangelische Kirche in Deutschland 1933–1944* (Gütersloh, 1948), pp. 64–65. For a comprehensive analysis of this document, see Arthur C. Cochrane, *The Church's Confession under Hitler* (Philadelphia, 1962).

37. See Franklin H. Littel, *The German Phoenix* (Garden City, 1960), p. 2.

38. Order to reform the administration of the German Evangelical Church, Apr. 19, 1934, in Beckmann, pp. 57–58.

39. "Message of the Confessing Synod of the Evangelical Church in the Old-Prussion Union to Its Congregations, Berlin-Dahlem, March 4–5, 1935," in Beckmann, pp. 85–86.

40. Quoted by Nathaniel Micklem, *National Socialism and the Roman Catholic Church* (London, 1939), p. 55.

41. See citations of Duncan B. Forrester, "Martin Luther and John Calvin," in Leo Strauss and Joseph Cropsey, *History of Political Philosophy* (Chicago, 1963), pp. 297–300.

42. Martin Luther, "Secular Authority: To What Extent It Should Be Obeyed," in *The Works of Martin Luther* (Philadelphia, 1915–1932), III, 230.

43. See *Reichsgesetzblatt.*

44. Hermann Rauschning, *Hitler Speaks* (London, 1939), p. 62.

45. See Hofer, p. 124.

46. Chancellery announcement of the temporary administration of the German Evangelical Church, Mar. 13, 1938, in Beckmann, p. 235; see also Conway, pp. 209–213.

47. Entry for Jan. 19, 1940, in Hans-Günther Seraphim, ed., *Das politische Tagebuch Alfred Rosenbergs* (Göttingen, 1956), p. 97.

48. *Ibid.*, p. 98.

49. For biographical data, see B. Friedberg, "Alfred Rosenberg Named Reichsminister for the Eastern Territories," (German ms.) in Yivo Institute for Jewish Research (File Occ E 3–47–53); see also Eugene Davidson, *The Trial of the Germans* (New York, 1966), pp. 127–129.

50. Alfred Rosenberg, *Memoirs* (Chicago, 1949), p. 28.

51. See Bullock, p. 122.

52. Rosenberg, *Memoirs,* pp. 72, 80.

53. Hans-Günther Seraphim, pp. 4–5.

54. Rosenberg, *Memoirs,* p. 104.

55. Hans-Günther Seraphim, p. 10. See also Report to Führer regarding confiscated art treasures, Mar. 20, 1941, in *TMWC* (014-PS).

56. Rosenberg, *Memoirs,* pp. 278–279.

57. Albert R. Chandler, *Rosenberg's Nazi Myth* (Ithaca, 1945), pp. 122–123.

58. Robert H. Jackson, *The Nürnberg Case* (New York, 1947), p. 143.

59. *Hitler's Table Talk,* p. 422.

60. Rosenberg, *Memoirs,* p. 83.

61. Hans-Günther Seraphim, pp. 199ff.

62. Alfred Rosenberg, *Der Mythus des 20. Jahrhunderts* (Munich, 1935), pp. 598ff.

63. Hans-Günther Seraphim, p. 56.

64. Note of the Holy See to the German Government, Jan. 29, 1936, in Neuhäusler, Part II, p. 199.

65. On Gestapo interventions, see *ibid.,* Part I, pp. 230–233.

66. Secret directive of the SD, Feb. 15, 1938, in *ibid,* Part I, p. 123. On the takeover of monasteries, see also SD reports of Apr. 9, 1940, and Sept. 12, 1940, in *ibid.,* Part I, pp. 125–126 and 155 respectively.

67. Hans-Günther Seraphim, pp. 56–57, 61.

68. Rosenberg, *Memoirs,* pp. 101–102.

69. Hans-Günther Seraphim, p. 63.

70. *Ibid.,* p. 204.

71. Rosenberg, *Memoirs,* p. 103.

72. Hans-Günther Seraphim, p. 87.

73. *Ibid.,* pp. 87–88.

74. On the bishops' awareness of this threat, see their pastoral letter of June 26, 1941, in Corsten, pp. 252ff.

75. Friedrich Heer, *Die Deutschen, der Nationalsozialismus und die Gegenwart* (Bielefeld, 1960)—cited in Rolf Hochhuth, *The Deputy* (New York, 1964), p. 305, though the source seems unavailable in U.S. libraries.

76. *Hitler's Table Talk,* p. 563.

77. Walter Hagen, *Die geheime Front* (Linz, 1950), pp. 34–35.

78. Dieter Schwarz, "The Big Lie of Political Catholicism," folios published in Berlin, 1938, cited by Hofer, pp. 133–134.

79. Martin Bormann, "Circular Letter to All Gauleiter on the Relation of National Socialism to Christianity," June 6, 1941, in *TMWC,* vol. 35, pp. 9–13 (075-D). See also Jackson, pp. 50, 130.

80. Hans-Günther Seraphim, pp. 42–44.

81. *Ibid.,* pp. 57–58.

82. Rosenberg, *Memoirs,* p. 100.

83. Hans-Günther Seraphim, pp. 168–171.

84. Chandler, pp. 122–123.

85. Rosenberg, *Memoirs,* pp. 191–192.

86. *Ibid.,* p. 100.

87. Cited in Micklem, p. 82.

88. Hans Günther Seraphim, p. 86; see also p. 165 for Kerrl's opposition in February 1940 to Rosenberg's new ideological assignment because it might lead to an intrusion into church affairs.

89. *Ibid.*, pp. 148–149.

90. *Ibid.*, pp. 168–171.

91. See n. 79, above.

92. Translation in Jackson, p. 50.

93. Memorandum on discussion between Rosenberg and Hitler, May 8, 1942, in *TMWC*, vol. 27, p. 286 (1520-PS).

Chapter 4. German Policy Toward the Orthodox Church: The Minister versus the Commissar

1. Hitler decree, Apr. 20, 1941, in *TMWC*, vol. 24, pp. 383–386 (865-PS).

2. Adolf Hitler, *Mein Kampf* (Munich, 1936), p. 742.

3. Henry Picker, ed., *Hitlers Tischgespräche im Führerhauptquartier, 1941–1942* (Stuttgart, 1965), p. 271.

4. "Führer's Decree on Administration," July 17, 1941, in *TMWC*, vol. 29, pp. 235–237 (1997-PS).

5. Entry for Jan. 19, 1940, in Hans-Günther Seraphim, ed., *Das politische Tagebuch Alfred Rosenbergs* (Göttingen, 1956), p. 97.

6. International Military Tribunal, *The Trial of German Major War Criminals: Proceedings of the International Military Tribunal Sitting at Nuremberg* (London, 1946–1950), VI, 221.

7. Alfred Rosenberg, *Memoirs* (Chicago, 1949), p. 277.

8. Wehrmacht Propaganda Branch, "Directives for Handling Propaganda in Project 'Barbarossa,'" June 9, 1941, in *TMWC*, vol. 34, pp. 191–195 (026-C).

9. Rafael Lemkin, *Axis Rule in Occupied Europe* (Washington, 1944), p. 9.

10. John A. Armstrong, *Ukrainian Nationalism* (New York, 1963), p. 170.

11. Adapted from Alexander Dallin, "Summary Statement of B-Schedule on Wartime Occupation" (Cambridge, Mass., n.d.), p. 4.

12. Stephen Graham, *Summing-Up on Russia* (London, 1951), pp. 51–52.

13. Fritz Lieb, *Russland unterwegs* (Berne, 1945), pp. 332–333.

14. Berthold Spuler, "Die orthodoxen Kirchen," *Internationale Kirchliche Zeitschrift* (Berne), 33 (1943), 34.

15. Metropolitan Seraphim, "Appeal to All Russian Believers" (Russian ms.), June 22, 1941, in Archive of Russian and East European History and Culture, Columbia University.

16. For the canonical contretemps of Seraphim's action, see Spuler, 30 (1940), 159–160.

17. See Alexander Svitich, "The Orthodox Church in Poland and Its Autocephaly" (Russian ms.), 1959, in Archive of Russian and East European History and Culture, Columbia University.

18. Harvard Refugee Interview Project, "Interview with Professor Markert" (Protocol G-10), n.d.

19. For abortive attempts by two temporary bishoprics in Belorussia to place themselves under Seraphim's jurisdiction, see Spuler, 32 (1942), 170; for a similar affair in Grodno, see 33 (1943), 34.

20. Ibid., 34, (1944), 64–65.

21. Graham, p. 52.

22. Memorandum on discussion between Rosenberg and Hitler, May 8, 1942, in *TMWC*, vol. 27, p. 289 (1520-PS).

23. Vladimir D. Samarin, *Civilian Life under the German Occupation, 1942–1944* (New York, 1954), p. 68 (in Russian).

24. Hermann Rauschning, *The Voice of Destruction* (New York, 1940), p. 132.

25. See Hans-Günther Seraphim, p. 69.

26. Letter of Schickedanz to Lammers, June 15, 1939 (doc. 1365-PS), cited in *ibid.*, pp. 141–147.

27. See Rosenberg memorandum, Apr. 2, 1941, in *TMWC*, vol. 36, pp. 547–554 (1017-PS).

28. Rosenberg memorandum, Apr. 29, 1941, in *TMWC*, vol. 26, p. 561 (1024-PS).

29. General instructions of Rosenberg to all Reich commissars in the occupied eastern territories, May 8, 1941, in *TMWC*, vol. 26, p. 579 (1030-PS); see "note 7" for deletions.

30. For censorship of Russian religious news for evidently the same reason by the Propaganda Ministry, see *Zeitschriftendienst*, Report No. 7060, June 26, 1942.

31. See Eugene Davidson, *The Trial of the Germans* (New York, 1966), p. 125.

32. See Peter Kleist, *Zwischen Hitler und Stalin, 1939–1945* (Bonn, 1950), pp. 145, 149–150.

33. For the short itinerary of his first visit to Belorussia and the Baltic states in May 1942, see *Deutsche Post aus dem Osten*, 14, no. 6 (June 1942); for his June 1943 tour of the Ukraine, during which he had to put up with Koch's insults, see Alexander Dallin, *German Rule in Russia, 1941–1945* (London, 1957), pp. 162–163.

34. See *ibid.*, pp. 84, 129, 136, 141, 160–161, 479; for an erroneous surmise that only two such meetings took place, cf. Davidson, p. 140.

35. Rosenberg, *Memoirs*, p. 279.

36. Kleist, p. 151.

37. See Brandenburg memoranda of June 12 and 14, 1944, in *TMWC*, vol. 25, pp. 88–92 (031-PS); see also Rosenberg letter to Lammers, July 20, 1944, in *ibid.*, pp. 362–365 (345-PS).

38. Rosenberg letter to Hitler, Oct. 12, 1944, in *TMWC*, vol. 41, pp. 185–194 (Rosenberg-14).

39. See U.S. National Archives and Records Service, "Records of the Reich Ministry for the Occupied Eastern Territories, 1941–45," microfilm (Washington, D.C., 1960), Roll 22, Frames 666–802.

40. Rosenberg testimony, *TMWC*, vol. 11, p. 462. But cf. Spuler, 32 (1942), 43, for an unsubstantiated report that the *Deutsche-Ukraine Zeitung*

(Lutsk) of Jan. 24, 1942, carried an announcement by Rosenberg and Koch that everyone could exercise his beliefs freely.

41. Ostministerium memorandum of Feb. 20, 1942, on conference of Jan. 27, in U.S. National Archives, "Records of the Reich Ministry," Frame 694.

42. *Ibid.*, Frames 666–668, 691–693, 695–696, 712, 732, 760–769.

43. Rosenberg instructions to a Reich commissar in the Ukraine, May 7, 1941, in *TMWC*, vol. 26, pp. 570-571 (1028–PS).

44. Rosenberg letter to Lohse and Koch, transmitting "Draft No. 16" of "Order Regarding Religious Freedom in the Occupied Eastern Territories," May 1942, in U.S. National Archives, "Records of the Reich Ministry," Frames 702–708.

45. *Ibid.*, Frame 707.

46. Alfred Rosenberg, "Speech at the Reception for Representatives of the German Administration in the Eastern Territories and Representatives of Latvian Economy, Science, and Art" (German ms.), May 15, 1942, in Yivo Institute for Jewish Research (File Occ E 3–53).

47. Alfred Meyer, ed., *Das Recht der besetzten Ostgebiete* (Munich, 1943), Section 0 i D4.

48. Kleist, pp. 159–160.

49. See Armstrong, p. 202.

50. Rosenberg, *Memoirs*, p. 185.

51. See Rosenberg memorandum, n.d., in *TMWC*, vol. 26, p. 595 (1056-PS).

52. Rosenberg speech of June 20, 1941, to his closest coworkers on the eastern problem, in *TMWC*, vol. 16, pp. 610–627 (1058-PS).

53. Rosenberg speech of August [?] 1942, to Reich commissars, in *TMWC*, vol. 39, pp. 412–425 (USSR-170).

54. Rosenberg, *Memoirs*, p. 185.

55. Cited by Victor H. Bernstein, *Final Judgment* (New York, 1947), p. 214. For text of top-secret memorandum of Dr. Otto Bräutigam, Oct. 25, 1942, see *TMWC*, vol. 16, pp. 332–342 (294-PS).

56. Sauckel speech at conference with Lohse (German ms.), Apr. 21, 1943, in Yivo Institute for Jewish Research (File Occ E 3–53).

57. Rosenberg speech of August 1942.

58. See Alexander Werth, *Russia at War, 1941–1945* (New York, 1964), p. 703.

59. Letter of Rosenberg to Keitel, Feb. 28, 1942, in *TMWC*, vol. 25, pp. 156–161 (081–PS).

60. Document 031–PS, cited in Robert H. Jackson, *The Nürnberg Case* (New York, 1947), p. 75; cf. *TMWC*, vol. 25, pp. 88–92.

61. Foreign Mail Censorship Office, Extract from current survey of opinion, Sept. 11–Nov. 11, 1942, in *TMWC*, vol. 25, pp. 77–78 (018–PS).

62. Cited in Bernstein, p. 37.

63. Harvard Refugee Interview Project, "Hans Koch," Protocol of June 1, 1951, p. 8.

64. "Minutes of the Conference of the Reich Minister for the Occupied Eastern Territories and Commanders of Army-Occupied Areas—Top Secret," Berlin (German ms.), Jan. 4, 1943.

65. Commander of the Security Police and the Security Service, Ostland, "Letter on Comments of Exarch Sergius in the *Deutsche Zeitung im Ostland*, Mar. 4, 1943" (German ms.).

66. Nicholas P. Vakar, *Belorussia* (Cambridge, Mass., 1956), p. 278.

67. See Armstrong, p. 209.

68. Reich Ministry for the Occupied Eastern Territories, Church Affairs Section, report to Rosenberg, June 30, 1944, as cited by Dallin, *German Rule*, p. 492.

69. Memorandum of July 16, 1941, on discussion by Hitler with Rosenberg, Lammers, Keitel, and Göring ("Aktenvermerk" of Bormann), in *TMWC*, vol. 38, pp. 86–93 (221–L).

70. Note of Altenstadt to Bräutigam, Apr. 11, 1943, and enclosure of Koch's speech in Kiev on Mar. 5, 1943, in *TMWC*, vol. 27, pp. 9–11 (1130–PS).

71. See Slawomir Orlowski, *Erich Koch pered polskim sudom* (Moscow, 1961), pp. 33–34.

72. See Kleist, pp. 180–181.

73. Orlowski, p. 203.

74. Hinrich Lohse, Speech at conference of Reichskommissariat Ostland, Dept. III, Feb. 23, 1943 (German ms.), in Yivo Institute for Jewish Research (File Occ E 3–53).

75. Cited in Meyer, *Das Recht*, Sections U i D2; O i D4.

76. Dienststelle Rosenberg, Memorandum on the "Ostland" (German ms.), November [?] 1942, in Yivo Institute for Jewish Research (File Occ E 20–23).

77. See Dallin, *German Rule*, p. 163.

78. See Kleist, pp. 181–182.

79. Hasso von Etzdorf, "Notes on Koch Speech at Rovno Conference, August 26, 1942" (German ms.); see also excerpts in *TMWC*, vol. 25, pp. 317–318 (264–PS).

80. Memorandum of July 16, 1941, in *TMWC*, vol. 38, p. 93, for Rosenberg's counter, see Memorandum of May 8, 1942, in *TMWC*, vol. 27, p. 286 (1520–PS).

81. Kleist, pp. 183–184.

82. Picker (1st ed., Bonn, 1951), p. 72.

83. *Ibid.* (2nd ed., Stuttgart, 1965), p. 150.

84. See Friedrich Heyer, *Die orthodoxe Kirche in der Ukraine von 1917 bis 1945* (Cologne, 1953), pp. 172–195.

85. See Dallin, *German Rule*, p. 482 n. 3; also Spuler, 32 (1942), 170–172. For a field survey by the *Einsatzgruppen*, see U.S. National Archives and Records Service, Reich Chief Security Office, *Ereignismeldungen. UdSSR*, microfilm (Washington, D.C. 1960), No. 117 (Oct. 18, 1941), Roll 234, Frames 2722943–2722950.

86. Harvard Refugee Interview Project, "Hans Koch," pp. 8–9. For the Gestapo version that finds Dr. Koch as well as Rosenberg "too accommodating to Ukrainian wishes," see U.S. National Archives and Records Service, Reich

Chief Security Office, *Ereignismeldungen,* No. 52 (Aug. 14, 1941), Roll 233, Frame 2721903.

87. See Heyer, pp. 213, 217–218.

88. *Ibid.,* p. 184; see also Armstrong, pp. 202–203.

89. Reich Ministry for the Occupied Eastern Territories, Press Chief, memorandum of March 1942, "Improvement of Enlightenment and Propaganda in the Eastern Space" (German ms.), in Yivo Institute for Jewish Research (File Occ E 15–16).

90. Reichskommissariat Ukraine, *Zentralblatt des Reichskommissars für die Ukraine* (marked "Confidential"), Edition "A" Nos. 34–35 (Rovno), Feb. 19, 1942.

91. See Spuler, 32 (1942), 172.

92. See Armstrong, p. 201.

93. Reichskommissariat Ukraine, *Zentralblatt,* I, 202, 495, Dec. 8, 1941.

94. Memorandum of Dr. Bräutigam, in *TMWC,* vol. 26, pp. 336–341.

95. See Orlowski, p. 35.

96. Memorandum on personnel for the East, from Rosenberg files, July 9, 1941 (doc. 1040–PS), cited in Armstrong, p. 199.

97. Memorandum on discussion between Rosenberg and Hitler, May 8, 1942, in *TMWC,* vol. 27, p. 286 (1520–PS).

98. See Orlowski, pp. 24, 42, 45, 56–58.

99. See Kleist, p. 192.

100. See Orlowski, p. 67.

101. Decree of July 27, 1941, in International Military Tribunal *Trials of War Criminals Before the Nürnberg Military Tribunals* (Washington, D.C., 1949–1954), vol. 13, p. 849 (NI-3777).

102. Speech of Aug. 26, 1942, in *TMWC,* vol. 25, p. 318 (264-PS).

103. Letter of Koch to Rosenberg, Mar. 6, 1943, in *TMWC,* vol. 25, pp. 255–288 (192-PS).

104. Koch's speech in Kiev, Mar. 5, 1943, in *TMWC,* vol. 27, pp. 9–11 (1130-PS).

105. Reich Ministry for Popular Enlightenment and Propaganda, "Entry No. 500/43g. in Diary of Press Section Chief—Secret: Report on the Trip of Dr. Kausch to the Ukraine and Crimea from June 3 to 22, 1943" (German ms.), Berlin, June 26, 1943, in Yivo Institute for Jewish Research (File Occ E 4–11).

106. Cited in Bernstein, p. 117.

107. See Reich Ministry for the Occupied Eastern Territories, Press Chief memorandum of May 1942; see also his "Situation Report," April 1942, in Yivo Institute for Jewish Research (File Occ E 15–16).

Chapter 5. German Policy Toward the Orthodox Church: The Ancillary Agencies

1. Walther Hofer, *Der Nationalsozialismus: Dokumente 1933–1945* (Frankfurt, 1957), pp. 274–275. For a microfilm record of Einsatzgruppen reports June 1941 to May 1943, see U.S. National Archives and Records Service, Reich

Chief Security Office, *Ereignismeldungen. UdSSR*, Nos. 1–195; *Meldungen aus den besetzten Ostgebieten*, Nos. 1–55 (Washington, 1960), Rolls 233–236.

2. U.S. Military Tribunals, Nuremberg, *Documents and Staff Evidence Analysis*, No. 2650 (Nuremberg, 1947–1948).

3. Heinrich Himmler, "Aktennotiz 5329. Führerhauptquartier, November 15, 1941" (German ms.), International Military Tribunal, Document NO-5329.

4. Heinrich Himmler, "Security Questions," Oct. 14, 1943, in *TMWC*, vol. 37, pp. 498–523 (070-L). For jurisdictional dispute at a subordinate level, see letter of Security Service, Ostland, to Reichskommissariat Ostland, Aug. 10, 1942, claiming that "work on sects and religious organizations" is its prerogative, in Yivo Institute for Jewish Research (File Occ E [Ch] 95).

5. See U.S. Military Tribunals, *Documents*, No. 4787, Dec. 5, 1941. See also U.S. National Archives and Records Service, *Ereignismeldungen. UdSSR*, No. 142 (Dec. 5, 1941), Roll 234, Frames 2723351–2723352.

6. See S. Raevski, *Ukrainskaya Avtokefalnaya Tserkov* (Jordanville, N.Y., 1948), p. 15; see also John A. Armstrong, *Ukrainian Nationalism* (New York, 1963), p. 206.

7. U.S. Military Tribunals, *Documents*, No. 4532, July 5, 1941. See also U.S. National Archives and Records Service, *Ereignismeldungen, UdSSR*, No. 13 (July 5, 1941), Roll 233, Frame 2721423.

8. See Armstrong, pp. 79–82. For biographies of Szepticky, see Stepan Baran, *Mitropolit Andrei Sheptitski* (Munich, 1947), and Gregor Propotschuk, *Der Metropolit* (Munich, 1955); for his abortive efforts to unify Ukrainian Orthodox and Uniates, see Berthold Spuler, "Die orthodoxen Kirchen," *Internationale Kirchliche Zeitschrift* (Berne), 32 (1942), 45, 173.

9. U.S. National Archives and Records Service, *Ereignismeldungen. UdSSR*, No. 52 (Aug. 15, 1941), Roll 233, Frame 2721903.

10. *Ibid.*, No. 60 (Aug. 22, 1941), Roll 233, Frames 2722046–2722047.

11. *Ibid.*, No. 86 (Sept. 17, 1941), Roll 233, Frames 2722365–2722366.

12. SS-Obergruppenführer Berger to Himmler, July 26, 1943, cited in Armstrong, p. 173.

13. SS-Obergruppenführer Berger to Brandt, July 22, 1943, *ibid.*

14. U.S. Military Tribunals, *Documents*, No. 36, July 28, 1941. See also U.S. National Archives and Records Service, *Ereignismeldungen. UdSSR*, No. 36 (July 28, 1941), Roll 233, Frames 2721692–2721694, and No. 43 (Aug. 5, 1941), Roll 233, Frames 2721778–2721781.

15. *Ibid.* No. 69 (Aug. 31, 1941), Roll 233, Frame 2722145, reporting on the Baltic states.

16. *Ibid.*, No. 73 (Sept. 4, 1941), Roll 233, Frame 2722179, reporting on Belorussia.

17. U.S. Military Tribunals, *Documents* No. 2954, July 26, 1941; see also U.S. National Archives and Records Service, *Ereignismeldungen. UdSSR*, No. 34 (July 26, 1941), Roll 233, Frame 2721671.

18. *Ibid.*, No. 89 (Sept. 20, 1941), Roll 233, Frame 2722461.

19. U.S. Military Tribunals, *Documents*, No. 4485, Aug. 31, 1941.

20. *Ibid.*, No. 2949, Aug. 5, 1941. See also U.S. National Archives and Records Service, *Ereignismeldungen. UdSSR*, No. 45 (Aug. 7, 1941), Roll 233, Frame 2721821.

21. Henry Picker, ed., *Hitlers Tischgespräche im Führerhauptquartier*, *1941–1942* (Stuttgart, 1965), p. 148.

22. U.S. Military Tribunals, *Documents*, No. 2950, Aug. 1, 1941.

23. U.S. National Archives and Records Service, *Ereignismeldungen. UdSSR*, No. 43 (Aug. 5, 1941), Roll 233, Frame 2721796.

24. *Ibid.*, No. 52 (Aug. 14, 1941), Roll 233, Frame 2721914; see also U.S. Military Tribunals, *Documents*, No. 4540, Aug. 14, 1941.

25. Rolf Hochhuth, *The Deputy* (New York, 1964), p. 309.

26. U.S. National Archives and Records Service, *Ereignismeldungen. UdSSR*, No. 73 (Sept. 4, 1941), Roll 233, Frame 2722179; No. 90 (Sept. 21, 1941), Roll 233, Frames 2722487–2722489; No. 122 (Oct. 23, 1941), Roll 234, Frame 2723019; No. 145 (Dec. 12, 1941), Roll 234, Frame 2723394.

27. For the later revision of Goebbels' views on Russia, see Curt Riess, *Joseph Goebbels* (Garden City, 1948), p. 212.

28. For Goebbels' comments on Rosenberg's incompetence, see Louis P. Lochner, ed., *The Goebbels Diaries* (Garden City, 1948), pp. 58, 84–85, 143, 331, 366, 516; for his dismay at Koch's rule by a "clout on the head," see p. 185.

29. See Riess, p. 97.

30. Reich Ministry for Popular Enlightenment and Propaganda, "Directives and Guidelines for Propaganda Work in the Occupied Eastern Areas—Strictly Confidential" (German ms.), 1st ed., April 1944, p. 26.

31. *Zeitschriftendienst*, Report No. 7060, June 26, 1942.

32. Alexander Dallin, *German Rule in Russia, 1941–1945* (London, 1957), p. 181.

33. See draft of memorandum by Goebbels to Hitler, May 22, 1943, in Yivo Institute for Jewish Research (File Occ E 18–19); for further evidence of Rosenberg's attempts to clip Goebbels' wings, see letter of Naumann to Schaub, June 5, 1943, *ibid.*

34. See memorandum of Lammers, Aug. 21, 1943, transmitting Führer order of Aug. 15, in Yivo Institute for Jewish Research (File Occ E 12).

35. See letter of Rosenberg to Lammers, Aug. 31, 1943, *ibid.*

36. Lochner, pp. 546–547.

37. *Ibid.*, p. 225.

38. *Ibid.*, pp. 201–202.

39. Eugen Hadamowsky and Eberhard Taubert, "Report on the Propaganda Situation in the East, September 17, 1942" (German ms.), in Yivo Institute for Jewish Research (File Occ E 18–19).

40. *Ibid.*, p. 40

41. See Dallin, *German Rule*, p. 330.

42. "To All Peoples of the East," n.d. (German ms.) in Yivo Institute for Jewish Research (File Occ E 18–19).

43. U.S. National Archives and Records Service, *Ereignismeldungen. UdSSR*, No. 89 (Sept. 20, 1941), Roll 233, Frame 2722458; No. 145 (Dec. 12, 1941), Roll 234, Frame 2723395.

44. Reichshauptamtsleiter Oberführer Scheidt, "Cultural-Political Tasks in the Occupied Eastern Areas," in *Probleme des Ostraumes* (Berlin, 1942).

45. Reich Ministry for the Occupied Eastern Territories, Press Chief, memorandum of March 1942, "Improvement of Enlightenment and Propaganda in the Eastern Space," (German ms.), in Yivo Institute for Jewish Research (File Occ E 15–16).

46. *Signal,* "Special Issue on Troops on the East Front," December 1943, pp. 33ff.

47. *Zeitschriftendienst,* Report No. 7060; Report No. 7113 (marked "Strictly Confidential"), June 26, 1942.

48. For an ambiguous photograph of soldiers said to be dismantling a wayside shrine (they could as well be assembling it), see Slawomir Orlowski, *Erich Koch pered polskim sudom* (Moscow, 1961), p. 104. Likewise of doubtful authenticity are the charges of desecration made by Nikolai, Metropolitan of Kiev and Galicia, in *The Russian Orthodox Church and the War against Fascism* (Moscow, 1943), pp. 26–27. See also O. Fjodorow, *Die Religion in der UdSSR* (Berlin, 1947), pp. 30–34.

49. Seventh Army Interrogation Center (APO 758), "Facts and Opinions as Reported by Field Marshal von Weichs" (October 12, 1945), No. SAIC/ FIR/ 55.

50. Heinz Guderian, *Panzer Leader* (London, 1952), p. 228.

51. Heinz Guderian, *Erinnerungen eines Soldaten* (Heidelberg, 1951), p. 40.

52. *Deutsche Post aus dem Osten* (Berlin), 13 (September 1941), 11–12.

53. See Dallin, *German Rule,* p. 478.

54. U.S. National Archives and Records Service, *Ereignismeldungen. UdSSR,* No. 43 (Aug. 5, 1941), Roll 233, Frame 2721781; No. 50 (Aug. 12, 1941), Roll 233, Frame 2721883; No. 73 (Sept. 4, 1941), Roll 233, Frames 2722179–2722180.

55. See, for example, *ibid.,* No. 128 (Nov. 3, 1941), Roll 234, Frames 2723085–2723086.

56. *Ibid.,* No. 90 (Sept. 21, 1941), Roll 233, Frames 2722487–2722489; No. 122 (Oct. 23, 1941), Roll 234, Frame 2723019; No. 145 (Dec. 12, 1941), Roll 234, Frames 2723394–2723395.

57. U.S. National Archives and Records Service, *Meldungen aus den besetzten Ostgebieten,* No. 25 (Oct. 6, 1942), Roll 236, Frame 2724966; No. 34 (Dec. 18, 1942), Roll 236, Frames 2725266–2725267.

58. Friedrich Heyer, *Die orthodoxe Kirche in der Ukraine von 1917 bis 1945* (Cologne, 1953), pp. 170–171; see also Spuler, 31 (1941), 160.

59. Oleg Anisimov, *The German Occupation in Northern Russia During World War II: Political and Administrative Aspects* (New York, 1954), pp. 24–25 (in Russian).

60. Vladimir D. Samarin, *Civilian Life under the German Occupation, 1942–1944* (New York, 1954), p. 51 (in Russian).

61. See Heyer, p. 171.

62. *Ibid.,* p. 216.

63. For an account of the two Galician regiments, see Armstrong, p. 75; for a report on the Kiev and Kharkov governments, p. 104; for Gestapo countermeasures, p. 106.

64. See Orlowski, p. 206.

65. See Dallin, *German Rule*, pp. 518–519.

66. U.S. National Archives and Records Service, *Ereignismeldungen. UdSSR*, No. 90 (Sept. 21, 1941), Roll 233, Frame 2722488.

67. Alfred Rosenberg, *Memoirs* (Chicago, 1949), p. 101.

68. August Haussleiter, *An der mittleren Ostfront* (Nuremberg, 1942), pp. 216, 246.

69. See Armstrong, pp. 101–102.

70. Paul Werner, *Ein schweizer Journalist sieht Russland* (Olten, 1942), p. 98.

71. Major O. W. Müller (Ostministerium Representative with Heeres Gruppe Mitte), "Report No. 21—Secret" (German ms.), Oct. 8, 1942, pp. 15–16.

72. U.S. National Archives and Records Service, *Ereignismeldungen. UdSSR*, No. 73 (Sept. 4, 1941), Roll 233, Frame 2722178.

73. Minutes of the conference of Dec. 18, 1942 (Jan. 4, 1943) (doc. NO-1481), as cited by Dallin, *German Rule*, pp. 152–154.

74. Memorandum of July 16, 1941, on discussion by Hitler with Rosenberg, Lammers, Keitel, and Göring ("Aktenvermerk" of Bormann), in *TMWC*, vol. 38, p. 39.

75. See, for example, Samarin, p. 13.

76. See Armstrong, p. 120; also Dallin, *German Rule*, pp. 320–373.

77. U.S. National Archives and Records Service, *Ereignismeldungen. UdSSR*, No. 190 (Apr. 8, 1942), Roll 235, Frame 2724162.

78. Cited in *TMWC*, vol. 39, p. 371.

79. Reich Ministry for the Occupied Eastern Territories (III Mi/i/), "Instructions on Attitudes Toward Eastern Peoples Employed in Economic Enterprises of the Occupied Eastern Territories" (German ms.).

80. Memorandum of Dr. Otto Bräutigam (marked "Secret"), Oct. 25, 1942, in *TMWC*, vol. 26, pp. 332–342 (294-PS).

81. Franz von Papen, *Memoirs* (London, 1952), pp. 179–182.

82. See Dallin, *German Rule*, pp. 40–42.

83. Memorandum of July 16, 1941, in *TMWC*, vol. 38, p. 93.

84. Dallin, *German Rule*, p. 475 n. 2.

85. Since 1939, by his own account, in Papen, p. 457.

86. Joachim von Ribbentrop, *Zwischen London und Moskau* (Leoni, 1954), p. 255.

87. U.S. National Archives and Records Service, *Meldungen aus den besetzten Ostgebieten*, No. 34 (Dec. 18, 1942), Roll 236, Frame 2725268.

88. Rosenberg, "Aktennotiz für den Führer," Aug. 22, 1941 (doc. 1053-PS), as cited by Dallin, *German Rule*, p. 478.

89. Ribbentrop, p. 130.

90. Reynolds and Eleanor Packard, *Balcony Empire* (New York, 1942), p. 230; see also Aldo Valori, *Campagna di Russia* (Rome, 1951), I, 244.

91. Lammers to Rosenberg, Oct. 18, 1942, in U.S. National Archives and Records Service, "Records of the Reich Ministry for the Occupied Eastern Territories, 1941–45" (Washington, 1960), Roll 22, Frames 825–827.

92. U.S. Military Tribunals, *Documents*, No. 4540, Aug. 14, 1941; see also U.S. National Archives and Records Service, *Ereignismeldungen. UdSSR*, No. 52 (Aug. 14, 1941), Roll 233, Frame 2721914.

93. U.S. Military Tribunals, *Documents*, No. 32, July 26, 1941.

94. U.S. National Archives and Records Service, *Ereignismeldungen. UdSSR*, No. 132 (Nov. 12, 1941), Roll 234, Frame 2722951.

95. U.S. Military Tribunals, *Documents*, No. 50, Aug. 12, 1941.

96. U.S. National Archives and Records Service, *Ereignismeldungen, UdSSR*, No. 132 (Nov. 12, 1941), Roll 234, Frame 2723148; No. 154 (Jan. 12, 1942), Roll 234, Frame 2723573.

97. Reich Minister and Chief of the Reich Chancellery, "To the Reich Minister for Foreign Affairs, Mr. von Ribbentrop" (German ms.), RK 6233A, May 3, 1942.

98. Ribbentrop to Lammers, May 10, 1942, in U.S. National Archives and Records Service, "Records of the Reich Ministry," Roll 22, Frame 810. For Rosenberg's peevish comment that this Foreign Office function was superfluous and his staff was capable of taking exclusive charge in the area, see Rosenberg to Lammers, May 27, 1942, *ibid.*, Frames 811–812.

99. See Dallin, *German Rule*, pp. 135–136; see also "Memorandum on Discussion Between Rosenberg and Hitler," May 8, 1942, in *TMWC*, vol. 27, p. 289 (1520-PS).

Chapter 6. The Popular Reaction to German Religious Policy in the East

1. For example, see O. Fjodorow, *Die Religion in der UdSSR* (Berlin, 1947), chap. iii.

2. David J. Dallin, *The Real Soviet Russia* (New Haven, 1944), p. 33.

3. See, for example, Vladimir D. Samarin, *Civilian Life under the German Occupation, 1942–1944* (New York, 1954), p. 11 (in Russian); see also Oleg Anisimov, *The German Occupation in Northern Russia During World War II: Political and Administrative Aspects* (New York, 1954), p. 4 (in Russian).

4. Samarin, p. 11.

5. Friedrich Heyer, *Die orthodoxe Kirche in der Ukraine von 1917 bis 1945* (Cologne, 1953), p. 171. See also Reich Ministry for the Occupied Eastern Territories, Press Chief, memorandum of March 1942, "Improvement of Enlightenment and Propaganda in the Eastern Space," in Yivo Institute for Jewish Research (File Occ E 15–16), p. 6.

6. Samarin, p. 11.

7. Alexander Dallin, "Popular Attitudes and Behavior under the German Occupation, 1941–1944" (Cambridge, Mass., Mar. 31, 1952), p. 39.

8. John A. Armstrong, *Ukrainian Nationalism* (New York, 1963), pp. 118–125.

9. U.S. National Archives and Records Service, Reich Chief Security Office, *Ereignismeldungen. UdSSR*, No. 19 (July 11, 1941), Roll 233, Frame 2721473.

10. See Vasili Alexeev, *Russian Orthodox Bishops in the Soviet Union, 1941–1953* (New York, 1954), p. 88 (in Russian); see also Heyer, p. 166.

11. Alexeev, pp. 91–92.

12. See Metropolitan Nikolai, *The Russian Orthodox Church and the War against Fascism* (Moscow, 1943), pp. 18–20; see also Russian Orthodox Church, *Patriarkh Sergi i ego dukhovnoe nasledstvo* (Moscow, 1947), p. 89.

13. For Reichskommissariat Ostland memorandum of May 26, 1942, backing Sergius as a means to avoid "Latvianization and Estonization" of the churches, see Files Occ E (Ch) 7–8, in Yivo Institute for Jewish Research; for Christmas Message, 1942, in which Sergius thanks the Army High Command for approving his diocesan authority, see File Occ E (Ch) 11.

14. Nikita Struve, *Christians in Contemporary Russia* (New York, 1967), pp. 69–72.

15. See U.S. National Archives and Records Service, *Ereignismeldungen. UdSSR*, No. 34 (July 26, 1941), Roll 233, Frame 2721671; No. 53 (Aug. 15, 1941), Roll 233, Frame 2721924; No. 162 (Jan. 30, 1942), Roll 234, Frame 2723742.

16. *Ibid.*, No. 165 (Feb. 6, 1942), Roll 234, Frame 2723797; for report of 60 priests in the mission, see Heyer, p. 166.

17. U.S. National Archives and Records Service, *Ereignismeldungen. UdSSR*, No. 96 (Sept. 27, 1941), Roll 233, Frames 2722662–2722663; No. 163 (Feb. 2, 1942), Roll 234, Frames 2723766–2723767.

18. *Ibid.*, No. 173 (Mar. 2, 1942), Roll 235, Frame 2723941; No. 182 (Mar. 18, 1942), Roll 235, Frame 2724020.

19. *Ibid.*, No. 195 (Apr. 24, 1942), Roll 235, Frames 2724311–2724312; *Meldungen aus den besetzten Ostgebieten*, No. 28 (Nov. 6, 1942), Roll 236, Frames 2725077–2725083.

20. Commander of the Security Police and the Security Service, Ostland, "Letter on Comments by Exarch Sergius in the *Deutsche Zeitung im Ostland*, March 4, 1943" (German ms.).

21. "Circular of 'Trustees' for the Russian Population in the General District of Lithuania, April 7, 1943" (Russian ms.), in Archive of Russian and East European History and Culture, Columbia University.

22. "Telegram from Lithuanian Metropolitan Sergius to Lithuanian Bishops, April 7, 1943" (Russian ms.), in *ibid.*

23. See Alexander Dallin, *German Rule in Russia, 1941–1945* (London, 1957), p. 490 n. 1.

24. Harvard Refugee Interview Project, "B-Schedules on Wartime Occupation," No. 67; for a version attributing the murder to Soviet agents, see I. Kasyak, *Z gistory Pravaslaunai Tsarkvi Belaruskaga Narodu* (New York, 1956), p. 103; for an open-ended account, see Heyer, p. 167.

25. Reichkommissariat Ostland, *Stimmen aus der Ostland Presse* (Riga), vol. III, No. 1 (1944).

26. Serge Bolshakoff, *The Christian Church and the Soviet State* (New York, 1942), pp. 69–71.

27. Msgr. A. M. [Bishop Athanasius], *Materialy da history Pravaslaunae Belaruskae Tsarkvy* (1948, n.p.).

28. See Nicholas P. Vakar, *Belorussia* (Cambridge, Mass., 1956), pp. 189–190.

29. U.S. National Archives and Records Service, *Ereignismeldungen. UdSSR*, No. 36. (July 28, 1941), Roll 233, Frame 2721693; see also Kasyak, p. 137.

30. Vakar, p. 278.

31. U.S. National Archives and Records Service, *Ereignismeldungen. UdSSR*, No. 180 (Mar. 13, 1942), Roll 235, Frame 2723995. See also Kasyak, p. 138.

32. See Dienststelle Rosenberg, memorandum "Ostland," November [?], 1942, in Yivo Institute for Jewish Research (File Occ E 20–23). For Gestapo moves against Catholic influence via Lithuania, see U.S. National Archives and Records Service, *Ereignismeldungen. UdSSR*, No. 145 (Dec. 12, 1941), Roll 234, Frame 2723395; No. 154 (Jan. 12, 1942), Roll 234, Frames 2723573–2723575; No. 191 (Apr. 10, 1942), Roll 235, Frame 2724204.

33. Walter Kolarz, *Religion in the Soviet Union* (New York, 1961), pp. 226–227; cf. Vakar, p. 278, for an account that puts the execution of Nemancevic 3 months earlier.

34. See Kasyak, pp. 42, 170–171.

35. U.S. National Archives and Records Service, *Ereignismeldungen. UdSSR*, No. 36 (July 28, 1941), Roll 233, Frame 2721693; No. 73 (Sept. 4, 1941), Roll 233, Frame 2722178; No. 90 (Sept. 21, 1941), Roll 233, Frames 2722488–2722489; No. 154 (Jan. 12, 1942), Roll 234, Frames 2723578–2723579.

36. See Dallin, *German Rule*, p. 486.

37. U.S. National Archives and Records Service, *Ereignismeldungen. UdSSR*, No. 154 (Jan. 12, 1942), Roll 234, Frames 2723576–2723577.

38. For attempts of the Warsaw diocese to dominate Panteleimon's hierarchy, see Berthold Spuler, "Die orthodoxen Kirchen," *Internationale Kirchliche Zeitschrift* (Berne), 32 (1942), 169.

39. See Kasyak, p. 84.

40. *Ibid.*, pp. 86–87, 91.

41. For German support of Belorussian autocephaly, see RKO memorandum, May 26, 1942, in Yivo Institute for Jewish Research (File Occ E [Ch] 7–8).

42. U.S. National Archives and Records Service, *Ereignismeldungen. UdSSR*, No. 180 (Mar. 13, 1942), Roll 235, Frames 2723995–2723996; No. 194 (Apr. 21, 1942), Roll 235, Frame 2724293; see also Kasyak, p. 97.

43. *Ibid.*, pp. 97–103.

44. U.S. National Archives and Records Service, *Meldungen aus den besetzten Ostgebieten*, No. 6 (June 5, 1942), Roll 235, Frames 2724450–2724451.

45. See Kasyak, p. 103.

46. *Ibid.*, pp. 99–109.

47. See Vakar, p. 278. For text of church statute, see Kasyak, pp. 173–188.

48. See Kasyak, p. 126.

49. See *Deutsche Post aus dem Osten* (Berlin), 14 (June 1942), 6.

50. Harvard Refugee Interview Project, "A-Schedules," No. 384 (n.d.).

51. As cited in Dallin, *German Rule*, p. 487 n. 1; see also U.S. National Archives and Records Service, *Meldungen aus den besetzten Ostgebieten*, No. 6 (June 5, 1942), Roll 235, Frame 2724450; No. 11 (July 10, 1942), Roll 235, Frames 2724568–2724569.

52. See Kasyak, pp. 92–93.

53. Reich Ministry for the Occupied Eastern Territories, "Memorandum of June 1, 1944" (German ms.).

54. See Vakar, pp. 203–206.

55. Harvard Refugee Interview Project, "A-Schedules," No. 141 (n.d.).

56. See Heyer, pp. 11–18.

57. See Merle Fainsod, *How Russia Is Ruled* (Cambridge, 1953), pp. 299–300.

58. See Heyer, pp. 34–37, 45–46.

59. See Kolarz, p. 106.

60. Serge Bolshakoff, *Russian Nonconformity* (Philadelphia, 1950), pp. 168–170.

61. See Kolarz, pp. 107–108.

62. See Bolshakoff, *Russian Nonconformity*, p. 169; cf. Kolarz for an estimate for only 2,000 parishes under the UAPTs.

63. See S. Raevski, *Ukrainskaya Avtokefalnaya Tserkov* (Jordanville, N.Y., 1948), pp. 3–7; see also Heyer, pp. 77–78.

64. See Kolarz, p. 109.

65. See Alex Inkeles and Raymond A. Bauer, *The Soviet Citizen: Daily Life in a Totalitarian Society* (Cambridge, Mass., 1959), p. 362.

66. Among the sources treating of this subject above, the most negative rendering of the UAPTs is by Bolshakoff, fairly critical ones by Heyer and Raevski, a more sympathetic one by Armstrong and Kolarz.

67. See Raevski, pp. 8–9.

68. On the initial welcome given by West Ukrainians to Red Army forces as liberators from the Polish Catholic "yoke," see Spuler, 30 (1940) 95, 154; 31 (1941), 49; for an account of Nikolai's mission, see Heyer, pp. 166–167.

69. See Armstrong, pp. 193–196.

70. U.S. National Archives and Records Service, *Ereignismeldungen. UdSSR*, No. 79 (Sept. 10, 1941), Roll 233, Frame 2722274.

71. See Raevski, pp. 9–10; see also Heyer, p. 164.

72. See U. S. National Archives and Records Service, *Ereignismeldungen. UdSSR*, No. 30, (July 22, 1941), Roll 233, Frame 2721613; No. 164 (Feb. 4, 1942), Roll 234, Frame 2723786.

73. See Armstrong, p. 194.

74. See Spuler, 31 (1941), 47.

75 *Ibid.*, pp. 47–48; see also *Who's Who in Occupied Europe* (London, 1944). For a report that the Kholm Cathedral had been a Catholic church "given" the Orthodox by Governor Frank, see Heyer, p. 164.

76. See Raevski, p. 13.

77. For protests by Bishop Dimitry (Magan) and Protopriest Vladimir Benevsky, see Heyer, p. 174.

78. *Ibid.*, p. 176; cf. U.S. National Archives and Records Service, *Ereignismeldungen. UdSSR,* No. 133 (Nov. 14, 1941), Roll 234, Frame 2723197.

79. Metropolitan Dionisius, "Memorandum, July 15, 1942" (Russian ms.), in Archive of Russian and East European History and Culture, Columbia University.

80. See Raevski, pp. 13–14. For estimates of strength of various Ukrainian church factions, see Spuler, 32 (1942), 170.

81. Heyer, pp. 163, 174.

82. Letter of Koch to Rosenberg, March 6, 1943, in *TMWC,* vol. 25, pp. 255–288 (192-PS).

83. See Raevski, p. 14.

84. See Heyer, pp. 213–216.

85. See Spuler, 33 (1943), 31.

86. John S. Curtiss, *The Russian Church and the Soviet State: 1917–1950* (Boston, 1953), p. 291.

87. Matthew Spinka, *The Church in Soviet Russia* (New York, 1956), p. 86. For condemnation of Nikolai by the Acting Patriarch on Mar. 20, 1943, see Russian Orthodox Church, *Patriarkh Sergi,* p. 89.

88. See Heyer, pp. 178ff.

89. Harvard Refugee Interview Project, "Hans Koch," Protocol of June 1, 1951, p. 9.

90. U.S. National Archives and Records Service, *Ereignismeldungen. UdSSR,* No. 155 (Jan. 14, 1942), Roll 234, Frames 2723627–2723629.

91. Harvard Refugee Interview Project, "Hans Koch," pp. 8–9.

92. U.S. National Archives and Records Service, *Meldungen aus den besetzten Ostgebieten,* No. 25 (Oct. 16, 1942), Roll 236, Frame 2724966.

93. Harvard Refugee Interview Project, "B-Schedules on Wartime Occupation," No. 96.

94. *Ibid.*, No. 314; see also Spuler, 32 (1942), 43.

95. U.S. National Archives and Records Service, *Meldungen aus den besetzten Ostgebieten,* No. 34 (Dec. 18, 1942), Roll 236, Frame 2725261; see also Heyer, p. 220.

96. See Armstrong, pp. 213–214.

97. Harvard Refugee Interview Project, "Interview with Professor Markert" (Protocol G-10).

98. See Raevski, pp. 14–15; see also Spuler, 33 (1943), 31; Heyer, p. 219.

99. See Armstrong, pp. 206–208; see also Spuler 33 (1943), 29.

100. See Raevski, p. 15.

101. U.S. National Archives and Records Service, *Ereignismeldungen. UdSSR,* No. 120 (Oct. 21, 1941), Roll 234, Frame 2722995.

102. See Armstrong, pp. 202–205.

103. See Heyer, pp. 176–178.

104. U.S. National Archives and Records Service, *Ereignismeldungen. UdSSR,* No. 191 (Apr. 10, 1942), Roll 235, Frames 2724228–2724229.

105. See Heyer, p. 206.

106. U.S. National Archives and Records Service, *Meldungen aus den besetzten Ostgebieten,* No. 34 (Dec. 18, 1942), Roll 236, Frame 2725265.

107. Heyer, p. 218; see also Raevski, p. 14.

108. See Armstrong, p. 205.

109. See Heyer, pp. 217–218.

110. For estimates based on émigré surveys, finding twice as many adherents of pro-Patriarchal than of Autocephalous churches, see Inkeles and Bauer, p. 363.

111. Harvard Refugee Interview Project, "B-Schedules on Wartime Occupation," No. 441 (n.d.).

112. Harvard Refugee Interview Project, "Interview with Professor Markert" (Protocol G-10).

113. See Raevski, p. 14.

114. Document CXLVa 474 (Centre de Documentation Juive Contemporaine, Paris), cited in Armstrong, pp. 201–212.

115. Reich Ministry for Popular Enlightenment and Propaganda, Department East, "Politics of the Ukraine. Report by Professor Pavel Saitsev to Taubert" (German ms.), Berlin, Mar. 29, 1943.

116. U.S. National Archives and Records Service: *Meldungen aus den besetzten Ostgebieten*, No. 34 (Dec. 18, 1942), Roll 236, Frames 2725260–2725265.

117. See Heyer, p. 218.

118. Document CXLVa 66 (Centre de Documentation Juive Contemporaine, Paris), cited in Dallin, *German Rule*, p. 492.

119. See Armstrong, p. 209; see also Heyer, pp. 222–223.

120. See Alexander Svitich, "The Orthodox Church in Poland and Its Autocephaly" (Russian ms.), in Archive of Russian and East European History and Culture, Columbia University.

121. Peter Kleist, *Zwischen Hitler und Stalin, 1939–1945*, (Bonn, 1950), p. 130.

122. Harvard Refugee Interview Project, "B-Schedules on Wartime Occupation," No. 182.

123. Harvard Refugee Interview Project, "Hans Koch," p. 10; for a Gestapo report implying that the Lavra's destruction was connected with a partisan plot against the visiting Slovakian president, Dr. Joseph Tiso, see U.S. National Archives and Records Service, *Ereignismeldungen. UdSSR*, No. 130 (Nov. 7, 1941), Roll 234, Frame 2723129.

124. Harvard Refugee Interview Project, "B-Schedules on Wartime Occupation," No. 141.

125. Vladimir Benevsky, "The Church Policy of Bolshevism. Report of October 12, 1941" (German ms.), Riga, 1942, p. 29.

126. See Heyer, p. 171.

127. Harvard Refugee Interview Project, "B-Schedules on Wartime Occupation," No. 96.

128. Struve, *Christians*, pp. 76–77.

129. Kolarz, p. 72.

130. Dallin, "Popular Attitudes," p. 39.

131. U.S. National Archives and Records Service, *Ereignismeldungen. UdSSR*, No. 81 (Sept. 12, 1941), Roll 233, Frames 2722311–2722313.

132. Pavel Slinsky, "Life in the Polotsk Area, 1941–44" (Russian ms.), 1952, n.p.

133. U.S. National Archives and Records Service, *Meldungen aus den besetzten Ostgebieten,* No. 55 (May 21, 1943), Roll 236, Frames 2725957–2725958.

134. Harvard Refugee Interview Project, "B-Schedules on Wartime Occupation," No. 96. For a report that the first Reichskommissariat Ukraine orders maintained Soviet proscriptions of religious instruction in schools and the celebration of church holidays, see Heyer, p. 218.

135. See Samarin, p. 55.

Chapter 7. Soviet Response: The "New Religious Policy" in Full Flower

1. Nikita Struve, *Les Chretiens en U.R.S.S.* (Paris, 1963), p. 341. For slightly higher counts of priests and bishops, as given by the Soviet Press Bureau, see Robert P. Casey, *Religion in Russia* (New York, 1946), p. 93, although even these show a 10-percent drop in number of clergy from pre-revolutionary days.

2. See Walter Kolarz, *Religion in the Soviet Union* (New York, 1961), p. 49.

3. See Matthew Spinka, *The Church in Soviet Russia* (New York, 1956), pp. 30–34.

4. See Wilhelm DeVries, *Kirche und Staat in der Sowjetunion* (Munich, 1959), pp. 32–33.

5. *Antireligioznik,* 1939, No. 4.

6. *Bezbozhnik,* 1938, No. 12.

7. *Pravda,* March 29, 1940; for a report that at the same time Stalin had allocated 20,000,000 rubles for a giant atheist congress scheduled for 1942, see Berthold Spuler, "Die orthodoxen Kirchen," *Internationale Kirchliche Zeitschrift* (Berne), 30 (1940), 95–96.

8. *Antireligioznik,* 1939, Nos. 1, 5.

9. N. S. Timasheff, *Religion in Soviet Russia: 1917–1942* (London, 1944), p. 123.

10. *Buryato-Mongolskaya Pravda,* April 18, 1939, cited in *ibid.*

11. Nikita Struve, *Christians in Contemporary Russia* (New York, 1967), pp. 57–58.

12. See William C. Fletcher, *A Study in Survival: The Church in Russia 1927–1943* (New York, 1965), pp. 98–99; for an estimate that 1,200 parishes were added by the former Polish territories alone, see Spuler, 30 (1940), 94; cf. Friedrich Heyer, *Die orthodoxe Kirche in der Ukraine von 1917 bis 1945* (Cologne, 1953), p. 162.

13. See Vasili Alexeev, *Russian Orthodox Bishops in the Soviet Union, 1941–1953* (New York, 1954), p. 83

14. S. Raevski, *Ukrainskaya Avtokefalnaya Tserkov* (Jordanville, 1948), p. 11.

15. See John A. Armstrong, *Ukrainian Nationalism* (New York, 1963), p. 67. For German acknowledgment that Volhynian and Podolian church life had not been greatly disturbed, see U.S. National Archives and Records Service, Reich Chief Security Office, *Meldungen aus den besetzten Ostgebieten*, No. 34 (Dec. 18, 1942), Roll 236, Frame 2725260.

16. See John S. Curtiss, *The Russian Church and the Soviet State: 1917–1950* (Boston, 1953), pp. 274–275.

17. See Timasheff, pp. 124–125.

18. See, for example, Alfred G. Meyer, *The Soviet Political System* (New York, 1965), p. 440, which further lists the failure of atheist campaigns as reason for the reversal. This also does not seem to be a sufficient and necessary cause, in light of (1) previous antireligious shortcomings that had not caused a reversal, and (2) the evident successes of the atheist drive among the youth.

19. See Russian Orthodox Church, *Pravda o religi v Rossii* (Moscow, 1942), pp. 15–17; for charges that the NKVD helped draft this appeal, see Milwe-Schröden, memorandum to Reichskommissariat Ostland, July 28, 1943, in Yivo Institute for Jewish Research (File OccE [Ch] 12); for a more credible account of the message composed by Sergius himself, see Heyer, p. 299.

20. See Struve, *Christians*, p. 61.

21. Russian Orthodox Church, *Pravda o religi*, pp. 83–94.

22. Metropolitan Nikolai, *Slova, rechi, poslaniya: 1941–1946* gg. (Moscow, 1947), I, 178.

23. Russian Orthodox Church, *Russkaya pravoslavnaya tserkov i velikaya otechestvennaya voina* (Moscow, 1943[?]), p. 6.

24. See Fletcher, *Study in Survival*, pp. 99–106.

25. See Timasheff, p. 138.

26. Russian Orthodox Church, *Patriarkh Sergi i ego dukhovnoe nasledstvo* (Moscow, 1947), pp. 85, 90.

27. *The New York Times*, Nov. 10, 1942.

28. Moscow Patriarchate, *The Truth about Religion in Russia* (London, 1942), p. 61.

29. *Ibid.*, p. 66. For evidence that in February Polykarp claimed that Sergius was impersonating the "real Sergius," who was in a Soviet jail, see Spuler, 32 (1942), 45.

30. Russian Orthodox Church, *Patriarkh Sergi*, p. 89.

31. See Spinka, *Church in Soviet Russia*, p. 86.

32. *The New York Times*, Oct. 1, 7, 1941.

33. See Leopold L. Braun, *Religion in Russia, from Lenin to Khrushchev: An Uncensored Account* (Patterson, N.J., 1959), p. 56. For an interpretation of this document as a response, at the instigation of U.S. Ambassador Joseph Davies, to American church attacks on Soviet atheism, see Heyer, p. 232.

34. Russian Orthodox Church, *Pravda o religi*, p. 9.

35. See Spuler, 31 (1941), 159.

36. For evidence of flights in June 1942, see Metropolitan Nikolai, *Slova*, pp. 243–244.

37. Russian Orthodox Church, *Patriarkh Sergi*, p. 90; cf. ROC, *Russkaya*, pp. 77–79.

38. "Decree of the Presidium of the Supreme Soviet of the USSR," Nov. 2, 1941, in *Soviet War Documents* (Washington, 1943), p. 157.

39. For a surmise that Molotov's charges of Nazi religious atrocities, in a note of Apr. 27, 1942, to President Roosevelt, were designed to overcome the scruples of American Catholics in aiding the Soviets, see Milwe-Schröden.

40. M. U. Nikitin and P. I. Vagin, *The Crimes of the German Fascists in the Leningrad Region* (London, n.d.), p. 63.

41. *Soviet Government Statements on Nazi Atrocities* (London, n.d.), p. 2.

42. U.S. National Archives and Records Service, *Meldungen aus den besetzten Ostgebieten*, No. 48 (Apr. 2, 1943), Roll 236, Frame 2725779.

43. Metropolitan Nikolai, *The Russian Orthodox Church and the War against Fascism* (Moscow, 1943), p. 27.

44. See, for example, Russian Orthodox Church, *Pravda o religi*, pp. 121–122.

45. Victor Kravchenko, *I Chose Freedom* (New York, 1946), p. 425.

46. *Sputnik Agitatora*, No. 10 (1943), 8.

47. *Zhurnal Moskovskoi Patriarkhi* (hereafter *Zh.M.P.*), 10 (1944), 3.

48. See Russian Orthodox Church, *Russkaya*, p. 95.

49. U.S. National Archives and Records Service, *Meldungen aus den besetzten Ostgebieten*, No. 46 (Mar. 19, 1942), Roll 236, Frame 2725689.

50. See Russian Orthodox Church, *Patriarkh Sergi*, pp. 287–294.

51. U.S. National Archives and Records Service, *Meldungen aus den besetzten Ostgebieten*, No. 50 (Apr. 16, 1943), Roll 236, Frame 2725822; No. 53 (May 7, 1943), Roll 236, Frames 2725904–2725905.

52. Russian Orthodox Church, *Patriarkh Sergi*, p. 44.

53. For the commencement of this in June 1944, see *ibid.*, p. 383.

54. For Karpov's estimate of 16,000 churches operating at the time, see *The New York Times*, June 7, 1945.

55. See Spinka, *Church in Soviet Russia*, p. 95.

56. For Karpov interview on this subject, see *The New York Times*, Aug. 18, 1944; also a second interview, Sept. 15, 1944.

57. See Simon Wolin and Robert M. Slusser, *The Soviet Secret Police* (New York, 1957), p. 23; see also Kolarz, p. 54.

58. See Alexander Werth, *Russia at War, 1941–1945* (New York, 1964), p. 433.

59. See Robert Magidoff, *The Kremlin vs. the People* (Garden City, 1953), p. 74.

60. *The New York Times*, Aug. 12, 1944.

61. Russian Orthodox Church, *Patriarkh Sergi*, pp. 45–46.

62. See Heyer, p. 233.

63. *Zh.M.P.*, 1 (1943), 16.

64. See Struve, *Christians*, p. 67.

65. See Kolarz, p. 56.

66. See Curtiss, *Russian Church*, p. 295.

67. See *Zh.M.P.* 3 (1944), 8–9; 1 (1944), 7–8; 4 (1944), 9; 1 (1945), 7–8.

68. See Armstrong, p. 297; see also Heyer, pp. 242–243.

69. On the defrocking of Vlasovites in September 1945, see Raymond A. Bauer, Alex Inkeles, Clyde Kluckhohn, *How the Soviet System Works* (Cambridge, Mass., 1956), p. 71; for transfers of priests ordained during the occupation, see Heyer, p. 239.

70. See Walter Birnbaum, *Christenheit in Sowjetrussland* (Tübingen, 1961), p. 189.

71. Russian Orthodox Church, *The Russian Orthodox Church, Organization, Situation, Activity* (Moscow, 1959), p. 78.

72. Semyon N. Khudyakov, *Vsegda li budet sushchestvovat religiya?* (Moscow, 1958), p. 17; see also F. Oleshchuk, "For Concreteness of Scientific-Atheistic Propaganda," in *Kommunist*, 5 (April 1958), 113; E. F. Muravev and Iu. V. Dmitriev, "On Concreteness in the Study and Overcoming of Religious Survivals," in *Voprosy Filosofi*, 3 (1961), 65–73; translated in *Soviet Review*, 2 (1961), 64.

73. See Russian Orthodox Church, *Pravda o religi*, p. 216. For a surmise that the curfew was lifted only to avert otherwise likely rioting, see William C. Fletcher, *Nikolai: Portrait of a Dilemma* (New York, 1968), p. 45.

74. *Orthodox Church Bulletin* (London), May 1943, p. 16.

75. Werth, pp. 433–434.

76. U.S. National Archives and Records Service, *Meldungen aus den besetzten Ostgebieten*, No. 53 (May 7, 1943), Roll 236, Frame 2725905; No. 55 (May 21, 1943), Roll 236, Frame 2725982.

77. Eve Curie, *Journey Among Warriors* (Garden City, 1943), pp. 145–146. For comments of Sergius on the paucity of youthful believers, see Wallace Carroll, *We're in This with Russia* (Boston, 1942), pp. 150–151.

78. *The New York Times,* Jan. 8, 1944.

79. *New York Herald-Tribune,* Sept. 25, 1943.

80. See Efraim Briem, *Kommunismus und Religion in der Sowjetunion, ein Ideenkampf* (Basel, 1948), p. 385.

81. Central Committee, Communist Party of the Soviet Union, "On the Organization of Scientific-Educational Propaganda," in *Propagandist*, 18 (1944), 1–5.

82. Regarding the import this had on the progressive secularization of Soviet society, see Alex Inkeles and Raymond A. Bauer, *The Soviet Citizen: Daily Life in a Totalitarian Society* (Cambridge, Mass., 1959), pp. 372, 380–381; see also Bauer, Inkeles, Kluckhohn, pp. 71–73.

83. See DeVries, *Kirche und Staat*, p. 20.

84. See Fletcher, *A Study*, p. 123.

85. Meyer, p. 440.

86. See Werth, p. 695.

87. See Fletcher, *Nikolai*, pp. 56–59, 67–69, 169.

88. Russian Orthodox Church, *Patriarkh Sergi*, pp. 135–136.

89. *Izvestiya*, Feb. 6, 1945, cited in Kolarz, p. 57.

90. *Zh.M.P.*, 3 (1945), 27–32.

91. "Document D," appendix of Struve, *Chrétiens*.

92. See Curtiss, *Russian Church*, pp. 308–309. For an account of the lag in building the proposed seminaries, see Heyer, p. 239.

93. See Struve, *Christians,* pp. 84–87.

94. *Zh.M.P.,* 2 (1945), 10–11.

95. *Ibid.,* 12 (1949), 7–11.

96. *Ibid.,* 4 (1953), 5–13.

97. *Izvestiya,* Feb. 10, 1945, cited in Curtiss, *Russian Church,* p. 248.

98. See Michael Bourdeaux, *Opium of the People: The Christian Religion in the U.S.S.R.* (Indianapolis, 1966), pp. 66, 223–231.

99. *Zh.M.P.,* 2 (1944), 28.

100. *Ibid.,* 12 (1945), 25.

101. *Ibid.,* 4 (1946), 35–37; see also Russian Orthodox Church, *Patriarkh Sergi,* p. 372.

102. See Kolarz, p. 234.

103. *Zh.M.P.,* 10 (1948); see also Heyer, pp. 243–245.

104. See Kolarz, p. 58.

105. *Zh.M.P.,* 11 (1945), 14–17.

106. See Bourdeaux, p. 64; also Heyer, pp. 240–241.

107. *Zh.M.P.,* 3 (1945), 4. For speculation that "Third Rome" ambitions had already motivated Soviet contact with the Ecumenical Patriarch in Constantinople by mid-1943, see Milwe-Schröden, p. 14. For a view that contact with the patriarchs of Antioch and Alexandria was primarily meant to block recognition of the UAPTs, see Heyer, p. 237.

108. See Kolarz, pp. 60–61.

109. *Zh.M.P.* (1948), special number; see also Paul B. Anderson, ed., *Major Portions of the Proceedings of the Conference of Heads and Representatives of Autocephalous Orthodox Churches in Connection with the Celebration of 500 Years of Autocephalicity of the Russian Orthodox Church, 8–18 July 1948* (Paris, 1952).

110. Serge Bolshakoff, *The Christian Church and the Soviet State* (New York, 1942), p. 69.

111. Miklos Nyarady, *My Ringside Seat in Moscow* (New York, 1952), pp. 171–178.

112. John S. Curtiss, "Non-Orthodox Religions in the U.S.S.R.," in *American Review on the Soviet Union,* 8, No. 1 (November 1946), p. 13.

113. N. S. Timasheff in Waldemar Gurian, ed., *The Soviet Union: Background, Ideology, Reality* (Notre Dame, 1951), pp. 176, 184.

114. *Zh.M.P.,* 8 (1944).

115. Stephen Graham, *Summing up on Russia* (London, 1951).

116. See Nyarady, p. 174.

117. Wilhelm DeVries, *Christentum in der Sowjetunion* (Heidelberg, 1950), p. 58.

118. See Nyarady, p. 174.

119. *Zh.M.P.,* 10 (1948), 39–48.

120. See Kolarz, pp. 92–93.

Index

Russian Research Center Studies

* Out of print.
† Publications of the Harvard Project on the Soviet Social System.
‡ Published jointly with the Center for International Affairs, Harvard University.